商务馆实用汉语听说教材
世界汉语教学学会审订

说话得体

Learn to Speak Chinese through Contextualized Dialogues

任长慧　朱敏琪　编著
Theresa Jen　Minqi Zhu

商务印书馆
2010年·北京

图书在版编目(CIP)数据

说话得体/任长慧，朱敏琪编著.—北京：商务印书馆，2008
商务馆实用汉语听说教材
ISBN 978-7-100-05407-2

I.说… II.①任…②朱… III.汉语—听说教学—对外汉语教学—教材 IV.
H195.4

中国版本图书馆CIP数据核字(2007)第026916号

所有权利保留。
未经许可，不得以任何方式使用。

SHUŌHUÀ DÉTǏ

说 话 得 体

任长慧　朱敏琪　编著

商 务 印 书 馆 出 版
（北京王府井大街36号　邮政编码100710）
商 务 印 书 馆 发 行
北京瑞古冠中印刷厂印刷
ISBN 978 - 7 - 100 - 05407 - 2

2008年6月第1版	开本 880×1230　1/16
2010年1月北京第3次印刷	印张 20¾
印数 5 000 册	
全套定价：99.00元	

以学生为中心组织教学
以交际任务为基点引导学生

Student-Centered & Task-Based Teaching and Learning

特别感谢

美国长堤市多元科技高中中文班学生
六年的合作和贡献

A special THANK YOU
to the Chinese Language students of
Long Beach Polytechnic High School
for their cooperation and
contributions over the last six years

教材编写说明

《说话得体》是为美国高中中文三、四年级或大学程度AP(Advanced Placement)中文课学生设计的听说教材，目的是强化口语表达的训练。通过高中阶段头两年的学习，学生积累了一定的汉语词汇量，掌握了一些基本的汉语语法和句型，对说汉语有了一定的语感，并且可以在课堂活动中作一些最基础的、有限的自由发挥。这本教材就是针对这类程度的学生而编写的。教材的编写采取"个案"教学方法，用引导和启发的方式，通过对常用词句和课文的操练与学习，启发学生举一反三地思维，培养学生分析问题、解决问题的能力。我们采用的方法是，要求学生在每一课开始的"开启思路"阶段完成10-3-1三个步骤的作业，即：设计10个场景（英文也行），用于开拓学生的思路；编写3个短小中文对话，使学生熟悉并掌握语言交流的技能。在学习常用词句部分之后，再让学生做场景对比，找出意义相近的词句，用在自己设计的10个场景上；最后选择主题，编写1个具有完整意义的短文。学生在听说训练的"开启思路"阶段对自己所提出的场景设计都会有很具体的语境概念。由于场景是学生自己设计的，贴近学生的实际生活，不仅鲜活，而且实用。对学生而言，因为容易上口，也就乐于学。至于课文部分，可以供学生在编写小品表演反馈时作为参考之用。当然教师也可以根据实际教学情况从课文学习入手。《说话得体》重点是培养学生的听说能力，同时兼顾阅读和理解能力的提高。《说话得体》不仅是学生用书，也可以作为中文听说课教师的手册，为教师在组织教学、课堂引导、与学生沟通等方面提供参考。

《说话得体》共分8个单元16课。全书以16个语言功能主题链接了64个场景，并列出了370多个句式。每一课有5个部分：常用词句、情景对话、看图说话、小品表演和练笔。每个单元有1个听力训练。《说话得体》是以学生为中心组织课堂教学，以交际任务为基点引导学生，打破了长期以来形成的词汇、语法教学的顺序。每一课情景对话是一个独立的教学单元，列有功能性常用词句，每个情景对话后配备词语表。教材的生词量并不刻意要求分布均匀，也不受句法或语法循序渐进的限制。听力训练部分配有双向交流听力练习图表，英文、中文相结合。如听力训练的内容部分，学生可以用英文记录，但是学生必须写下小品表演中使用的新学到的常用词语和句子。总的目的是让学生看懂、听懂表演的小品，与表演者有交流，相互学习，避免学生开小差。

《说话得体》的每一课情景对话部分都有四个层次的对话：基本用法、实用用法、复杂用法和特殊用法。这是根据美国加利福尼亚教育委员会2003年通过的《加

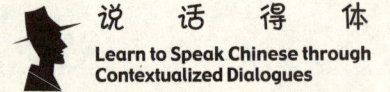

利福尼亚州公立学校外语学习准则》中"外语学习五个阶段准则[①]"的前四个准则所编排的，同时也体现了著名教育心理学家维高斯基有关学习的"相近开发区域"的理念（Vygosky's "the Zone of Proximal Development"[②]），目的是为了调动不同程度学生的学习参与积极性。《说话得体》在编写过程中也考虑到了学生的不同情况，汉语水平参差不一，学习目的也不一样等诸多因素。既然是以学生为中心，教师也必须相应地变换教材的内容和教学方法。比如常用句应答部分，原本就是参考性质的，各种不同的回应可能性很多，完全由教师根据学生和课堂教学实际情况掌控，需要不时地筛减或增补学习内容。

在多年的教学经验积累中，我们注意到了形象在语言学习过程中具有特殊的地位，是开发学生潜在记忆的一种有效方法。借助图画的帮助，学生能够充分发挥观察力和想象力，有益于学生创作合乎逻辑的词句和语段。此外，系列图画还能够提供一个运用语言的明确语境或想象方向。活泼有趣的图画也有益于激发学生学习中文的兴趣和积极性。为此《说话得体》设计了16组各自内部有连贯性、可叙述的图画，每组4幅，结合每一课最后的练笔部分，旨在培养学生的表述能力，让学生学会用汉语作成段的、意义完整的口头或书面表达。

《说话得体》选择了16个语言功能主题，组成8个学习单元：问候、告别、介绍、推荐、询问、要求、拒绝、接受、告诫、建议、许诺、致歉、同情、安慰、恭维、抱怨。这些语言现象都是日常生活中经常遇到的，学生一旦掌握了便能应付日常生活的需求。每一课的常用词句、情景对话、小品表演、听力训练、练笔都是围绕语言功能而展开的。课文中所选择的场景和例句，特别是"学生生活中常用的120句话"，都是源自于学生所熟悉的学习、工作和生活，当然也包含了中国人的日常生活、社会交际以及与中国文化相关的话题，所选择的场景尽可能涵盖AP中文课程以及大学一、二年级中文课程的语境：在家、在街上、在学校、在教室、在工作场所、在图书馆、在宿舍、在饭馆、在飞机场、在商店、在电话里或在其他的公共场合；内容包括了购物、问路、访友、学习、聚会、运动、交友、聊天、开会、娱乐、旅行、参观、订票、婚姻、健康、教育、选专业、找工作、商务会谈以及其他社会文化主题。

[①] Foreign Language Framework for California Public Schools, published by California Department of Education, Sacramento, 2003, pp. 9-14.

[②] Vygosky defined the Zone of Proximal Development as "the distance between the actual development level as determined by independent problem solving and the level of potential development as determined through problem solving under adult guidance or in collaboration with more capable peers" Mind in Society, 1978, p. 86.

教材编写说明
Preface

《说话得体》的编写和教学实践力求遵循美国外语教学学会(ACTFL)的检测标准，即美国外语教师都熟悉的 5 Cs 和 3 Modes。5 Cs 是五大外语教学目标，即：沟通 (Communication)、文化(Cultures)、连贯(Connections)、比较(Comparisons)和社区(Communities)。教师在课程设计和组织教学活动时，要尽可能地针对这 5 个目标，至少每课必须突显 1~2 个主要目标。3 Modes 指的是学习语言沟通的 3 种模式，即：互动交流(Interpersonal)，通过使用所学的外语进行交谈、交换意见、表达情感；理解诠释(Interpretive)，通过使用所学语言对接受的口语或文字进行信息分析、理解、诠释；表达演示(Presentational)，通过使用所学语言进行口语及书写方式的信息传递、概念陈述和思想表达。除此以外，本教材还列入了高级口语教学实践中强调的综合(Synthesizing)、分析(Analyzing)、假设(Hypothesizing)、结论(Concluding)、总体结构(Organization)等认知能力的检测标准。这些标准基本反映了美国外语教学学会（ACTFL)所制定的外语面谈口语能力考试 (Oral Proficiency Interview)的教学要求。

编著者

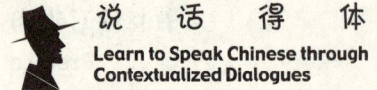

Preface

Learn to Speak Chinese through Contextualized Dialogues is a textbook designed for 3rd and 4th level and AP (Advanced Placement) Chinese students in the United States with emphasis on listening and speaking. The objective is to strengthen students' speaking proficiency. Through the previous two years of Chinese language learning in high school, the students would have accumulated a certain amount of Chinese vocabulary, developed a basic command of Chinese grammar and sentence patterns, and have developed some sense of the language. With all these aspects, students may produce the most fundamental, but restricted, compositions at will during classroom activities. This textbook was compiled with students at these levels in mind.

This textbook has adopted the "case study" approach: with the application of guiding and inspiring methods and providing practice and study of Common Expressions and Texts, students are encouraged to learn from the thinking process, and are trained to develop their ability to analyze issues and solve problems. The method is to assign students a 10-3-1 step course work, namely: designing 10 (using English language is fine) situations for exploring ideas; preparing 3 short dialogues for familiarizing themselves with and practicing the learned communicative skills and writing of one short paragraph based on the subject matter. After learning Common Expressions, students are required to make comparison with scenes and to apply similar expressions for the scenes they have designed. Finally, students select one topic and write a short, complete and meaningful paragraph. Students have always demonstrated concrete and contextualized concepts when putting forth the scene designs at the brainstorming stage. Because all scenes are designed by students based on their own life experiences, they are both vivid and practical. It is also easy for students to work with this method, and students are happy to learn. As for the text port, it can be used as reference for the students when they prepare for the skit performance, a feedback project. Of course, teachers may start with learning the texts in accordance with actual instructional circumstances.

The primary aim of *Learn to Speak Chinese through Contextualized Dialogues* is to train students in listening and speaking abilities, but it also takes into account the improvement of students' reading comprehension. *Learn to Speak*

教材编写说明
Preface

Chinese through Contextualized Dialogues is not only a textbook for students, but also an instructional manual for teachers. Teachers may use it as a reference book for lesson organization, classroom direction, and a means of communication with students.

Learn to Speak Chinese through Contextualized Dialogues consists of 16 lessons divided into 8 units. The whole textbook contains 64 contextualized dialogues with 16 functional themes, and gives more than 370 sentence patterns. Each lesson has 5 components: 1. Common Expressions; 2. Texts (in dialogue form); 3. Story Narration; 4. Skit Performance Hints; 5. Writing Exercise. Since *Learn to Speak Chinese through Contextualized Dialogues* is student-centered and task-based, it deviates from the conventional vocabulary-grammar order pedagogy; each lesson is an independent instructional unit with a list of functional words and expressions, and a vocabulary list after each text (dialogue). The distribution of new words is not uniform, nor the order restricted for grammar and syntax.

Listening Comprehension is provided with a two-way communicative practice chart in both Chinese and English. Students may take notes in English when listening. However, students must create their skits with the newly acquired common expressions and sentences. The overall goal is to enable students to understand the performance pieces and exchange feedback with the performers, so as to learn from each other, and avoid the exclusion of students from participation.

In *Learn to Speak Chinese through Contextualized Dialogues*, every text section has four levels: Essential Delivery, Practical Delivery, Complex Delivery and Special Delivery. This is based on the Foreign Language Learning Continuum in the Foreign Language Framework for California Public Schools, published by California Department of Education, 2003. These four delivery levels reflect the first four of the five continuum, which also demonstrates the well known educational psychologist Vygosky's theory The Zone of Proximal Development. There is nothing more important than to facilitate active participation of students at all levels of learning.

The composition of *Learn to Speak Chinese through Contextualized*

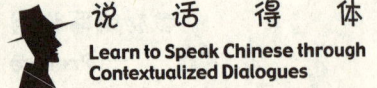

Dialogues has taken into account the factors of students' different circumstances, various Chinese standards, and their study motivations. Since the approach is designed around the students, teachers also need to change the teaching content and adopt new teaching methods accordingly. For example, the Responses to Common Expressions were designed as a reference because of the possibility of many different responses. It is entirely up to teachers to adjust to changing classroom circumstances. It is essential for teachers to reduce and add instructional contents from time to time.

Throughout years of teaching experience, we have noticed that the use of images in the process of learning a language plays a special role. It is an effective way to develop students' potential memory. With the help of pictures, students may exercise their power in observation and imagination to a great extent. Reading pictures is conducive to creativity among students for logical expressions in sentences and paragraphs. In addition, the use of a series of pictures can also provide a clear context and creative direction. Lively and interesting pictures are also conducive to stimulating the interest and enthusiasm of students studying Chinese. Therefore, *Learn to Speak Chinese through Contextualized Dialogues* has designed, altogether, 16 series of pictures, each having 4 pictures, easy to describe in words. Combined with the Writing Exercise at the end of each lesson, students will learn how to present themselves with a complete and well-organized paragraph in both oral and written formats.

Learn to Speak Chinese through Contextualized Dialogues has selected 16 themes based on language function comprising 8 units: Greetings, Saying Farewell, Introducing, Recommending, Inquiring, Requesting, Refusing, Accepting, Cautioning, Suggesting, Promising, Apologizing, Showing Sympathy, Giving Comfort and Reassurance, Complimenting and Complaining. These linguistic phenomena are often encountered in daily life. Once students have a good command of the above communicative skills, they can meet their daily needs. Each lesson's Common Expressions, Texts (dialogues), Skit Performance Hints, Listening Comprehension, Story Narration and Writing Exercise, all develop with the focus on language function. Contexts and listed expressions selected for the texts, especially the "120 Popular Expressions in Daily Life Among Students" originate from students' personal experiences: study, work and life. It also embraces Chinese people's daily life, social interaction, and some other issues related to Chinese culture. All selected scenes cover the contexts in a second year Chinese language course at the university levels and they are appropriate for AP Chinese study: at home, on the streets, in schools, in the classroom, in the office, at the library, in the dormitory, at restaurants, at airports, at stores, on the telephone, or in other public places. The contents include shopping, asking for directions, visiting friends, learning, gatherings, exercising, making friends, chatting, attending meetings, entertaining, traveling and visiting, booking tickets, marriage, health, education, major election, job searching, business meetings and other social and cultural themes.

The composition of *Learn to Speak Chinese through Contextualized Dialogues* and teaching with it should seek to follow the standards of teaching foreign language in the United States familiar to American foreign-language teachers: that is the five Cs and three Modes. The 5 Cs are five foreign language teaching objectives, namely: Communication, Culture, Connecting, Comparison and Community. When teachers design curriculum and organize class activities, they should achieve these five goals to the extent possible, and each lesson should at least stress on one or two main objectives. The Three Modes refers to the communicative modes essential to language learning: Interpersonal (through the use of the target language for conversation, exchanging views, and expressing emotions); Interpretive (through the use of what have been learned to accept the spoken or written language for information analysis, understanding, interpretation); Presentational (through the use of spoken and written forms of language learning for information transmission, the concept of representation and expression of ideas). In addition, the textbook has also included advanced comprehensive oral proficiency standards with the emphasis on synthesizing, analyzing, hypothesizing, concluding, and organization. These cognitive assessment standards generally reflect the criteria for Oral Proficiency Interview of the American Council on the Teaching Foreign Languages (ACTFL).

目 录
Contents

第一单元　Unit 1

★ 第一课 问候
Lesson One　Greetings 3

★ 第二课 告别
Lesson Two　Saying Farewell 13

常用词句 Common Expressions

情景对话 Contextualized Dialogues

　　对话一：您说着了
　　Dialogue I: You Are Right

　　对话二：恭喜，贺喜
　　Dialogue II: Congratulations

　　对话三：欢迎光临
　　Dialogue III: Welcome

　　对话四：稀客
　　Dialogue IV: What a Rare Visitor

看图说话 Story Narration

小品表演 Skit Performance

练笔 Writing Exercise

常用词句 Common Expressions

情景对话 Contextualized Dialogues

　　对话一：时间不早了
　　Dialogue I: It's Getting Late.

　　对话二：接着聊
　　Dialogue II: Continue to Talk

　　对话三：保持联系
　　Dialogue III: Keep in Touch

　　对话四：尽管来找我
　　Dialogue IV: Feel Free to Visit Me

看图说话 Story Narration

小品表演 Skit Performance

练笔 Writing Exercise

第一单元听力练习　Listening Comprehension Unit 1

说 话 得 体
Learn to Speak Chinese through
Contextualized Dialogues

第二单元 Unit 2

★ 第一课 介绍
Lesson One   Introducing 27

★ 第二课 推荐
Lesson Two   Recommending 39

常用词句 Common Expressions

情景对话 Contextualized Dialogues

　　对话一：不必客套
　　Dialogue I: No Need to Be So Formal.

　　对话二：听好消息
　　Dialogue II: Hearing Good News

　　对话三：自我介绍
　　Dialogue III: Self-Introducing

　　对话四：逛商场
　　Dialogue IV: Shopping

看图说话 Story Narration

小品表演 Skit Performance

练笔 Writing Exercise

常用词句 Common Expressions

情景对话 Contextualized Dialogues

　　对话一：读个痛快
　　Dialogue I: Read with Pleasure

　　对话二：不会让你失望
　　Dialogue II: You Won't Be Disappointed.

　　对话三：北京特产
　　Dialogue III: Beijing Specialties

　　对话四：必不可少
　　Dialogue IV: Absolutely Necessary

看图说话 Story Narration

小品表演 Skit Performance

练笔 Writing Exercise

第二单元听力练习   Listening Comprehension Unit 2

第三单元 Unit 3

★ 第一课 询问
Lesson One　Inquiring 57

★ 第二课 要求
Lesson Two　Requesting 71

常用词句 Common Expressions

情景对话 Contextualized Dialogues

 对话一：对不起，请问
 Dialogue I: Excuse Me, May I Ask...

 对话二：有何贵干
 Dialogue II: What Kind of Business Do You Have?

 对话三：申请工作
 Dialogue III: Applying for a Job

 对话四：你几岁了
 Dialogue IV: How Old Are You?

看图说话 Story Narration

小品表演 Skit Performance

练笔 Writing Exercise

常用词句 Common Expressions

情景对话 Contextualized Dialogues

 对话一：家常饭菜
 Dialogue I: Homemade Meal

 对话二：洗耳恭听
 Dialogue II: Listening Devoutly and Respectfully

 对话三：请你转告
 Dialogue III: Please, Pass the Word

 对话四：赏光
 Dialogue IV: Will You Honor Me?

看图说话 Story Narration

小品表演 Skit Performance

练笔 Writing Exercise

第三单元听力练习 Listening Comprehension Unit 3

3

说 话 得 体
Learn to Speak Chinese through
Contextualized Dialogues

第四单元 Unit 4

★ 第一课 拒绝
Lesson One　Refusing 87

★ 第二课 接受
Lesson Two　Accepting 99

常用词句 Common Expressions

情景对话 Contextualized Dialogues

  对话一：恕不远送
  Dialogue I: Sorry for not Escorting You any Further

  对话二：看你怎么办
  Dialogue II: What Will You Do?

  对话三：情我领了
  Dialogue III: Appreciate the Kindness

  对话四：销售代理
  Dialogue IV: Becoming a Sales Representative

看图说话 Story Narration

小品表演 Skit Performance

练笔 Writing Exercise

常用词句 Common Expressions

情景对话 Contextualized Dialogues

  对话一：多买便宜
  Dialogue I: The More, the Cheaper

  对话二：祝贺生日
  Dialogue II: Celebrating a Birthday

  对话三：接受任职
  Dialogue III: Accepting a Job Offer

  对话四：接受建议
  Dialogue IV: Taking a Suggestion

看图说话 Story Narration

小品表演 Skit Performance

练笔 Writing Exercise

第四单元听力练习 Listening Comprehension Unit 4

第五单元 Unit 5

★ 第一课 告诫
Lesson One　Cautioning 113

★ 第二课 建议
Lesson Two　Suggesting 126

常用词句 Common Expressions

情景对话 Contextualized Dialogues

 对话一：预防万一
 Dialogue I: Prepare for the Worst

 对话二：第一次开车
 Dialogue II: First Time Driving

 对话三：别惹麻烦
 Dialogue III: Don't Look for Trouble

 对话四：权衡得失
 Dialogue IV: Weighing Gains and Losses

看图说话 Story Narration

小品表演 Skit Performance

练笔 Writing Exercise

常用词句 Common Expressions

情景对话 Contextualized Dialogues

 对话一：我感冒了
 Dialogue I: I Have a Cold

 对话二：去哪儿玩
 Dialogue II: Where to Have Fun

 对话三：温故而知新
 Dialogue III: Review What has been Learned so as to Learn Something New

 对话四：减肥要领
 Dialogue IV: Key to Dieting

看图说话 Story Narration

小品表演 Skit Performance

练笔 Writing Exercise

第五单元听力练习 Listening Comprehension Unit 5

说 话 得 体
Learn to Speak Chinese through Contextualized Dialogues

第六单元 Unit 6

★ 第一课 许诺
Lesson One   Promising 143

★ 第二课 致歉
Lesson Two   Apologizing 155

常用词句 Common Expressions

情景对话 Contextualized Dialogues

    对话一：不再失信
    Dialogue I: No More Breaking Promises

    对话二：修理电脑
    Dialogue II: Repairing a Computer

    对话三：额外加分
    Dialogue III: Extra Credit

    对话四：促销期间
    Dialogue IV: Sales Promotion

看图说话 Story Narration

小品表演 Skit Performance

练笔 Writing Exercise

常用词句 Common Expressions

情景对话 Contextualized Dialogues

    对话一：隐私权
    Dialogue I: Right to Privacy

    对话二：坏记性
    Dialogue II: A Poor Memory

    对话三：又迟到了
    Dialogue III: Being Late Again

    对话四：收回所说的话
    Dialogue IV: Taking Back What was Said

看图说话 Story Narration

小品表演 Skit Performance

练笔 Writing Exercise

第六单元听力练习 Listening Comprehension Unit 6

第七单元　Unit 7

★ 第一课 同情
Lesson One Showing Sympathy 171

★ 第二课 安慰
Lesson Two Giving Comfort and Reassurance 184

常用词句 Common Expressions

情景对话 Contextualized Dialogues

    对话一：谈学业
    Dialogue I: Talking about College Study

    对话二：探望受伤者
    Dialogue II: Visiting the Injured

    对话三：等待大学入学通知
    Dialogue III: Waiting for College Admission

    对话四：最需要的关心
    Dialogue IV: The Most Needed Care

看图说话 Story Narration

小品表演 Skit Performance

练笔 Writing Exercise

常用词句 Common Expressions

情景对话 Contextualized Dialogues

    对话一：违规受罚
    Dialogue I: Fine for Traffic Violation

    对话二：发挥正常
    Dialogue II: Performing Normally

    对话三：你们尽力了
    Dialogue III: You Did All You Could

    对话四：振作起来
    Dialogue IV: Pull Yourself Together

看图说话 Story Narration

小品表演 Skit Performance

练笔 Writing Exercise

第七单元听力练习 Listening Comprehension Unit 7

说 话 得 体
Learn to Speak Chinese through
Contextualized Dialogues

第八单元　Unit 8

★ 第一课 恭维
Lesson One Complimenting 201

★ 第二课 抱怨
Lesson Two Complaining 214

常用词句 Common Expressions

情景对话 Contextualized Dialogues

　　对话一：托你的福
　　Dialogue I: Thanks to You

　　对话二：找舞伴
　　Dialogue II: Looking for a Prom Date

　　对话三：乔迁之喜
　　Dialogue III: Congratulations on Moving to a New Home

　　对话四：名师出高徒
　　Dialogue IV: A Great Master Brings up Brilliant Disciples.

看图说话 Story Narration

小品表演 Skit Performance

练笔 Writing Exercise

常用词句 Common Expressions

情景对话 Contextualized Dialogues

　　对话一：不能随便
　　Dialogue I: Can't Do as You Wish

　　对话二：怎么回事
　　Dialogue II: What's the matter?

　　对话三：人影都没有
　　Dialogue III: Can't Find Him

　　对话四：习惯了就行
　　Dialogue IV: You Will Get Used to It

看图说话 Story Narration

小品表演 Skit Performance

练笔 Writing Exercise

第八单元听力练习 Listening Comprehension Unit 8

学生生活中常用的120句话
120 Popular Expressions in Daily Life Among Students 229

附录一：外语学习阶段准则(简介)
Appendix I: The Language Learning Continuum 239

附录二：《说话得体》教学安排
Appendix II: Instructional Plan for Speaking Chinese through Contextualized Dialogues 254

附录三：《说话得体》教学课时安排(仅供参考)
Appendix III: Daily Agenda for Teaching and Learning(for reference only) 267

附录四：《说话得体》总体教学要求参考与自我检测
Appendix IV: General Instructional Requirement and Self-Evaluations 272

附录五：听力练习文本
Appendix V: Text for Listening Comprehension 279

词语总表 Vocabulary 284

第一单元
Unit 1

第一课 问候
Lesson One Greetings

常用词句
Common Expressions

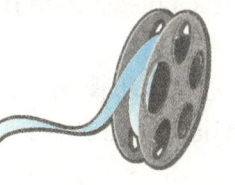

常用词句 Common Expressions	回应提示参考 Suggested Responses
1 你好! Hello!	你好!Hello! 好!Hi.
2 你好吗? How are you?	我很好。I am very well! 还不错。Pretty good. 马马虎虎。I'm fine.
3 早上好!(晚上好!) Good morning! / Good evening! 早! Morning!	早上好!(晚上好!) Good morning! / Good evening! 早! Morning!
4 你吃饭了吧? Have you eaten yet?	刚吃完,你呢? Yes, I have. How about you?
5 你这是去上班吧? Are you going to work?	就是啊。 Yes. 你是怎么知道的? How did you know?

3

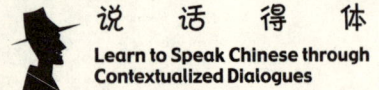

说 话 得 体
Learn to Speak Chinese through Contextualized Dialogues

常用词句 Common Expressions	回应提示参考 Suggested Responses
6 啊!你就是陈功先生。 久仰!久仰! Wow! You are Mr. Chen Gong. It's a pleasure to finally meet you.	幸会!幸会! It's nice to meet you.
7 见到你很高兴! Glad to meet you.	见到你我也很高兴。 I am also glad to meet you./Glad to meet you too.
8 你近来怎么样? How are you doing?	不错,谢谢你的关心。 Pretty well. Thank you for asking!
9 你身体好吗?(别来无恙吧?) How is your health?	托你的福,还不错。 Thank you, not bad.
10 最近你忙吗? Have you been busy recently?	是啊!有点忙。你呢? Yes, I've been a bit busy. How about you?
11 李先生,你这一阵子去哪儿了? 久违了! Mr. Li, where have you been these days? I haven't seen you for a long time.	是啊。好久不见了。 That's right. We haven't seen each other for a long time.
12 是什么风把您吹来的? What brings you here?	你没想到吧。我这是临时决定的,没来得及通知你。 You probably weren't expecting me. I just decided to come at the last minute and didn't have time to tell you.
13 稀客,稀客! What a surprise!	是啊。我好不容易才找到你。 Indeed, it took me a long time to find you.
14 好久不见,你可发了! It's been so long since we've seen each other. You look great.	哪里,哪里!那是托你的福。 Thanks. So do you.

4

第一单元 第一课 问候
Unit 1　Lesson One　Greetings

常用词句 Common Expressions	回应提示参考 Suggested Responses
15 一路上好吗？ Did you have a good trip?	很好。旅途很轻松。 Very good! The trip was very relaxed.
16 昨晚睡得好吗？ Did you sleep well last night?	很好！躺下就睡着了。一觉睡到天亮。 Very well. I fell asleep as soon as I lay down, and didn't wake up until this morning.
17 请代我向你父母亲问好！ Please give my regards to your parents.	一定，一定！谢谢，谢谢！ I will. Thanks!
18 欢迎！欢迎！（欢迎光临！） Welcome!	谢谢！ Thank you!
19 恭喜发财！ Wishing you happiness and prosperity!	发财，发财！大家都发财！ Same to you. Good fortune to all.
20 祝你生日快乐！ Happy Birthday!	谢谢！ Thank you so much!

情景对话
Contextualized Dialogues

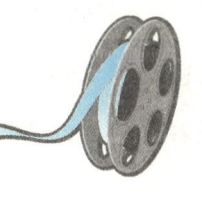

 对话一：您说着了
Dialogue 1: You Are Right

人物 Characters	甲：李先生，一位老人 A: Mr. Li, an old man	乙：陈先生，一位年轻人 B: Mr. Chen, a young man

5
Unit 1　Lesson One　Greetings

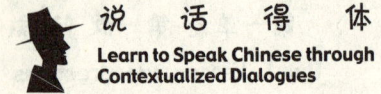

关 系 Relationship	在两位邻居之间 Between two neighbors
情 景 Location	在街上 In the street

甲：早上好，老李。
A：Good morning, Lao Li.

乙：早上好，小陈。
B：Good morning, Xiao Chen.

甲：您这是去哪儿？
A：Where are you going?

乙：我去街口买早点。你呢？你是去公园打太极拳吧？
B：I am going to the street corner to get some breakfast. How about you? Are you going to the park to practice Tai-Chi?

甲：真叫您给说着了。
A：Yes, I am.

 词语表　New Words

您	nín	you (polite)
街口	jiē kǒu	street corner
早点	zǎodiǎn	breakfast
太极拳	tàijíquán	Tai-Chi, traditional Chinese shadowboxing
说着了	shuō zháo le	What you say is correct.

 对话二：恭喜，贺喜
Dialogue II: Congratulations

人 物 Characters	甲：一位高中生 A：A high school student	乙：一位大学生 B：A college student

6

Unit 1　Lesson One　Greetings

关 系 Relationship	在两位以前的邻居之间 Between two former neighbors
情 景 Location	在图书馆 In the library

甲：你这是在干什么呢?
A：What are you doing?

乙：马上要考试了，我在复习。好久没见到你了，最近忙什么呢?
B：I have a test coming up soon, and I am reviewing. Haven't seen you for a long time. How have you been?

甲：我爸爸妈妈刚买了新房子，我现在正忙着帮他们搬家呢。
A：My parents have just bought a new house. I am busy helping them move now.

乙：住新房，这可是大喜事。恭喜，贺喜啦!请代我向你父母亲问好!
B：Moving to a new house, how exciting! Congratulations! Please give my regards to your parents.

甲：一定，一定。
A：I will.

 词语表　New Words

最近	zuìjìn	recently
喜事	xǐshì	joyous occasion; happy event
恭喜	gōngxǐ	congratulate
代	dài	in place of; on behalf of
一定	yīdìng	surely; certainly

 对话三：欢迎光临
Dialogue III：Welcome

人物 Characters	甲：一位歌唱家 A：A singer	乙：一位电影明星 B：A movie actor

7

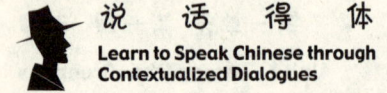
说话得体
Learn to Speak Chinese through Contextualized Dialogues

关 系 Relationship	在两位名人之间 Between two celebrities
情 景 Location	在庆祝会上 At a celebration

甲：先生，贵姓？
A：Sir, what's your name?

乙：姓陈，我是陈功。
B：My last name is Chen. I am Chen Gong.

甲：啊，您就是陈功先生啊！久仰，久仰！
A：Wow! You are Mr. Chen Gong. It's a pleasure to finally meet you.

乙：不敢，不敢。请问，先生，您尊姓大名？
B：It's very kind of you. What is your name?

甲：姓刘，名华德。
A：My last name is Liu and my first name is Huade.

乙：幸会，幸会！刘先生，欢迎大驾光临。
B：It's great to meet you, Mr. Liu.

 词语表　New Words

久仰	jiǔyǎng	It's a pleasure to finally meet you.
不敢（当）	bù gǎn (dāng)	It's very kind of you.
尊姓大名	zūnxìng dàmíng	What is your name?
幸会	xìnghuì	It's great to meet you.
大驾光临	dàjià guānglín	your gracious presence

Unit 1　Lesson One　Greetings

 对话四：稀客
Dialogue IV：What a Rare Visitor

人　物 Characters	甲：一位大学老教授 A：An old university professor	乙：一位美国学者 B：An American scholar
关　系 Relationship	在两位很久没见面的学者之间 Between two scholars who haven't seen each other for a long time	
情　景 Location	在中国人的家中 At a residence in China	

甲：哎哟！稀客，稀客！怎么会是你呢？
A：Look! What a surprise! What brings you here?

乙：没想到吧。
B：You must not have had the faintest idea.

甲：什么风把你吹来了？
A：What brings you here?

乙：我刚从美国来。很高兴又见到您了。您好！
B：I just came from the United States. I am glad to see you again. How are you?

甲：谢谢！好久不见了，你身体怎么样？
A：Thank you. I haven't seen you for a long time. How is your health?

乙：还不错。您呢？
B：Pretty good. How about you?

甲：我？硬朗着呢。快！请进屋说话吧。
A：Very good. Please, come in. Let's chat inside.

 词语表　New Words

稀客	xīkè	rare guest
风	fēng	wind
吹	chuī	blow
身体	shēntǐ	health; body
不错	búcuò	pretty well; not bad
硬朗	yìnglang	strong and healthy; sprightly

9

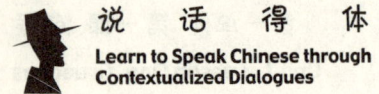

看图说话
Story Narration

按照以下图画顺序及各幅图画所提示的情景，叙述一个有始有终的完整故事。

Based on the order of the following pictures and the situations presented in each, narrate a story including a beginning and an end.

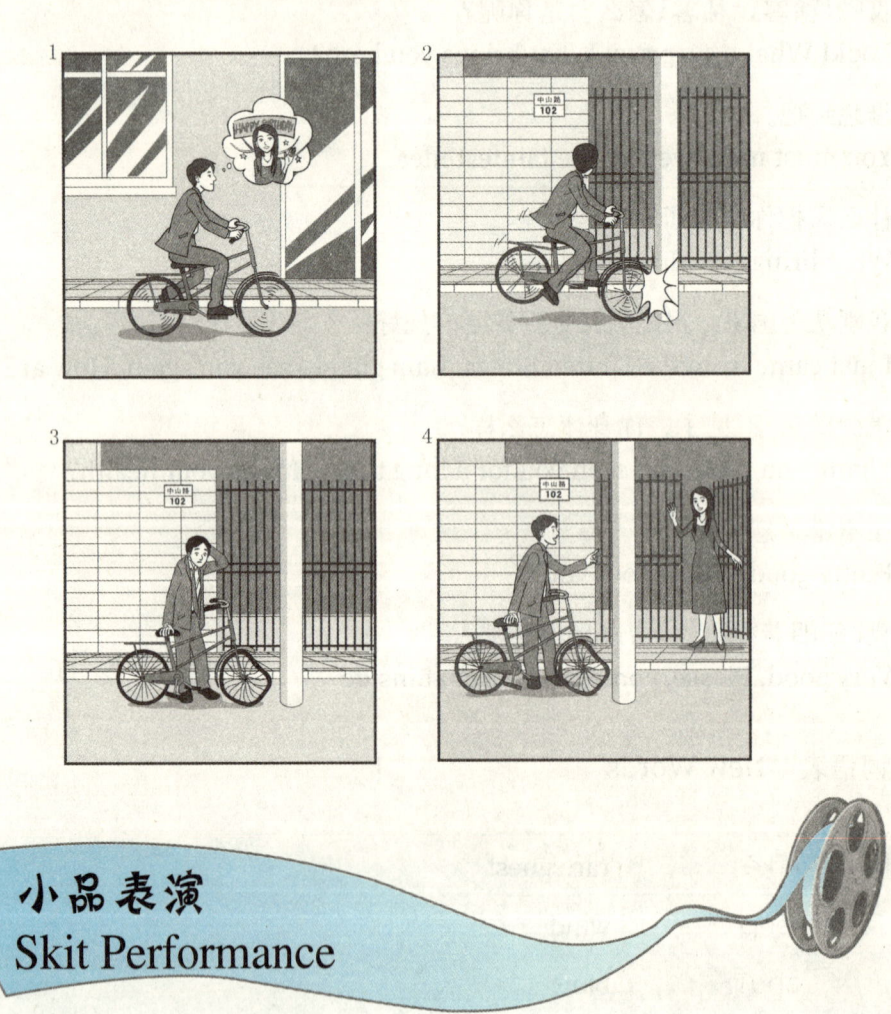

小品表演
Skit Performance

学生创作对话小品时尽可能使用本单元列出的和学生学到的新词、新句。小品主题选择应该得到老师首肯，以免重复。

10

Unit 1　Lesson One　Greetings

Create situational dialogues with topics approved by the teacher to avoid repetition. Use as many expressions listed/learned in this unit as possible.

对话地点（时间） Place (Time) of Dialogue	对话情景 Context	对话者之间的关系 Relation Between Speakers
1　在学校家长会上 at a parent-teacher conference	认出对方 recognizing the other party	在两位学生家长之间 between two parents
2　在医生诊所里 at a clinic	看病 visiting a doctor	在医生和病人之间 between a doctor and a patient
3　在超级市场里 inside a supermarket	购物 shopping	在街坊邻居之间 between two neighbors
4　在饭馆里 at a restaurant	用餐 dining	在客人和服务员之间 between a guest and a waiter/waitress
5　在健身房锻炼身体时 at the gym while exercising	遇见一位名人 meeting a celebrity	在仰慕者和电影明星之间 between an admirer and a movie star
6　在街头巷尾 in the street (or in an alley)	遇见以前的同学 meeting a former classmate	在两位老同学之间 between two former classmates
7　在公车上 on a bus	遇见老熟人 meeting an old acquaintance	在两位邻居（同学、同事）之间 between neighbors (classmates or colleagues)
8　在电影院门口 at the entrance of a movie theater	相见 meeting someone	在两位朋友之间 between two friends
9　在白宫参观入口处 at the entrance to the White House	安全检查 passing security check	在警察和观光客之间 between a policeman and a tourist
10　在商场里 at a shopping mall	寻找厕所 looking for a restroom	在营业员和顾客之间 between a salesperson and a customer

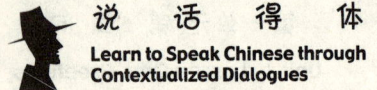

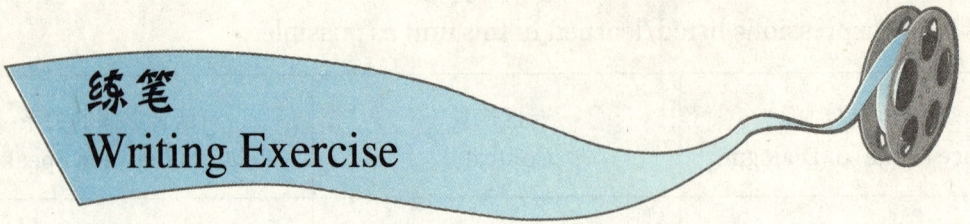

根据要求写一篇短文,尽可能用上本单元学到的词句。

Write a short passage on the given topic. Do your best to use words and expressions from the sentence patterns you have learned in this unit.

留言 (Write a short message for someone who can't be reached at the moment.)

第二课 告别
Lesson Two   Saying Farewell

常用词句
Common Expressions

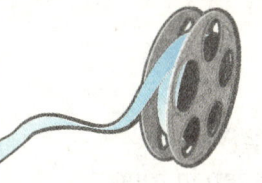

常用词句 Common Expressions	回应提示参考 Suggested Responses
1 再见！ Goodbye!	再见！ Goodbye!
2 回头见！ See you around!	回见！ See you later.
3 我们就到那个时候再见面吧。 We will meet then.	好，一言为定。 Good. It's settled.
4 我在学校大门那儿等你。 I will wait for you at the school's main gate.	不见不散！ OK. I will wait for you there.
5 祝你玩得痛快！ Have fun!	那是一定的啦！ Certainly!
6 祝你称心如意！ Hope you have a good time!	谢谢。 Thanks!
7 祝你学习顺利！ Hope you do well with your studies!	一定不辜负你的期望。 I won't let you down. / I'll try my best.

13

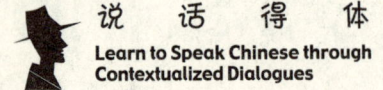

常用词句 Common Expressions	回应提示参考 Suggested Responses
8 我是来向你告别的。 I came to say goodbye.	怎么,你要走了?你应该早一点告诉我,我也好给你饯行。 Why do you have to leave? You should have told me earlier, then I could have had a farewell party for you.
9 经常联系。 Keep in touch!	我会的。 I will.
10 常来电话(写信、发电子邮件)。 Call me./Write me./Send me emails.	我记住了。 I will.
11 欢迎你再来。 You are welcome to visit again.	那是一定的。我也请你方便时去我那儿坐坐。 Thanks. You are also welcome to visit my place any time.
12 时间不早了,我得走了。咱们改天再聊吧。 It's getting late. I should get going. We will chat later.	时间过得真快。好,我们今天就谈到这儿。后会有期。 Time flies! Okay. See you next time.
13 咱们真是相见恨晚。 I wish I could have known you before.	我也同样有这种感觉。 Me, too. / I feel the same way.
14 以后你就是我这儿的常客了。 From now on, you are my guest.	对对对!一回生,二回熟嘛。以后我们就是朋友了。 That's right. From now on, we are friends.
15 有问题,尽管来找我。千万别见外。 Don't hesitate to drop by if you have any trouble. Don't be a stranger.	有你这句话,我就放心了。 Thanks. I appreciate it.
16 我真舍不得离开老朋友。 I hate to leave you.	后会有期,我们还会见面的。 See you later. We will meet again soon.

14

Unit 1 Lesson Two Saying Farewell

常用词句 Common Expressions	回应提示参考 Suggested Responses
17 不要送了，请留步。 You don't need to see me off.	没关系啦。 It's fine.
18 恕不远送。 Sorry for leaving you here.	好，咱们就在这儿分手吧。 I guess we should part here.
19 天下没有不散的筵席，我们就各奔前程吧！ Good things always come to an end. We have to take our leave.	对，来日方长！再见！ Right, we will have quite a few opportunities in the future. Goodbye!
20 请多多保重！一路平安！ Take care! Bon voyage!	你也保重。请回吧。 You take care, too. Please go back.

情景对话
Contextualized Dialogues

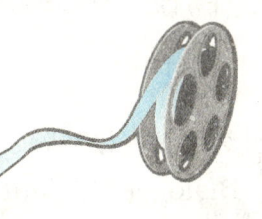

对话一：时间不早了
Dialogue I：It's Getting Late.

人物 Characters	甲：妹妹 A：Younger sister	乙：哥哥 B：Elder brother
关系 Relationship	在兄妹之间 Between a brother and a sister	
情景 Location	在家中 At home	

15

说 话 得 体
Learn to Speak Chinese through Contextualized Dialogues

甲：时间不早了，你应该去上班了。
A：It's getting late. You should go to work.

乙：你也应该去学校上课了。
B：You should go to school for class as well.

甲：再见。
A：Good-bye!

乙：再见。
B：Good-bye!

词语表　New Words

时间	shíjiān	time
应该	yīnggāi	should; must
上（下）班	shàng(xià) bān	go to work (get off work)
上（下）课	shàng(xià) kè	go to or attend class (dismiss or finish class)

对话二：接着聊
Dialogue II: Continue to Talk

人物 Characters	甲：一位高中生 A：A high school student	乙：一位高中生 B：A high school student
关系 Relationship	在两位同学之间 Between two classmates	
情景 Location	在学校 At a high school	

甲：对不起，我得马上去上课了。
A：I am sorry. I have to go to class right now.

乙：我也得走。咱们放学后再接着聊吧。
B：I also have to leave. How about we continue our chat after school?

第一单元 第二课 告别
Unit 1　Lesson Two　Saying Farewell

甲：好哇！那放学以后，我在学校门口等你。我们去喝咖啡。
A：Wonderful! I will wait for you at the school gate. We can go for coffee.

乙：好，好！回头见。
B：Excellent! We will meet each other then.

甲：不见不散。
A：I'll wait for you there.

词语表　New Words

马上	mǎshàng	immediately
接着	jiēzhe	go on; continue
聊	liáo	to chat
回头见	huítóujiàn	see you later
不见不散	bù jiàn bù sàn	not leave without seeing each other

对话三：保持联系
Dialogue III：Keep in Touch

人物 Characters	甲：一位实验室技术员 A：A lab technician	乙：一位从外地来的技术员 B：A technician from another place
关系 Relationship	在两位刚认识的工作人员之间 Between two technicians who had just met each other	
情景 Location	在实验室门口 At the door of a lab	

甲：很幸运认识你。希望不久能再见到你。
A：It was great to meet you. I hope to see you again soon.

乙：我也是。咱们是不是有点儿相知恨晚？
B：Me too. I wish we have known each other earlier.

甲：没关系，一回生，二回熟嘛。我们以后保持联系。

17

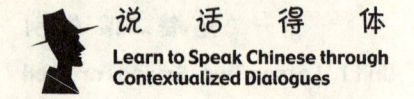

说 话 得 体
Learn to Speak Chinese through Contextualized Dialogues

A: It doesn't matter. We didn't know each other well, but we will be friends soon. From now on we will keep in touch.

乙：当然啦！咱们一言为定。
B: Of course. It's settled.

甲：好，后会有期。
A: Great! We will meet again.

乙：再见！
B: Goodbye!

词语表　　New Words

幸运	xìngyùn	fortunate; lucky
希望	xīwàng	to hope
不久	bùjiǔ	before long
相知（见）恨晚	xiāng zhī (jiàn) hèn wǎn	too late to know each other
生	shēng	unacquainted; new; strange(r)
熟	shú	familiar; experienced

对话四：尽管来找我
Dialogue IV：Feel Free to Visit Me

人物 Characters	甲：一位资深教授 A：A senior professor	乙：一位从外地来的年轻教授 B：A junior professor from another place
关系 Relationship	在两位刚认识的教授之间 Between two professors who had just met each other	
情景 Location	在办公室门口 At the door of an office	

甲：希望不久能在这儿再见到你。
A: I hope to be able to meet you here again.

18

Unit 1 Lesson Two Saying Farewell

乙：我也欢迎丁教授有机会去我们那儿看看，指导指导。
B： I also welcome you, Prof. Ding, to come to my place when you have the chance. I'd appreciate some pointers.

甲：有机会我一定去。你有问题尽管来找我，打电话写信都行。
A： Whenever I have the opportunity, I will certainly come. Please feel free to visit me when you have any problems, or call me or send me a letter (e-mail). It's all fine by me.

乙：有问题一定会来请教。非常感谢您！
B： If I have any question, I will certainly turn to you for help. I am grateful to you.

甲：没关系。这都是我应该做的。
A： No problem. I am here to help.

乙：不要送了，请留步。
B： You don't need to see me out.

甲：恕不远送，你走好，多保重，祝你一路平安。
A： Sorry for not escorting you any further. Take care! Have a good trip.

词语表 New Words

机会	jīhuì	opportunity
指导	zhǐdǎo	to direct; to instruct
尽管	jǐnguǎn	feel free; not hesitate to
请教	qǐngjiào	ask for advice; consult
留步	liúbù	don't bother to come any further
恕不远送	shù bù yuǎn sòng	sorry not to escort you further
走好	zǒuhǎo	walk with care
保重	bǎozhòng	take care
平安	píng'ān	safe and sound

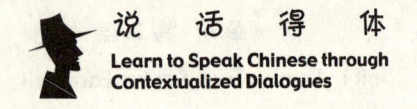

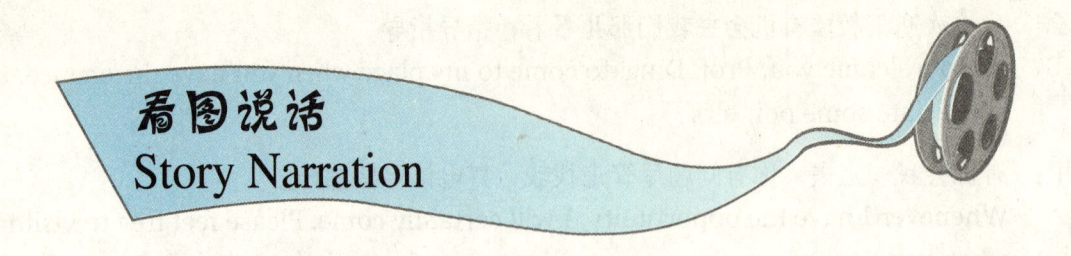

说话得体
Learn to Speak Chinese through Contextualized Dialogues

看图说话
Story Narration

按照以下图画顺序及各幅图画所提示的情景，叙述一个有始有终的完整故事。

Based on the order of the following pictures and the situations presented in each, narrate a story including a beginning and an end.

第一单元 第二课 告别
Unit 1 Lesson Two Saying Farewell

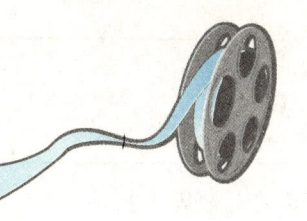

小品表演
Skit Performance

学生创作对话小品时尽可能使用本单元列出的和学生学到的新词、新句。小品主题选择应该得到老师首肯，以免重复。

Create situational dialogues with topics approved by the teacher to avoid repetition. Use as many expressions listed/learned in this unit as possible.

对话地点（时间） Place (Time) of Dialogue	对话情景 Context	对话者之间的关系 Relation Between Speakers
1 在出租车上 in a taxi	到了目的地 having arrived at the destination	在司机和乘客之间 between a taxi driver and a passenger
2 在机场候机室 at the waiting room of an airport	送别朋友 seeing off a friend	在两位同学之间 between two classmates
3 在家门口 at the gate of one's house	送客 saying farewell to a visitor	在两位老师之间 between two teachers
4 在教室里 in the classroom	课刚结束 right after class	在老师和学生之间 between a teacher and a student
5 在办公室里 in the office	同事找到新工作 a colleague has found a new job	在两位同事之间 between two colleagues
6 在电话里 on the phone	约会 making an appointment	在两位同学之间 between two classmates
7 在大剧院门口 at the entrance of a grand theater	音乐会散场 a concert has just ended	在两位音乐爱好者之间 between two music lovers
8 在毕业典礼结束时 at the commencement after it has ended	相互告别 bidding farewell to each other	在两位毕业生之间 between two graduates

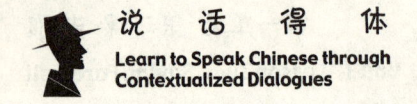

9	在火车上 on a train	到站了 having arrived at the destination	在两位乘客之间 between two passengers
10	在轮船码头上 at the pier	父母坐游轮去欧洲度假 parents going on a cruise to Europe	在子女和父母之间 between a child and his/her parents

练笔
Writing Exercise

根据要求写一篇短文。尽可能用上本单元学到的词句。

Write a short passage on the given topic. Do your best to use words and expressions from the sentence patterns you have learned in this unit.

告别高中时代演说辞 (Write a commencement speech to bid farewell to your high school.)

第一单元听力练习
Listening Comprehension Unit 1

听完以下各项听力练习的内容，先回答理解提示中的问题，再识别句子或语段的语境，然后尽可能使用本单元列出的和学到的新词、新句作出适当的回应。

After listening to the sentences given, identify a proper context and response in each situation, using as many expressions listed/learned in this unit as possible.

	1. 理解提示 Comprehension	2. 情景识别 Context Identification	3. 学生回应 Student's Response
1	Where is Mr. Li going?		是啊！你也是去吃饭吧？
2	What happened?		
3	What does the speaker ask about?		
4	Who came to school?		
5	What has the listener just accomplished?		
6	Where will the listener live next time he visits?		
7	Who is speaking?		
8	Where does the listener go?		
9	What is the speaker going to do?		
10	What will the listener do?		

23

第二单元
Unit 2

第一课 介绍
Lesson One Introducing

常用词句
Common Expressions

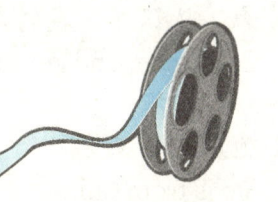

常用词句 Common Expressions	回应提示参考 Suggested Responses
1 我是张儒思。 I am Zhang Rusi.	你好！我是白一道。 How do you do! I am Bai Yidao.
2 我姓黄，叫黄大中。 My last name is Huang. My full name is Huang Dazhong.	你好！我姓洪，叫晓凤。 How do you do! My last name is Hong. My full name is Hong Xiaofeng.
3 我今年三十七岁。 I am 37 years old [of age].	你看上去很年轻。 You look very young.
4 他的名字叫王中华。 His name is Wang Zhonghua.	谢谢你告诉我。 Thank you for telling me.
5 我来自我介绍一下。 Let me introduce myself.	好，请，请。 That's good. Please!
6 我姓李，木子李。 My last name is Li. The character of Li consists of components "mu" and "zi".	幸会！幸会！很高兴认识你。 How fortunate! Nice to meet you.
7 我是随访问团来这儿的。 I am here with the delegation.	欢迎，欢迎！ Welcome!

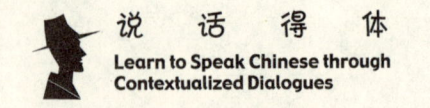

说 话 得 体
Learn to Speak Chinese through Contextualized Dialogues

常用词句 Common Expressions	回应提示参考 Suggested Responses
8 你有没有见过林教授? Have you met Prof. Lin before?	没有。请你为我引见一下。 No, will you please introduce me to him?
9 来,认识一下我的老板。 Come over and get to know my boss.	这位先生是姚经理吧? Is this Mr. Yao, the manager?
10 他从中国来。 He is from China.	欢迎远道来的客人。 Welcome our guest from afar.
11 我住在苏州。 I live in Suzhou.	听说过,那是一个好地方。 I was told that is a good place.
12 我在北京大学念书(工作)。 I study (work) at Peking University.	那可是一个好学校。我曾经去过。 That's a good university. I have been there before.
13 我喜欢看京剧。 I like to watch Peking Opera.	是吗?我也喜欢。 Really? I like it, too.
14 我是上海话剧团的,慕名而来取经。我是不请自来啊。 I'm from Shanghai Modern Drama Troupe. I've heard about your fame in the field and come here to learn from you. I am here unexpectedly.	欢迎,欢迎! Welcome!
15 我从事传媒工作。 I work in mass media.	那可不是一般的工作。一定很有意思。 That is not an ordinary job. It must be very interesting.
16 让我来(为你俩)介绍一下。 Allow me to introduce you (two) to each other.	太好了! Wonderful!
17 这(位)是李杰先生。 This is Mr. Li Jie.	李先生,久仰,久仰! Mr. Li, It's a pleasure to finally meet you.

Unit 2 Lesson One Introducing

常用词句 Common Expressions	回应提示参考 Suggested Responses
18 我们很荣幸请到了杨教授。 It is a great honor to have (invite) Professor Yang here.	欢迎！欢迎！ Welcome!
19 我代表可口可乐公司。 I represent the Coca Cola Company.	欢迎光临，指导工作。 You are welcome to inspect and direct our work.
20 这是我的名片。 This is my business card.	谢谢！可是我没有准备名片。 Thank you, but I haven't prepared my business cards.

情景对话
Contextualized Dialogues

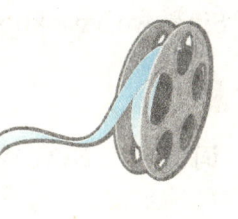

对话一：不必客套
Dialogue I：No Need to Be So Formal.

人物 Characters	甲：某公司代表　　　　　　乙：另一家公司代表 A：A company's representative　B：Another company's representative
关系 Relationship	在两位商务代表之间 Between two business representatives
情景 Location	在会客厅 At a reception room

29

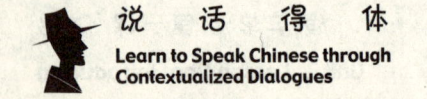

说　话　得　体
Learn to Speak Chinese through Contextualized Dialogues

甲：您好！我猜您是孔方圆先生吧？
A: How are you! I guess you must be Mr. Kong Fangyuan.

乙：正是，我是孔方圆。先生，您贵姓？
B: That's me. I am Kong Fangyuan. Can I get your surname, Sir?

甲：我姓李，叫李强，是大兴公司的代表。欢迎，欢迎。
A: My last name is Li, and I am Li Qiang. I represent the Daxing Company. Welcome.

乙：谢谢！很高兴在这儿见到您。虽说这是我们第一次见面，其实我们早就是老朋友了。
B: Thank you! I am glad to meet you here. Although this is our first meeting, we are actually old friends.

甲：是的，是的。我们在电子邮件交往中打过交道，只是从未见过面。
A: Oh! Yes! We have been in contact through exchanging emails, but had never met each other.

乙：既然是熟人，咱们就不必客套了。
B: Since we have known each other well, let's cut out the formality.

词语表　New Words

猜	cāi	to guess
正	zhèng	just; exactly; precisely
代表	dàibiǎo	representative; to represent; on behalf of
虽说	suīshuō	although
其实	qíshí	in fact
电子邮件	diànzǐ yóujiàn	email
打交道	dǎ jiāodao	to come into contact; have dealings with
见面	jiànmiàn	to meet
不必	búbì	needn't
客套	kètào	courteous

Unit 2 Lesson One Introducing

第二单元 第一课 介绍

对话二：听好消息
Dialogue II：Hearing Good News

人 物 Characters	甲：一位老师 A：A teacher	乙：一位年轻男士 B：A young man	丙：一位年轻女士 C：A young woman
关 系 Relationship	婚姻介绍 Match Making		
情 景 Location	在公园门口 At the entrance of a park		

甲：首先让我来为你们俩介绍一下。这是林文静小姐，东亚系讲师。这位是秦志豪先生，我的好朋友。

A：First, let me introduce you to each other. This is Ms. Lin Wenjing, a lecturer at the East Asian Studies Department. This is Mr. Qin Zhihao, my good friend.

乙：林小姐，您好！我在福特汽车公司公关部门工作。

B：Hi! Ms. Lin. I work at the Public Relations Division of Ford Automobile Company.

丙：您好！很高兴认识你，秦先生。

C：Hi! Glad to meet you, Mr. Qin.

甲：你们俩就慢慢儿谈吧。我有事先告辞了。回头听你们的好消息。

A：You two may take your time chatting. I am a bit busy and have to leave first. I am looking forward to hearing the good news from you later.

丙：谢谢！王老师，您走好！

C：Thank you, Mr. Wang. Take care.

乙：王思贤，辛苦你了。改日再谢你。

B：Wang Sixian, I appreciate your efforts. I will find some other day to say thanks.

词语表　New Words

首先	shǒuxiān	first
介绍	jièshào	to introduce
讲师	jiǎngshī	lecturer

31

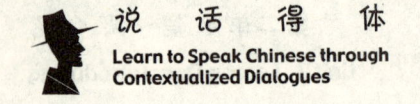

说话得体
Learn to Speak Chinese through
Contextualized Dialogues

部门	bùmén	department; division; section
告辞	gàocí	take leave; farewell
消息	xiāoxī	news; information
辛苦	xīnkǔ	effort; hardworking
改日	gǎirì	some other day

对话三：自我介绍
Dialogue III: Self-Introducing

人物 Characters	甲：一位学生代表 A: A student representative	乙：一位教师 B: A teacher
关系 Relationship	演讲者自我介绍 Speaker's self-introduction	
情景 Location	在演讲会上 At a lecture	

甲：今天我们很荣幸请到了李老师。现在请李老师跟大家讲几句话。

A: Today we have the great honor of having invited Mr. Li. Now let's welcome Mr. Li to give us a talk.

乙：谢谢！首先请允许我作一个自我介绍。我姓李，木子李。我叫李瑞杰。我以前是文化大学的讲师，在那儿教中文。后来我去了贝尔电话公司，被派往中国负责市场调查。两年前我受聘于华美商学院，一直在那儿工作到现在。我除了教中文以外，还讲授"中国企业管理"和"中国市场"两门课。最近我写了一本书，书名是《美中贸易前景》。

B: Thank you for your attendance. First please allow me to introduce myself. My last name is Li. The character "li" consists of two radical components, "mu" and "zi". I am Li Ruijie. I used to be a lecturer at Wenhua University. I was teaching Chinese there. Later I turned to Bell Telephone Company, and was sent to conduct their market research in China. Sino-America Business Institute hired me two years ago, and I have been working there till now. Besides teaching Chinese, I also teach two courses, "Business Management in China" and "Chinese Marketing". Recently I wrote a book. The title is *Prospects of Sino-US Trade*.

Unit 2　Lesson One　Introducing

甲：李老师，您能不能跟我们讲讲这本书？
A：Mr. Li, can you please talk about this book?

乙：当然可以。我来这儿就是要向你们介绍这本书的。
B：Of course. I am here for no other purpose but to introduce this book.

词语表　New Words

荣幸	róngxìng	be honored
讲话	jiǎnghuà	to speak; speech
允许	yǔnxǔ	allow; permit
自我	zìwǒ	oneself; self
文化	wénhuà	culture
派往	pàiwǎng	be sent to/for
负责	fùzé	be in charge of; responsible for
市场调查	shìchǎng diàochá	market research
讲授	jiǎngshòu	to lecture on
企业管理	qǐyè guǎnlǐ	business management
贸易	màoyì	trade
前景	qiánjǐng	prospect; vista
当然	dāngrán	of course

对话四：逛商场
Dialogue IV: Shopping

人　物 Characters	甲：顾客甲 A：Customer A	乙：顾客乙 B：Customer B
关　系 Relationship	在两位顾客之间 Between two customers	
情　景 Location	在购物中心 At a shopping center	

33

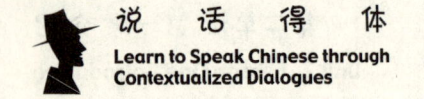

说话得体
Learn to Speak Chinese through Contextualized Dialogues

甲：友谊商城真大！我们先去哪个部门？
A: The Friendship Mall is really huge. Which department shall we visit first?

乙：看，这是一张商城导购图，上面有详细的介绍。
B: Look! Here is a Shopping Directory of the Mall. There is a detailed introduction to it.

甲：底层是食品、医药、烟酒等柜台。
A: The lobby has a food court, counters for medicines, tobacco and alcoholic drinks.

乙：二楼是服装商场。三楼是皮革制品、鞋帽部门。
B: The second floor is for clothing. The third floor has a department for leather goods, shoes and hats.

甲：四楼专卖化妆品和健身器材。五楼正在展销新式家具。
A: The fourth floor specifically sells cosmetics and fitness facilities. The fifth floor is conducting a sales exhibition for modern furniture.

乙：六楼有传统手工艺品，还有古董调剂市场。七楼有文具办公用品。
B: There are traditional arts and crafts products on the sixth floor. In addition, there is also an antiques market. On the seventh floor there are stationery and office supplies.

甲：八楼是家用电器部门。九楼是新华书店。
A: The eighth floor is the household electronic appliances department. There is a Xinhua Bookstore on the ninth floor.

乙：十楼是旋转餐厅，供应世界各国的饭菜点心和各种饮料。
B: The tenth floor is the rotating cafeteria, which provides dishes and snacks from all over the world, and various beverages, too.

甲：我们先坐电梯去十楼吃饭，然后慢慢儿地往下走，一层一层地逛。
A: Let's first take the elevator and go up to the tenth floor for a meal. After that, we can take our time going down, browsing one floor after another.

乙：好极了！我们吃饱了，喝足了，逛商场就更有劲儿了。
B: Terrific. When we have had food and drinks to our hearts' content, then we will have more fun (energy) visiting the mall.

词语表 New Words

| 友谊 | yǒuyì | friendship |
| 商城 | shāngchéng | shopping center; mall |

Unit 2 Lesson One Introducing

导购图	dǎogòutú	shopping guide; directory
详细	xiángxì	detailed
食品	shípǐn	food
医药	yīyào	medicine
烟酒	yānjiǔ	tobacco and alcoholic drinks
服装	fúzhuāng	clothing; fashion
皮革制品	pígé zhìpǐn	leatherwear
鞋帽	xiémào	shoes and hats
化妆品	huàzhuāngpǐn	cosmetics
健身器材	jiànshēn qìcái	fitness facilities
展销	zhǎnxiāo	sales exhibition
新式	xīnshì	new fashion; new style
家具	jiājù	furniture
传统	chuántǒng	tradition; traditional
手工艺品	shǒugōngyìpǐn	arts and crafts product
古董	gǔdǒng	antique
调剂	tiáojì	exchange and sell
文具	wénjù	stationery
办公用品	bàngōng yòngpǐn	office supply
家用电器	jiāyòng diànqì	household electrical appliances
新华书店	Xīnhuá Shūdiàn	Xinhua Bookstore
旋转餐厅	xuánzhuǎn cāntīng	rotating cafeteria
供应	gōngyìng	to supply
电梯	diàntī	elevator
逛	guàng	stroll; wander about
饱	bǎo	have eaten one's fill; be full
足	zú	sufficient
有劲	yǒujìn	energetic; interesting

看图说话
Story Narration

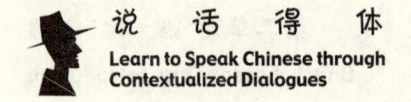

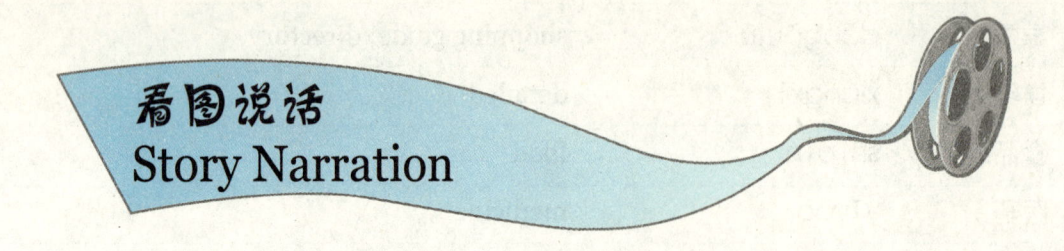

按照以下图画顺序及各幅图画所提示的情景，叙述一个有始有终的完整故事。

Based on the order of the following pictures and the situations presented in each, narrate a story including a beginning and an end.

小品表演
Skit Performance

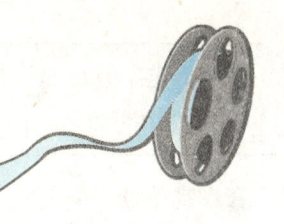

学生创作对话小品时尽可能使用本单元列出的和学生学到的新词、新句。小品主题选择应该得到老师首肯，以免重复。

Create situational dialogues with topics approved by the teacher to avoid repetition. Use as many expressions listed/learned in this unit as possible.

	对话地点（时间） Place (Time) of Dialogue	对话情景 Context	对话者之间的关系 Relation Between Speakers
1	在毕业班升学指导会上 at a high school recruitment advisory meeting	介绍一个高中 introducing a high school	在高中生和初中生之间 between a high school student and a middle school student
2	在家里 at home	向父母介绍新认识的朋友 introducing a new friend to parents	面对父母和朋友 facing parents and his/her friend
3	在旅游行程中 on a guided tour	介绍一个历史景观 introducing a historical site	在导游和旅游者之间 between a tour guide and a tourist
4	在电器商店购物时 when shopping at an electrical appliance store	介绍如何使用电脑 introducing how to use the computer	在营业员和顾客之间 between a salesperson and a customer
5	在逛商城时 shopping at a mall	介绍一个商业中心 introducing a shopping center	在服务台经理和顾客之间 between a service desk manager and a customer
6	在公园里 at a park	为朋友介绍对象 introducing a date	面对两位被介绍者 between a matchmaker and two people on a date
7	在返校日那天晚上 at the homecoming night	向父母介绍自己的老师 introducing the teacher to parents	面对父母和老师 between a student and his/her parents and teacher

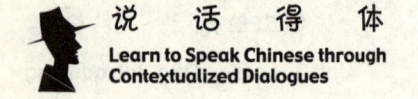

说 话 得 体
Learn to Speak Chinese through Contextualized Dialogues

8	在大街上 in the street	指点一条最便捷的路途 pointing out a short cut	在两位陌生人之间 between two strangers
9	在咖啡馆里 at a coffee shop	介绍当地的一个地标 introducing a local landmark	与来访的亲戚朋友交谈 talking to a relative or a friend
10	在办公室里 at the office	申请工作面谈：自我介绍 introducing oneself when applying for a job	在业主和申请者之间 between an employer and an applicant

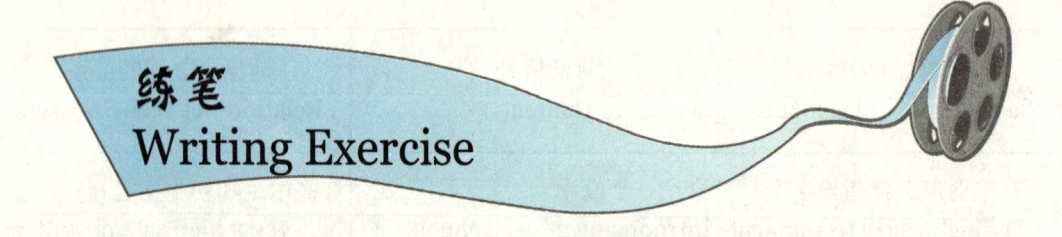

练笔
Writing Exercise

根据要求写一篇短文。尽可能用上本单元学到的词句。

Write a short passage on the given topic. Do your best to use words and expressions from the sentence patterns you have learned in this unit.

竞选学生会主席的演说辞(Write a speech on the topic of running for the president of the student union.)

第二课 推荐
Lesson Two Recommending

常用词句
Common Expressions

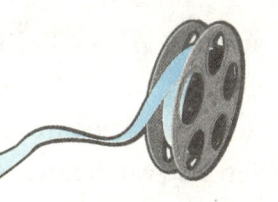

常用词句 Common Expressions	回应提示参考 Suggested Responses
1 今天我向大家推荐一个新建的游乐中心。 Today I present everyone with a newly built entertainment center.	那我倒要好好听听。 Then I think this will be good.
2 这儿是故宫，又叫紫禁城，是明清两个朝代的皇宫。 Here is the Imperial Palace, which is also called the Forbidden City. It was the palace for both the Ming and Qing dynasties.	我是第一次看到这么大的宫殿。 This is my first time visiting such a big palace.
3 这是（那是）一个杂技城。 This is (That is) an acrobatic center.	我早就知道了。 I already knew that.
4 这本书讲的是伦理道德。 This book is about moral principles.	我没有兴趣。 I am not interested in it.
5 这门课是必修课。 This is a required course.	一定很难吧。 It must be very difficult.
6 下一个产品是百事可乐公司推出的新型饮料。	那会是什么东西呢？ What product could it be?

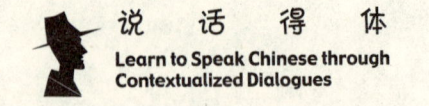

说 话 得 体
Learn to Speak Chinese through Contextualized Dialogues

常用词句 Common Expressions	回应提示参考 Suggested Responses
The next product is a new beverage recently introduced by the Pepsi-Cola Company.	
7　他是从(在)一百位候选者中挑选出来的。 He was selected from among one hundred candidates.	真的吗? Really?
8　这是一种新的教学方法,其特点是学生不必死记硬背。 This is a new pedagogical method. Its special feature is that students don't have to use rote memorization.	听起来有点儿意思。 It sounds interesting.
9　他的专长是计算机图像设计,优点是乐于接受他人意见。 His specialty is designing computer graphics, and he is willing and happy to accept suggestions.	不错。 Not bad.
10　这位学生唯一的缺点是与人交往时不够主动。 This student's only shortcoming is not having enough initiative while associating with others.	那也不一定是缺点。 It is not necessarily a shortcoming.
11　李先生做事认真负责,值得信赖。 Mr. Li is serious and responsible in doing things, therefore he is trustworthy (reliable).	我欣赏的就是这种人。 I think highly of people like him.
12　你先试试看,我想你会喜欢的。 Please try it. I am sure you will like it.	好,我就先试试看。 Fine, let me try it.
13　我给你买的礼物是不会让你失望的。 The gift I bought for you will not	但愿如此。 I hope not.

40

常用词句 Common Expressions	回应提示参考 Suggested Responses
disappoint you.	
14 我向你介绍的这台电视机，包你满意。 You are guaranteed satisfaction with the television set I recommend.	好，我相信你。 Fine, I trust you.
15 林中天是徐教授推荐的人，绝对错不了。 Lin Zhongtian is the candidate recommended by Prof. Lin. He is absolutely perfect.	那是当然。 Of course.
16 北京全聚德饭店是以烤鸭而出名的。 Beijing's Quan Ju De Restaurant is known for its roast duck.	让我们进去看一看。 Let's go in and have a look.
17 这种酒杯是用特选的玛瑙制成的。 This wine cup is made of (specially selected) agate.	看上去不错。 It looks pretty good.
18 在电视塔塔顶你可以看到这个城市的全景。 You may have a bird's eye view of the city from the top of the TV tower.	真的吗？ Are you sure?

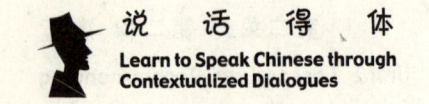

情景对话
Contextualized Dialogues

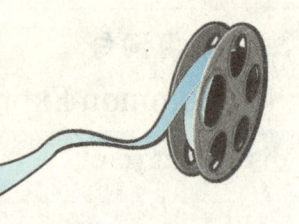

对话一：读个痛快
Dialogue I: Read with Pleasure

人 物 Characters	甲：一位读者 A: A reader	乙：一位图书馆馆员 B: A librarian
关 系 Relationship	在图书馆馆员和读者之间 Between a librarian and a reader	
情 景 Location	在图书馆 At the library	

甲：这是一本什么书？
A: What is this book?

乙：这是中国四大古典名著之一的《三国演义》，作者是明代初期的罗贯中。
B: This is *The Romance of Three Kingdoms*, one of the four well-known Chinese classics. The author is Luo Guanzhong who lived during the early days of the Ming Dynasty.

甲：书里面讲的是什么？
A: What is the book about?

乙：这本书所讲述的是公元三世纪时魏、蜀、吴鼎足三分的故事。
B: This book tells about a situation dominated by three powerful rivals, the warring States of Wei, Shu and Wu during the 3rd century AD.

甲：原来这是一本历史小说啊。值得读一读吗？
A: It is a historical novel then. Is it worth reading?

乙：非常值得，《三国演义》这本书文字精练，结构宏大，人物众多，情节曲折，是中国历朝小说中艺术成就最高的著作之一。
B: It really is worth reading. *The Romance of Three Kingdoms* is characterized by refined writing, grand structure, numerous characters, and complicated plots. It is

one of the greatest works, reaching the highest artistic achievement throughout all Chinese dynasties.

甲：那我今天就把《三国演义》借回家，读个痛快。

A：I will borrow it today and enjoy the pleasure of reading it.

词语表　New Words

古典	gǔdiǎn	classical
名著	míngzhù	masterpiece; famous work
作者	zuòzhě	writer; author
(朝)代	(cháo)dài	dynasty
初期	chūqī	prime; initial stage
讲述	jiǎngshù	tell about; give an account of
公元	gōngyuán	the Christian era; AD
世纪	shìjì	century
鼎足三分	dǐngzú sān fēn	a situation dominated by three powerful rivals
故事	gùshi	story
值得	zhídé	worthy; worth
文字	wénzì	characters; script; writing
精练	jīngliàn	refine; concise
结构	jiégòu	structure
宏大	hóngdà	grand; immense; vast
众多	zhòngduō	numerous; multitudinous
情节	qíngjié	plot; story; details
曲折	qūzhé	tortuous; complicated; twists and turns
艺术	yìshù	art
成就	chéngjiù	achievement; accomplishment; success
著作	zhùzuò	literary works
痛快	tòngkuài	joyful; to one's great satisfaction

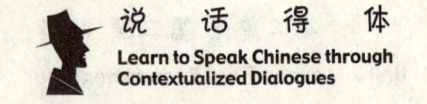

说 话 得 体
Learn to Speak Chinese through Contextualized Dialogues

对话二：不会让你失望
Dialogue II: You Won't Be Disappointed.

人 物 Characters	甲： 一位项目经理 A： A project manager	乙： 一位中文老师 B： A Chinese teacher
关 系 Relationship	在两位老朋友之间 Between two old friends	
情 景 Location	在办公室 At the office	

甲： 刘老师，我们展览会下个月开幕，急需一个中文讲解员。您是否能从高级中文班里挑选一个学生推荐给展览会？
A： Mr. Liu, our exhibition will open next month, but we are badly in need of a guide who speaks Chinese. Can you select a student from your advanced Chinese class and recommend him for the exhibition?

乙： 你们有什么具体要求吗？
B： Do you have any specific requirements for the student?

甲： 要求并不高，只要能与厂商沟通就行。不过，最好能懂一点儿电脑。
A： We don't have high requirements. It will be fine as long as the student is able to communicate with the manufacturers. However, it's better for the student to have some knowledge of computer.

乙： 这不难。我这儿现成有一位，包你满意。
B： This is not difficult. I have a student right at hand. I guarantee you will be satisfied.

甲： 那太好了。请你把这个同学的情况给我简单说一说。
A： Great! Will you please give me a brief description of the student?

乙： 这是一个男同学，叫郑聪明，是计算机专业三年级的学生。他跟我学中文已经三年了。这个学生勤奋好学，做事认真负责，可信赖，人也随和，很合群。唯一的缺点是跟女同学交往时他会很害羞。不过，我相信他不会让你失望的。
B： He is a boy. His name is Zheng Congming, and he is a junior student of computer science. He has been studying Chinese with me for three years. This student is diligent and good at learning. He is responsible in any undertaking, and very reliable. He is amiable and easy to get along with. His only flaw is shyness when he has social contact with female students. But, I am sure he will not disappoint you.

Unit 2 Lesson Two Recommending

甲： 那还用说?刘老师推荐的人绝对错不了。
A： Needless to say. Whoever is recommended by Mr. Liu will certainly not disappoint me.

词语表　New Words

展览会	zhǎnlǎnhuì	exhibition
开幕	kāimù	open; inaugurate
急需	jíxū	be badly in need of
讲解员	jiǎngjiěyuán	guide; interpreter
高级	gāojí	advanced; senior; high-ranking; superb
挑选	tiāoxuǎn	select; choose
推荐	tuījiàn	recommend
具体	jùtǐ	concrete; specific
要求	yāoqiú	require; requirement
厂商	chǎngshāng	manufacturer; firm
沟通	gōutōng	communicate
电脑	diànnǎo	computer
满意	mǎnyì	satisfactory; satisfaction
简单	jiǎndān	simple; easy to handle
计算机专业	jìsuànjī zhuānyè	computer science
勤奋	qínfèn	diligent
好学	hàoxué	be good at learning
认真	rènzhēn	earnest; serious
可信赖	kě xìnlài	reliable; dependable
随和	suíhé	amiable; easy going; easy to get along with
合群	héqún	be gregarious; get on well with others
唯一	wéiyī	only
缺点	quēdiǎn	defect; weakness
交往	jiāowǎng	associate with; contact

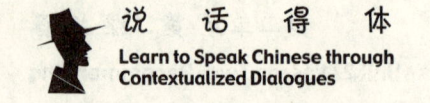

害羞	hàixiū	shy; bashful
失望	shīwàng	disappoint
绝对	juéduì	absolutely
错不了	cuò bù liǎo	unlikely to go wrong

对话三：北京特产
Dialogue III：Beijing Specialties

人物 Characters	甲：一位顾客 A：A customer	乙：一位服务员 B：A waiter or waitress
关系 Relationship	在顾客和服务员之间 Between a restaurant guest and a waiter or waitress	
情景 Location	在饭馆 At a restaurant	

甲：我们是第一次来你们饭店，请问你们的招牌菜是什么？

A：It is our first time dining at your restaurant. May I ask if you have any house specials?

乙：我向几位推荐烤鸭吧。本店就是以北京的特产烤鸭而闻名的。

B：I recommend the roast duck. This restaurant is known for the specialty of Beijing styled roast duck (Peking Duck).

甲：你可不可以向我们介绍一下烤鸭的吃法？

A：Would you please give us an introduction on the proper way to eat it?

乙：当然可以。你先拿一张薄饼抹上甜面酱，再在上面撒上葱段，然后把切成片的鸭皮卷在薄饼中就可以吃了。

B：Of course. You first take a pancake, spread the special sauce and sprinkle some diced scallion. You then place the sliced duck skin on the pancake and roll it up for serving.

甲：只吃鸭皮吗？

A：Do I only eat the duck skin?

乙：当然不。在我们这儿吃北京烤鸭，最大的特点就是一鸭三吃。鸭皮卷薄饼，鸭肉作主

46

第二单元 第二课 推荐
Unit 2 Lesson Two Recommending

菜，鸭骨头熬汤喝。

B：Of course not. The greatest part of having Beijing roast duck here is one duck being cooked three ways. The skin is served with the pancakes; the duck meat is the main course; and the duck bones are used for stewing soup.

甲：真是物尽其用。我们就吃烤鸭吧。

A：This really makes the best use of everything. Let's then have roast duck.

……

乙：烤鸭的味道怎么样？

B：How does it taste?

甲：味道好极了。鸭子这么做，又嫩又脆，我是第一次吃。

A：It tastes extremely delicious. The duck cooked in this way tastes both tender and crispy. This is a first for me.

乙：我们的烤鸭是用特选的木柴烤炙的，用料精致，特点就是皮脆肉嫩。

B：Our ducks are roasted with specially selected firewood, marinated with fine seasonings. It's distinctive for being tender and crispy.

甲：你说的完全对。

A：You are absolutely right.

词语表　New Words

招牌菜	zhāopaicài	house special (at restaurants)
烤鸭	kǎoyā	roast duck
特产	tèchǎn	special product
闻名	wénmíng	well-known; famous
吃法	chīfǎ	eating method
薄饼	báobǐng	pancake
抹	mǒ	to put on; to spread
甜面酱	tiánmiànjiàng	a sweet sauce made of fermented flour
撒	sǎ	spread; scatter
葱	cōng	scallion
段	duàn	section; part; cut

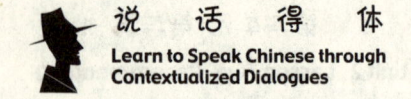

说 话 得 体
Learn to Speak Chinese through Contextualized Dialogues

切片	qiēpiàn	slice
皮	pí	skin
卷	juǎn	roll
主菜	zhǔcài	main course; main dish
骨头	gǔtou	bone
熬	āo	to stew; to cook
物尽其用	wù jìn qí yòng	to make the best use of everything
味道	wèidào	taste
好极了	hǎo jí le	extremely good
又嫩又脆	yòu nèn yòu cuì	both tender and crispy
木柴	mùchái	firewood
烤炙	kǎozhì	to roast; to bake
用料	yòngliào	condiments; seasoning; ingredient
精致	jīngzhì	fine; delicate
完全	wánquán	absolutely; whole; complete

对话四：必不可少
Dialogue IV: Absolutely Necessary

人 物 Characters	甲：一位导游 A：A tour guide	乙：一位游客 A：A tourist
关 系 Relationship	在导游和游客之间 Between a tour guide and a tourist	
情 景 Location	在北京故宫入口 At the entrance of the Palace Museum in Beijing	

甲：来中国北京，参观故宫是必不可少的。
A：When coming to Beijing, visiting the Imperial Palace is a must.

乙：为什么参观故宫那么重要呢？故宫是哪一年建造的？

48

第二单元 第二课 推荐
Unit 2 Lesson Two Recommending

B： Why is it so important to visit the Imperial Palace?

甲： 故宫又叫紫禁城，最初建于1420年，曾经是明、清两个朝代的皇宫，也是中国现存最大、最完整的古代宫殿建筑群。

A： The Imperial Palace is also called the Forbidden City. Construction was started in 1420. It was once the palace for the emperors of two dynasties. Currently it is also the biggest and the most intact ancient palace complex.

乙： 有多少个皇帝在这儿住过？

B： How many emperors lived here?

甲： 明代有十四个皇帝，清代有十个皇帝在这里居住过，先后统治了中国四百九十一年。

A： There lived 14 emperors of the Ming Dynasty and 10 emperors of Qing Dynasty. They successively ruled China for 491 years.

乙： 真是不可思议。现在故宫被用来做什么呢？

B： Incredible! What is the Imperial Palace now?

甲： 现在这儿是中国最大的博物馆——故宫博物馆的所在地。

A： It is the location for China's biggest museum, the Palace Museum.

词语表　New Words

参观	cānguān	to visit
故宫	Gù Gōng	the Palace Museum
必不可少	bì bù kě shǎo	indispensable; essential
紫禁城	Zǐjìn Chéng	Forbidden City
最初	zuìchū	first; prime
建	jiàn	build; establish
于	yú	in (the year of)
现存	xiàncún	be extant
完整	wánzhěng	intact; complete
古代	gǔdài	ancient
宫殿	gōngdiàn	palace
建筑群	jiànzhùqún	building complex
皇宫	huánggōng	imperial palace
居住	jūzhù	to reside; to live

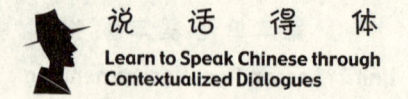

说话得体
Learn to Speak Chinese through Contextualized Dialogues

先后	xiānhòu	successively; one after another
统治	tǒngzhì	to rule; to dominate
博物馆	bówùguǎn	museum
所在地	suǒzàidì	site; location

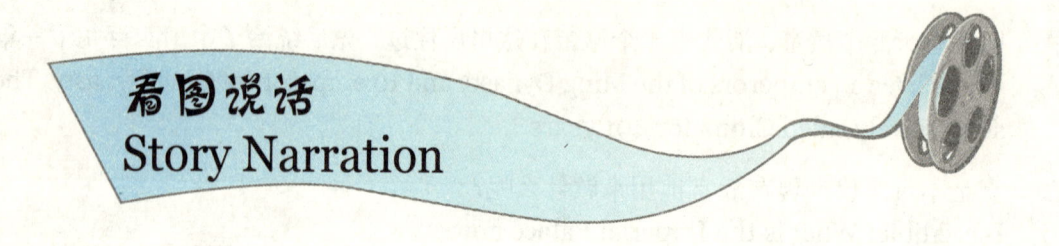

看图说话 Story Narration

按照以下图画顺序及各幅图画所提示的情景，叙述一个有始有终的完整故事。

Based on the order of the following pictures and the situations presented in each, narrate a story including a beginning and an end.

Unit 2　Lesson Two　Recommending

小品表演
Skit Performance

学生创作对话小品时尽可能使用本单元列出的和学生学到的新词、新句。小品主题选择应该得到老师首肯，以免重复。

Create situational dialogues with topics approved by the teacher to avoid repetition. Use as many expressions listed/learned in this unit as possible.

	对话地点（时间） Place (Time) of Dialogue	对话情景 Context	对话者之间的关系 Relation Between Speakers
1	在展销会上 at a sales promotion	推荐一种新型饮料 recommending a new beverage	在推销员和客户之间 between a salesperson and a customer
2	在图书馆里 at the library	推荐一本自传书 recommending an autobiographical book	在图书馆管理员和读者之间 between a librarian and a reader
3	在电话里 on the phone	推荐一个人才 recommending a gifted person	在推荐者与用人单位主管之间 between a recommender and the manager of a personnel department
4	在校园里 on the campus	推荐学生中心 recommending a student center	在两位学生之间 between two students
5	在学生餐厅用餐时 dining at a student cafeteria	推荐一门课（中文课） recommending a course (Chinese class)	在两位学生之间 between two students
6	在递电子邮件时 typing an Email	推荐一个学生申请奖学金 recommending a student applying for a scholarship	在两位教授之间 between two professors
7	在饭馆点菜时 ordering food at a restaurant	推荐一个招牌菜 recommending a house special	在服务员和顾客之间 between a waiter/waitress and a customer

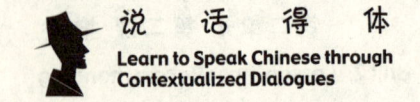

说话得体
Learn to Speak Chinese through Contextualized Dialogues

8	在旅行社里 at a travel agency	推荐一个去中国的旅游计划 recommending a tour package to China	在旅行社代理和顾客之间 between an agent and a customer
9	在教室里 in the classroom	推荐一个电视栏目（新电影） recommending a new TV program (new movie)	在两位同学之间 between two students
10	在租房子的时候 renting a place to live	推荐一处住所 recommending a place to live	在房东和未来的房客之间 between a landlord and a would-be tenant

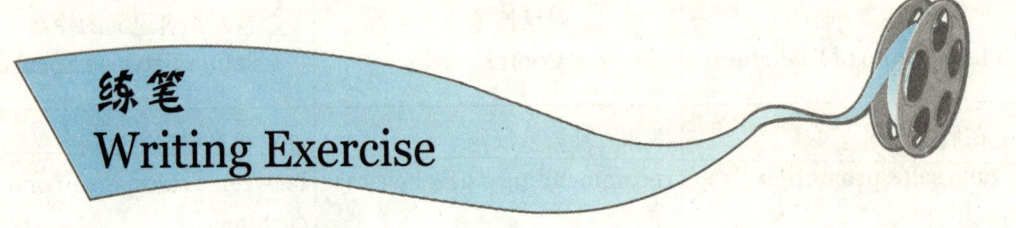

练笔
Writing Exercise

根据要求写一篇短文。尽可能用上本单元学到的词句。

Write a short passage on the given topic. Do your best to use words and expressions from the sentence patterns you have learned in this unit.

推荐我的学校 (Write a letter recommending the school you attend.)

第二单元 听力练习
Listening Comprehension Unit 2

听完以下各项听力练习的内容，先回答理解提示中的问题，再识别句子或语段的语境，然后尽可能使用本单元列出的和学到的新词、新句做适当的回应。

After listening to the sentences given, identify a proper context and response in each situation, using as many expressions listed/learned in this unit as possible.

	1. 理解提示 Comprehension	2. 情景识别 Context Identification	3. 学生回应 Student's Response
1	Who is the speaker?		
2	Do Lao Li and Xiao Zhang know each other?		
3	What is Li's job?		
4	Who is the speaker?		
5	What is the book about?		
6	What does the speaker want to know?		
7	What is the speaker going to talk about?		
8	What is the special of this restaurant?		
9	What is the speaker doing?		你推荐的人，错不了！
10	Say three things about this tower.		

第三单元 Unit 3

第一课 询问
Lesson One Inquiring

常用词句
Common Expressions

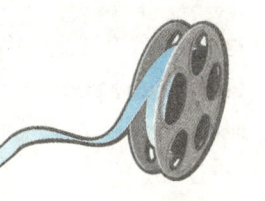

常用词句 Common Expressions	回应提示参考 Suggested Responses
1 请问，这儿是不是王经理的办公室？ If you don't mind me asking, is this Manager Wang's office?	是的。请进！ Yes, come in please.
2 对不起，附近有没有厕所？ Excuse me! Is there a toilet nearby?	前面就有一个。 There is one ahead.
3 请问，北京大学在哪儿？ Excuse me! Where is Peking University?	对不起，我也不知道。 I am sorry. I don't know, either.
4 打搅一下，去人民广场怎么走？ Sorry to bother you, but how can I get to the People's Square?	从这儿一直往前走，过三个红绿灯就到了。 Go straight from here. You will get there in three blocks.
5 这儿就是地铁出（入）口吧？ Is this the subway's exit / entrance?	是啊。你没见到那个地铁标志吗？ Yes. The sign is right there.
6 赵先生，您在哪儿高就？ Where do you work, Mr. Zhao?	我在沃尔玛商场上班。 I work at Wal-Mark.

57

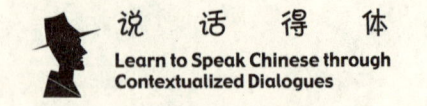

说 话 得 体
Learn to Speak Chinese through Contextualized Dialogues

常用词句 Common Expressions	回应提示参考 Suggested Responses
7 花旗银行的刘总裁住几号房间? Which room is President Liu of Citibank staying in?	1234号房间。 Room 1234.
8 这个会议室能坐几(多少)个人? How many people can this conference room hold?	六十个人没问题。 It is fine for 60 people.
9 你好,李小姐在吗? Hello! Is Miss Li there?	她不在,你是哪位? She is out. Who is this?
10 你什么文化程度? What is your educational experience?	我高中毕业,现在在社区大学荣誉班念书。 I graduated from high school, and I am attending an honors class at a community college now.
11 你会不会在视窗下编写程序? Can you write programs in Windows?	当然会。这对我来说太简单了。 Of course I can. It is easy for me.
12 他会打高尔夫球吗?打得怎么样? Does he know how to play golf? How well does he play?	他打是会打,可是打得不太好。 He knows how to play, but he doesn't play well.
13 这是用什么做成的? What is this made of?	这是废物利用的再生原料。 It is made of recycled materials. (Waste materials are reused again.)
14 你的病好点儿了吗? Are you feeling better now?	好多了,谢谢你。 I feel much better now. Thank you!
15 先生,高见?(你是怎么想的?) What is your opinion?	我还是先听听大家的想法吧。 I should first listen to everyone.
16 你喜欢吃什么?西餐还是中餐? What do you like to eat? Western food or Chinese food?	吃什么都行。 Anything is fine with me.

第三单元 第一课 询问
Unit 3　Lesson One　Inquiring

常用词句 Common Expressions	回应提示参考 Suggested Responses
17 这个假期你打算怎么过？ What do you plan to do during this vacation?	我还没有想好呢，你有什么打算呢？ I haven't decided yet. What have you decided?
18 你为什么对本公司感兴趣？ Why are you interested in our company?	因为贵公司重视人才，员工都有机会发挥个人的才干。 Because your company gives premier consideration to talented people, so the employees have the opportunity to demonstrate their talents.
19 我已经等了半个多钟头，车还没来。怎么回事？ I have been waiting for half an hour, but the bus still hasn't come. What's the matter?	请耐心一点。车马上就来了。 Please be patient. The bus will come soon.
20 老天为什么要这样对待我？ Oh, God! Why was I treated this way?	那你有没有做过什么亏心事呀？ Have you done anything that makes you feel guilty?

情景对话 Contextualized Dialogues

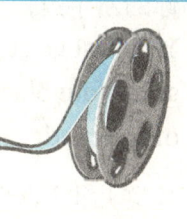

对话一：对不起，请问
Dialogue I：Excuse Me, May I Ask…

人 物 Characters	甲：一位外来者 A：An outsider	乙：当地路人 B：A local passer-by
关 系 Relationship	路人与当地人之间 between an outsider and a local passer-by	

59

说话得体
Learn to Speak Chinese through Contextualized Dialogues

情景	在街上
Location	In the street

甲：对不起，请问，附近有没有银行？
A：Excuse me. Is there a bank nearby?

乙：很对不起，附近没有。
B：I am sorry. There aren't any banks nearby.

甲：先生，那您能不能告诉我哪儿有银行？
A：Will you please tell me where there is one?

乙：假日宾馆对面有一个。
B：There is one opposite the Holiday Inn.

甲：那假日宾馆在哪条街上？
A：Then, where is the Holiday Inn?

乙：就在新华路和龙门路的交叉口。
B：It is at the intersection of Xinhua Road and Longmen Road.

甲：去那儿该怎么走呢？
A：How can I get there?

乙：你先一直往前走，在第二个红绿灯处向右拐，然后往前走四条街就到了。假日宾馆在你的右手边，华夏银行在马路的左边。
B：You first go straight, and turn right at the second traffic signal. You will find it after going four blocks. The Holiday Inn is on your right, and Huaxia Bank is on the left side of the road.

甲：离这儿很远吧？
A：Is it far from here?

乙：不算太远，步行大概二十分钟。
B：It's not very far. It probably takes 20 minutes to walk there.

甲：坐公交车是否方便？
A：Is it convenient to take a bus?

乙：方便极了。你往回走一条街，那儿有45路公交车车站。上车坐三站，一下车就能看见华夏银行了。
B：Extremely convenient. You walk back one block, and there is a Route 45 bus stop. Take the bus for three stops. You will see Huaxia Bank as soon as you get off the bus.

Unit 3 Lesson One Inquiring

甲：真不好意思，耽搁您这么长时间。
A：I am sorry to take so much of your time.

乙：没关系，你请走好。
B：It's OK. Take care.

词语表　New Words

请问	qǐng wèn	May I ask ...
附近	fùjìn	vicinity; nearby
假日宾馆	Jiàrì Bīnguǎn	Holiday Inn
街	jiē	street; block
龙门	lóngmén	Dragon Gate
交叉口	jiāochākǒu	crossroads
红绿灯	hónglǜdēng	traffic light
处	chù	place
拐	guǎi	turn
右手边	yòushǒubiān	right (hand) side
华夏	Huáxià	China; Cathy
步行	bùxíng	go on foot; walk
大概	dàgài	perhaps; probably
方便	fāngbiàn	convenient
公交车	gōngjiāochō	public bus
车站	chēzhàn	bus stop
上车	shàng chē	get on/into vehicle
下车	xià chē	get off/out of vehicle
不好意思	bù hǎoyìsi	feel embarrassed; impolite (to do something)
耽搁	dānge	delay; hold up; stop over

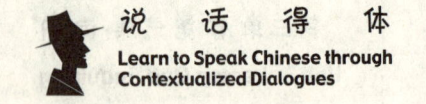

说 话 得 体
Learn to Speak Chinese through Contextualized Dialogues

对话二：有何贵干
Dialogue II：What Kind of Business Do You Have?

人 物 Characters	甲：一位从美国来的客人 　　A：A guest from America	乙：一位教授太太 　　B：A professor's wife
关 系 Relationship	请求登门拜访 Asking for permission to visit	
情 景 Location	在电话里 On the phone	

甲：喂！请问，这儿是不是李保胜先生的家？
A：Hello! May I ask if this is Mr. Li Baosheng's residence?

乙：是的。请问您是哪位？有何贵干？
B：Yes. May I have your name please? What is this regarding?

甲：我姓肖，刚从美国来。我的导师季传贤教授托我给李老先生带了点东西，我想当面交给他，不知道他什么时候方便见我？
A：My last name is Xiao. I just came from the United States. My teacher, Mr. Ji Chuanxian had entrusted me to bring something to him. I wish to give it to him personally, but I don't know when it is convenient for him to see me.

乙：李先生现在正在午睡。请稍等，我去把他叫醒。
B：Mr. Li is taking a nap right now. Please wait for a moment. I will go wake him up.

甲：请不要叫醒他，别打搅老人家休息。我能不能下午晚点儿到府上登门拜访？
A：Please don't wake him up. Don't disturb his rest. Can I visit your home later this afternoon?

乙：行。李先生一醒来我就告诉他。
B：That's fine. As soon as Mr. Li awakes, I will let him know.

甲：我来之前要不要再打个电话？
A：Do I need to call again before I come over?

乙：不必了。
B：No, it's OK.

甲：谢谢！一会儿见！
A：Thank you! See you in a while.

Unit 3 Lesson One Inquiring

乙：再见！
B：Good-bye!

词语表 New Words

有何贵干	yǒu hé guì gān	What can I do for you?
导师	dǎoshī	tutor or supervisor (at high learning institutes)
托	tuō	entrust
带	dài	bring; bring to someone
当面	dāngmiàn	in sb's presence; face to face
午睡	wǔshuì	nap
稍等	shāo děng	wait a moment
叫醒	jiàoxǐng	to awake
打搅	dǎjiǎo	disturb; trouble
休息	xiūxi	to rest
府上	fǔshàng	your home (family)
登门拜访	dēngmén bàifǎng	come (go) on a visit to sb's house

对话三：申请工作
Dialogue III：Applying for a Job

人物 Characters	甲：工作申请者 A：A job applicant	乙：公司人事主管 B：A director in charge of human resources department
关系 Relationship	在人事主管和工作申请者之间 Between a job applicant and a director of personnel department	
情景 Location	在人事处办公室 At the office of personnel department	

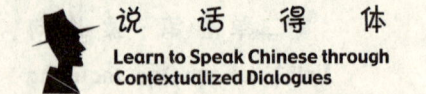

说 话 得 体
Learn to Speak Chinese through Contextualized Dialogues

甲：我是林中天，前来申请贵公司会计一职。
A：I am Lin Zhongtian. I am here to apply for the accountant position.

乙：好，林先生。我是公司人事处主管，姓田。你请坐。请问林先生多大了？在哪儿上的学？
B：Good, Mr. Lin. I am the Director of the Human Resources Department. My last name is Tian. Please take a seat. May I know your age? Which school did you attend?

甲：我今年二十二岁，三年前从旅游专科学校毕业。后来通过自学考试获得了中级会计师资格证书。
A：I am 22 years old, and graduated from a vocational college specializing in tourism 3 years ago. Later I passed the self-taught test and obtained the certificate for intermediate accountant.

乙：你为什么不愿做导游工作了呢？
B：Then why did you give up your job as a tour guide?

甲：我认为我的性格比较内向，更适合在办公室工作。
A：I believe that I'm rather introverted. I find it more suitable working in an office.

乙：不知道林先生会不会使用电脑？
B：Is Mr. Lin good at operating computers?

甲：我修过初级计算机课程。对电脑虽然懂得不多，可是上机在视窗下操作是绝对没有问题的。
A：I had taken an elementary computer class. Although I don't know too much about computers, I have no difficulty at all operating computers using Windows.

乙：那就请你现在在我这儿演示一下，行不行？
B：Can you give me a demonstration here?

甲：行。
A：Fine.

词语表　New Words

申请	shēnqǐng	to apply for
职	zhí	position
人事处	rénshìchù	human resources department
主管	zhǔguǎn	person in charge

Unit 3 Lesson One Inquiring

旅游	lǚyóu	tour; tourism
专科学校	zhuānkē xuéxiào	vocational college
毕业	bìyè	to graduate
通过	tōngguò	pass (test)
自学	zìxué	self-taught; self-learning
获得	huòdé	to obtain; achieve
中级	zhōngjí	intermediate
会计师	kuàijìshī	accountant
资格证书	zīgé zhèngshū	certificate of qualification
导游	dǎoyóu	tourist guide
性格	xìnggé	temperament; character
内向	nèixiàng	introvert; uncommunicative
适合	shìhé	suitable for
修	xiū	to take (courses)
初级	chūjí	elementary; primary; initial
课程	kèchéng	course (for learning); curriculum
虽然	suīrán	although
懂	dǒng	to understand
上机	shàngjī	to run (machine); to work with a computer
视窗	shìchuāng	Windows
操作	cāozuò	to operate
演示	yǎnshì	to demonstrate
一下	yīxià	once (measure word for verb)

对话四：你几岁了
Dialogue IV: How Old Are You?

人物 Characters	甲：一位外国同事 A：A foreign colleague	乙：一位中国同事 B：A Chinese colleague

65

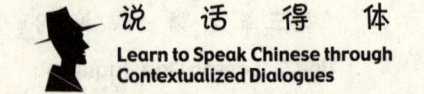

说 话 得 体
Learn to Speak Chinese through Contextualized Dialogues

关 系 Relationship	在中外同事之间 Between Chinese and foreign colleagues
情 景 Location	在一次聚会上 At a social gathering

甲：李先生，我有个问题想请教你，不知道……
A：Mr. Li, I have a question to ask you, but...

乙：请说吧，别客气。
B：Please tell me. No need to be polite.

甲：中国人所谓的"爱人"是什么意思？
A：What does the so-called "airen" mean in Chinese?

乙："爱人"指的是妻子或者丈夫，现在一般都管结了婚的女士叫夫人，管男士叫先生。
B："Airen" indicates wife or husband. However, nowadays people generally address married women as "furen", and married men as "xiansheng".

甲：那怎么称呼还没有结婚的人呢？
A：Then how do you address those who are not married?

乙：男士还是叫先生，女士可以叫小姐，当然得因人而异，年纪大一点的还叫小姐就不大贴切了。
B：For men, they are still called "xiansheng", while ladies may be called "xiaojie". Of course, it varies with individuals. It will not be appropriate to say "xiaojie" for those who are of an old age.

甲：我可不可以问中国人年龄？
A：May I ask a Chinese person for his age?

乙：当然可以。要是对方是老年人，你可以问"您高寿了"或者"您多大年纪了"。
B：Of course you may. If the addressed is an old person, you may ask "Nin gaoshou le" or "Nin duo da nianjile".

甲：对小孩儿呢？
A：How about little kids?

乙：你可以直接问："你几岁了？"
B：You may directly ask: "Ni ji sui le?"

甲：那你几岁了？
A：Then, Ni ji sui le?

第三单元 第一课 询问
Unit 3 Lesson One Inquiring

乙：我……
B：I...

词语表   New Words

所谓	suǒwèi	so-called
意思	yìsi	meaning
指	zhǐ	to indicate; to mean
妻子	qīzi	wife
丈夫	zhàngfu	husband
一般	yībān	common; ordinary; general
管	guǎn	a preposition (like "把") used with "叫"
结婚	jiéhūn	to marry; marriage
女士	nǚshì	Ms.; Miss
夫人	fūrén	Lady; Madame; Mrs.
称呼	chēnghu	call; form of address
因人而异	yīn rén ér yì	vary with each individual
年纪	niánjì	age
贴切	tiēqiè	appropriate; suitable
年龄	niánlíng	age
老年人	lǎoniánrén	the aged; old people
高寿	gāoshòu	long life; longevity
小孩儿	xiǎoháir	little kids
直接	zhíjiē	directly

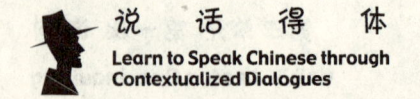

说话得体
Learn to Speak Chinese through Contextualized Dialogues

看图说话
Story Narration

按照以下图画顺序及各幅图画所提示的情景，叙述一个有始有终的完整故事。

Based on the order of the following pictures and the situations presented in each, narrate a story including a beginning and an end.

Unit 3　Lesson One　Inquiring

小品表演
Skit Performance

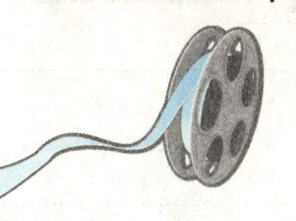

学生创作对话小品时尽可能使用本单元列出的和学生学到的新词、新句。小品主题选择应该得到老师首肯，以免重复。

Create situational dialogues with topics approved by the teacher to avoid repetition. Use as many expressions listed/learned in this unit as possible.

	对话地点（时间） Place (Time) of Dialogue	对话情景 Context	对话者之间的关系 Relation Between Speakers
1	在街上迷路时 having gotten lost on the street	打听去某个地方的路 asking for directions	在两位路人之间 between two pedestrians
2	在学校注册上课时 when registering for classes at school	打听学习中文的方法 inquiring about a way to learn Chinese	在两位同学之间 between two students
3	在图书馆里 at the library	打听下学期历史课的情况 inquiring about a history class for next semester	在两位同学之间 between two students
4	在商店里 at a store	打听购买某商品的信息 inquiring about the information regarding a commodity	在营业员和顾客之间 between a clerk and a customer
5	在电话里聊天时 when chatting on the phone	打听某人的性格和为人 inquiring about one's personality and attitude towards life	在两位朋友之间 between two friends
6	在中国领事馆问讯处 at the information desk of the Chinese Consulate	打听去中国留学的细则 inquiring about the detailed rules for studying in China	在学生和签证领事之间 between a student and the consul in charge of visa application
7	办理护照申请时 when processing the application for a passport	打听办护照的方法 inquiring about passport application	在官员和学生之间 between an official and a student

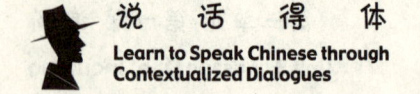

说话得体
Learn to Speak Chinese through Contextualized Dialogues

8	在邮局里 at the post office	打听邮局的某项业务 inquiring about a particular service at the post office	在邮局职员和顾客之间 between a post office clerk and a customer
9	在机场（火车站）里 at the airport (train station)	打听飞机（火车）的时刻 inquiring about the schedule of a plane (train)	在机场(火车站)职员和旅客之间 between an airport (train station) clerk and a customer
10	在办公室里 at the office	打听别人对你的看法 inquiring about how other people think of you	在两位同事之间 between two colleagues

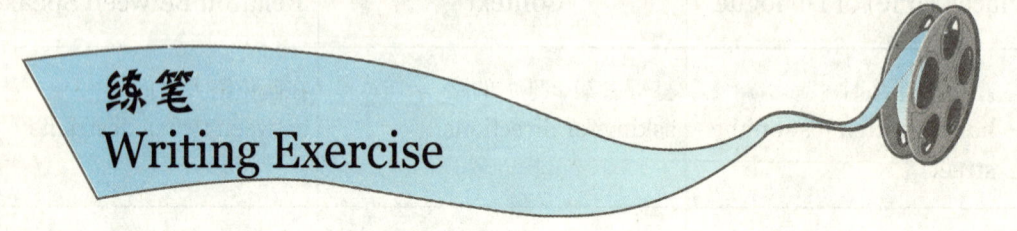

练笔
Writing Exercise

根据要求写一篇短文。尽可能用上本单元学到的词句。

Write a short passage on the given topic. Do your best to use words and expressions from the sentence patterns you have learned in this unit.

写信打听去中国留学的规定 (Write a letter to inquire about the detailed rules regarding studying in China.)

第二课 要求
Lesson Two Requesting

常用词句
Common Expressions

常用词句 Common Expressions	回应提示参考 Suggested Responses
1 别动！ Don't move!	我没动啊！ I didn't move at all.
2 请到这儿来一下。 Please come here.	有什么事？ What's the matter?
3 我需要你帮（我一个）忙。 I need your help.	好，没问题。你说吧，要我做什么？ Fine, no problem. Tell me what to do.
4 你还是去看一看的好。 You'd better go and have a look.	发生了什么大不了的事？ Is something serious happening?
5 如果有人打电话找我，请给我记一下留言，好吗？ If anybody calls, would you please take a message?	当然可以。 No problem.
6 不知能不能借你的笔用一下？ I wonder if I could borrow your pen?	对不起，我自己要用。 I am sorry. I have to use it myself.

71

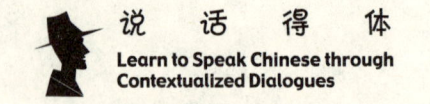

说 话 得 体
Learn to Speak Chinese through Contextualized Dialogues

常用词句 Common Expressions	回应提示参考 Suggested Responses
7 不要客气，请多提意见（请指教）。 Please be frank, and give more suggestions.	好的，我会的。我是一个直性子，有什么就说什么。 Okay, I will. I am straight forward, so I won't hide anything from you.
8 麻烦你，请把糖递给我。 Excuse me, will you please pass me the sugar?	好的，接着。 Certainly, here you are.
9 借光，让我过去。 Excuse me, can I get by? / Make way please.	对不起，请吧！ I'm sorry. Please!
10 我要求你立即答复。 I demand an immediate response from you.	我会尽力而为的，但是要看你的要求是否合理。 I will do my best, but I have to make sure it is reasonable.
11 请您把这个问题再解释一遍。 Will you please explain this problem again?	好，这次我讲慢一点。 Fine, I will speak slowly this time.
12 麻烦，请你帮我叫一辆计程车，好吗？ I wonder if you would help me call a taxi?	没问题！请问，去哪儿？ No problem. May I ask where you will go?
13 今晚七点半我有客人，请准备十二个人的饭菜。 I have guests at seven thirty this evening. Please prepare a dinner for a party of 12.	好，七点半，十二个人。您就放心吧。 Of course. Seven thirty and twelve people. You may rest assured.
14 请你在电脑上演示一下操作程序，行不行？ Would you please demonstrate the operating procedure on the computer?	行，就在这儿吗？ Yes. Shall I do it here?

常用词句 Common Expressions	回应提示参考 Suggested Responses
15 我把窗户打开，你介意吗? Do you mind me opening the window?	不介意。请吧! I don't mind. Please go ahead.
16 我想请你到我家来喝几杯，给不给面子? It would honor me if you would have a couple of drinks at my home. What do you think?	你真是太客气了。好，你什么时候在家? You are too polite. Okay, when will you be at home?
17 你这也是去城里吗?请带我一块儿去吧。 Are you also going to the town? Please take me with you.	好，上车吧。 Good. Come with us, please.
18 你看看，你做的是什么作业，乱七八糟的。拿回去，重做! Look at your homework. It's a mess. Take it back and re-do it.	真那么糟糕吗?重做就重做吧。 Is it really bad? I will re-do it, since you want me to.
19 请先填写外币兑换单，然后再交钱。 Please fill in the Foreign Currency Exchange Form, and then deposit your money.	好，我照你的意思办。 Fine. I will follow your instructions.
20 我要预订两张下个星期二早上直达香港的头等舱飞机票。 I want to reserve two first class airline tickets for next Tuesday's non-stop flight to Hong Kong.	请稍候、我帮您查一下。 Please wait a minute. I'll help you with that.

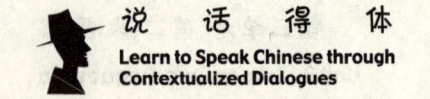

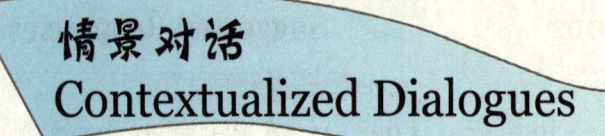

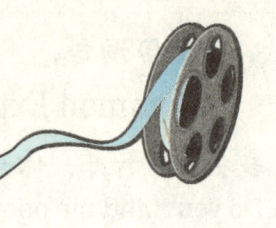

说 话 得 体
Learn to Speak Chinese through
Contextualized Dialogues

情景对话
Contextualized Dialogues

对话一：家常饭菜
Dialogue I: Homemade Meal

人 物 Characters	甲：主人 A: A host	乙：客人 B: A guest
关 系 Relationship	在朋友之间 Between friends	
情 景 Location	在饭桌上 At a dinner table	

甲：都是些家常饭菜，请大家随便用。
A: All the dishes are homemade. Please eat as you please.

乙：你也入座吧。对不起，请把醋递给我。
B: Please sit down as well. Excuse me, will you please pass me the vinegar?

甲：没关系。噢，对了，这种酱油味道很特别，很鲜。要不要尝尝？
A: Sure. Oh, right, this soy sauce tastes special, very delicious. Would you like to try it?

乙：好，让我试试吧。……嗯，甜甜的，辣辣的，果然不错，在哪儿买的？
B: Good. Let me have a taste. …Mmm, it's kind of sweet, and spicy, too. It is pretty good. Where can I buy it?

词语表　New Words

家常	jiācháng	the daily life of a family
饭菜	fàncài	food

74

Unit 3　Lesson Two　Requesting

随便	suíbiàn	informal; do as one pleases
用	yòng	to eat or drink
入座	rùzuò	be seated
递	dì	to pass
酱油	jiàngyóu	soy sauce
特别	tèbié	special
鲜	xiān	tasty; delicious
尝	cháng	to taste
试	shì	to try
甜	tián	sweet
辣	là	(spicy) hot
果然	guǒrán	really; as expected

对话二：洗耳恭听

Dialogue II：Listening Devoutly and Respectfully

人　物 Characters	甲：一位高中生　　　乙：一位高中生 A：A high school student　B：A high school student
关　系 Relationship	在高中生之间 Between high school students
情　景 Location	在教室里 In the classroom

甲：这本书很有教育意义，适合咱们高中生。你不妨也读一读。

A：This book is very educational, and suitable for high school students like us. I suggest that you read it.

乙：真的?能否请你先谈谈你的读后感，我洗耳恭听。

B：Really? Would you please tell me your impression of the book, and I will listen attentively.

75

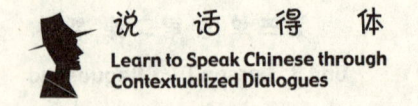

说 话 得 体
Learn to Speak Chinese through Contextualized Dialogues

甲：还是你先看书吧。等你看完了，咱们再一块儿讨论不是更好吗？
A：It's better for you to read the book first. We can have a discussion when you finish reading.

乙：你说得倒也是。那我就先拿去看了？
B：You're right. Good idea! Then I will read the book first.

甲：我拿来就是要借给你看的。
A：I brought this book here so that you could borrow it.

词语表　New Words

教育	jiàoyù	education
意义	yìyì	significance
不妨	bùfáng	there is no harm (in doing sth.)
读后感	dúhòugǎn	impression of a book or an article
洗耳恭听	xǐ ěr gōng tīng	listen respectfully
讨论	tǎolùn	to discuss
倒	dào	used to denote a transition or concession

对话三：请你转告
Dialogue III：Please, Pass the Word

人物 Characters	甲：一位求助者 　A：A person requesting help	乙：一位助人者 　B：A helper
关 系 Relationship	在两位同屋之间 Between two roommates	
情 景 Location	在学生宿舍里 In the student dormitory	

甲：我明天考试，现在得去图书馆查点资料。你不出去吧？
A：I have a test tomorrow, and have to go to the library to look up some materials. You

are not leaving, are you?

乙：我哪儿都不去。你什么时候回来？有事可以交代给我。

B：I will not go anywhere. When will you be back? If you have anything to do, you may count on me.

甲：哦，对了，九点钟左右，也许有人会打电话找我，请你转告他我十点半回来；要不，请你帮我记一下留言，好吗？

A：Oh, yes. Someone will call me around 9 o'clock. Please tell him that I will come back at 10:30, or please take down a message. Is that OK?

乙：那还用说？你就尽管放心去看书吧。

B：Of course. Don't worry and go study.

甲：真不知道该怎么谢你才好啊！你真是个大好人。

A：I really don't know how to thank you. You are truly a good man.

乙：哪里，哪里。瞧你说的！

B：Not really, you are too nice.

词语表　New Words

查	chá	to check; to look up
资料	zīliào	data; material
交代	jiāodài	to give an account of; to make clear
也许	yěxǔ	perhaps
转告	zhuǎngào	to pass on
要不	yàobù	otherwise; or else
记	jì	to write down
留言	liúyán	words (message) written; to leave message
放心	fàngxīn	feel at ease
大好人	dàhǎorén	person of fine quality
哪里	nǎlǐ	not really
瞧	qiáo	to look

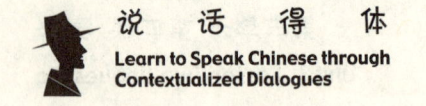

说 话 得 体
Learn to Speak Chinese through Contextualized Dialogues

对话四：赏光
Dialogue IV: Will You Honor Me?

人 物 Characters	甲：校长助理 A: An assistant principal	乙：校长的客人 B: A guest
关 系 Relationship	在校长助理和校长的客人之间 Between the assistant principal and the principal's guest	
情 景 Location	在住处 In the residence	

甲：王先生，李校长让我来请您今天晚上观看昆剧《牡丹亭》。
A: Mr. Wang, Principal Li asked me to come and invite you to watch the *Kunqu* opera, "*Peony Pavilion*", this evening.

乙：他想得真周到，知道我是昆曲迷，每戏必看。好，我去。
B: He is very considerate. He knows I am a *Kunqu* fan. Whenever there is a play I must go and watch. Good, I will go.

甲：他还请了几位票友，不知您是否愿意跟他们认识一下？
A: He also has invited several amateur performers, and he wonders if you would like to meet them.

乙：那还用说？和行家们聚在一块，何乐而不为呢？
B: That goes without saying. I don't see any reason not to get together with the experts.

甲：那我晚上六点半开车来接您，怎么样？
A: Then, I will drive and come pick you up at 6:30. How about that?

乙：好，我等你。
B: Good! I will wait for you.

词语表 New Words

观看	guānkàn	to watch
昆剧	kūnjù	*Kunqu* opera

第三单元 第二课 要求
Unit 3 Lesson Two Requesting

《牡丹亭》	Mǔdān Tíng	*Peony Pavilion* (a traditional Chinese drama)
周到	zhōudào	thoughtful; considerate
迷	mí	fans
戏	xì	theatrical play; drama
票友	piàoyǒu	amateur performer (of traditional Chinese theater)
愿意	yuànyì	be willing to
行家	hángjia	expert; connoisseur
聚	jù	to get together
何乐而不为	hé lè ér bù wéi	I don't see any reason why not.

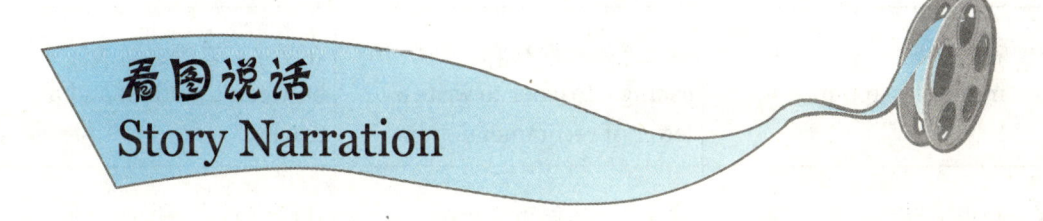

看图说话
Story Narration

按照以下图画顺序及各幅图画所提示的情景，叙述一个有始有终的完整故事。

Based on the order of the following pictures and the situations presented in each, narrate a story including a beginning and an end.

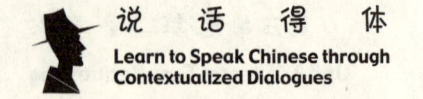

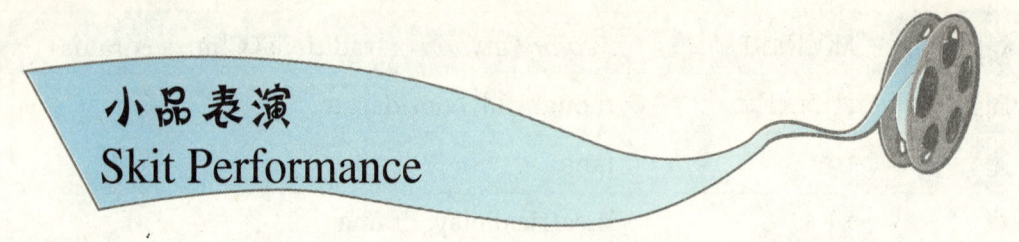

说话得体
Learn to Speak Chinese through Contextualized Dialogues

小品表演
Skit Performance

学生创作对话小品时尽可能使用本单元列出的和学生学到的新词、新句。小品主题选择应该得到老师首肯，以免重复。

Create situational dialogues with topics approved by the teacher to avoid repetition. Use as many expressions listed/learned in this unit as possible.

对话地点（时间） Place (Time) of Dialogue	对话情景 Context	对话者之间的关系 Relation Between Speakers
1 在教室里 in the classroom	请求老师写推荐信 asking a teacher to write a letter of recommendation	在学生和老师之间 between a student and a teacher
2 在电话里 on the phone	请求搭车去超市买东西 requesting a ride to go shopping at the supermarket	在两位邻居（朋友）之间 between two neighbors (friends)
3 在宿舍里 in the dormitory	借用计算器参加数学竞赛 intending to borrow a calculator for a math competition	在两位同屋（同学）之间 between two roommates (classmates)
4 在学校门口 at the school gate	邀请同学参加生日晚会 inviting a classmate to a birthday party	在两位同学之间 between two classmates
5 在家中 at home	邀请来访的客人看歌剧 inviting a visitor to watch an opera	在主人和客人之间 between a host/hostess and a visitor
6 在家门口 at the door of a residence	邀请男（女）友吃饭 inviting your boy (girl) friend to dinner	在男女朋友之间 between a boy friend and a girl friend
7 在老师办公室里 at the teacher's office	要求学生重做功课 requesting a student to redo the homework	在老师和学生之间 between a teacher and a student

Unit 3 Lesson Two Requesting

8	在警察局里 at the police station	要求配合案件调查 requesting cooperation during an investigation	在警察和犯罪嫌疑人之间 between a police officer and a suspect
9	在电影院售票处 at the box office of a movie theater	要求没票的观众离开 requesting those who don't have tickets to leave	在电影院职员和观众之间 between a theater clerk and an audience
10	在电话里 on the phone	饭店订位、音乐会订座、旅行社订飞机票、旅馆订房 making a reservation for a restaurant table, concert tickets, airline tickets, or hotel rooms	在职员和客人之间 between a clerk and a customer

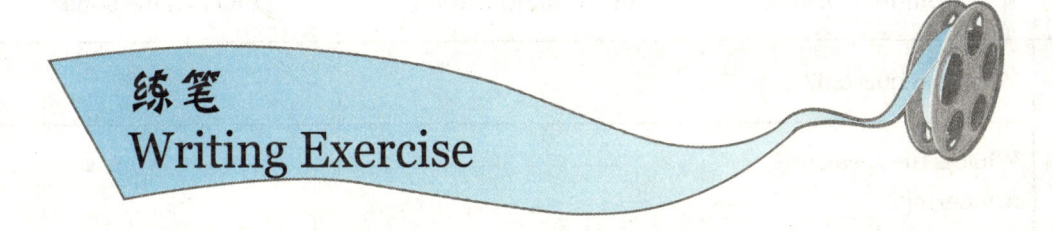

练笔 Writing Exercise

根据要求写一篇短文。尽可能用上本单元学到的词句。

Write a short passage on the given topic. Do your best to use words and expressions from the sentence patterns you have learned in this unit.

委托朋友预订飞机票 (Write a note asking your friend to help you book airline tickets.)

第三单元听力练习
Listening Comprehension Unit 3

听完以下各项听力练习的内容,先回答理解提示中的问题,再识别句子或语段的语境,然后尽可能使用本单元列出的和学到的新词、新句做适当的回应。

After listening to the sentences given, identify a proper context and response in each situation, using as many expressions listed/learned in this unit as possible.

	1. 理解提示 Comprehension	2. 情景识别 Context Identification	3. 学生回应 Student's Response
1	What is requested?		
2	What is the speaker wondering?		
3	What should the listener do after the conversation?		
4	Who is most probably the listener?		
5	Who is requesting an autograph?		
6	What is the object made for?		
7	What will the listener do for the speaker?		没问题,你放心去吧。
8	Describe the relationship between the speaker and the listener.		

第三单元 听力练习
Listening Comprehension Unit 3

（续表）

	1. 理解提示 Comprehension	2. 情景识别 Context Identification	3. 学生回应 Student's Response
9	Please take notes for the reservation.		
10	Please take notes for the reservation.		

第四单元
Unit 4

第一课　拒绝
Lesson One　Refusing

常用词句
Common Expressions

常用词句 Common Expressions	回应提示参考 Suggested Responses
1　不。 No.	一点商量的余地都没有了吗? Isn't there any room for negotiation?
2　不必破费了。 You needn't go to any trouble./ You don't have to pay for me.	对我来说这不算什么。 It's no big deal.
3　对不起，不可以。 Sorry, no.	再考虑考虑吧! Please reconsider.
4　谢谢你的好意，不过我已经吃过午饭了。 It's very kind of you, but I already had lunch.	那就算了吧。 OK then.
5　我看免了吧。（我看算了吧。） Let's not be bothered.	那我也就不勉强了。 Then I will not insist.
6　我能不能不回答? Can I not answer?	你自己看着办吧。 Do as you wish.
7　不行啊，我自己得用。 No, I need it.	没关系，我还可以去找别人。 It's fine. I'll ask someone else.

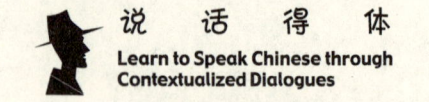

说 话 得 体
Learn to Speak Chinese through Contextualized Dialogues

常用词句 Common Expressions	回应提示参考 Suggested Responses
8 无功不受禄，这怎么可以呢？ I don't deserve this award.	这只是一点小意思，不成敬意。 It's just a small token of appreciation, not really indicative of our true heartfelt respect.
9 钱我不能收，（你的）情我领了。 I can't take your money, but I appreciate your kindness.	那我以后给你买礼物吧。 I will buy you some gifts later.
10 真遗憾，我已经跟别人约好了。 I'm sorry but I already made plans.	没关系，我们还会有机会。 It doesn't matter. We will have another opportunity.
11 我很愿意去，不过现在我必须做功课。 I'd like to go (with you), but I must do homework right now.	你说得对，做功课要紧。 You are right. It's important to do your homework.
12 很抱歉，这个商品暂时缺货。 Sorry, it is temporarily out of stock.	你们什么时候进货呢？ When will you order more?
13 真不好意思，这张桌子已经有人订位了。 I'm sorry, but this table has been reserved.	那一张呢？ How about that one?
14 如果你们坚持这个价格，我们很难成交（达成协议）。 If you insist on this price, we can't reach an agreement.	那我也没有办法了。 Then there's nothing I can do, either.
15 现在谈这种问题，恐怕还为时过早。 I am afraid it is too early to talk about this.	你认为什么时候比较合适呢？ When do you think it will be convenient for you?
16 今天看来不大可能，不打扰了，改天再说吧。	谢谢光临！我们改日再见。 Thank you for coming. We will meet

Unit 4　Lesson One　Refusing

常用词句 Common Expressions	回应提示参考 Suggested Responses
It probably won't work today, so let's not bother. We'll try another day.	next time.
17　坦率跟你讲，我不会让我女儿嫁给你。 Honestly, I will never let my daughter marry you.	难道我就那么让您讨厌吗？ Do you mean that you dislike me so much?
18　你还是另请高明吧。 You're better off finding someone better qualified.	好，咱们走着瞧。 Fine, we will wait and see.
19　这一次我不能满足你的要求。 I can not satisfy your needs.	太遗憾了。 I am sorry.
20　我是力不从心，爱莫能助。 I would help you if I could.	没关系！你已经尽力了。 It's fine. You have done your best.

情景对话
Contextualized Dialogues

对话一：恕不远送
Dialogue I：Sorry for not Escorting You any Further

人物 Characters	甲：主人 A: A host	乙：客人 B: A visitor
关系 Relationship	在两位老朋友之间 Between two old friends	
情景 Location	在朋友家 At a friend's home	

89

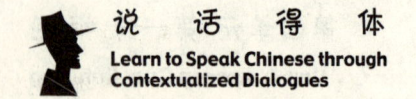

说话得体
Learn to Speak Chinese through Contextualized Dialogues

甲：时间还早，你再坐一会儿吧。
A: It's still early. Please sit for a while longer.

乙：不打扰了，我们改天再聊吧。
B: I don't want to bother you. We can find some other day to chat.

甲：那我送送你。
A: Fine. I'll see you off.

乙：不必了，我能找到回去的路。请留步吧。
B: It is not necessary. I can find the way back home. Please don't bother to escort me.

甲：恭敬不如从命，恕不远送。再见！
A: To comply with your wish is better than showing courtesy. I am sorry I cannot escort you further. Good-bye!

词语表　New Words

打扰	dǎrǎo	to bother
改天	gǎitiān	another day; some other day
送	sòng	to escort
恭敬	gōngjìng	respectful; with great respect
不如	bùrú	not as
从命	cōngmìng	comply with someone's wish

对话二：看你怎么办
Dialogue II：What Will You Do?

人　物 Characters	甲：同学甲 　A：Student A	乙：同学乙 　B：Student B
关　系 Relationship	在两位同屋之间 Between two roommates	
情　景 Location	在宿舍 In the dormitory	

Unit 4 Lesson One Refusing

甲：今天你帮我打扫屋子吧。
A：Will you help me clean the house?

乙：不，明天才轮到我，我不干。
B：No. It will be my turn tomorrow, so I can't do it for you.

甲：今天是应该我打扫屋子，整理房间，可是我现在得去图书馆预备下个礼拜的中文考试。
A：I should clean the house and clean the room today, but I have to go to the library and prepare for the Chinese test next week.

乙：你老是偷懒，找借口。今天你不打扫不行。
B：You always loaf about on the job and find excuses. But you're not getting away today if you don't clean.

甲：你要我干，我偏不干，看你能把我怎么样？
A：Because you want me to do that, I will purposely not do anything. I will see what you can do about it.

词语表 New Words

打扫	dǎsǎo	to clean
轮(到)	lún(dào)	it's someone's turn
整理	zhěnglǐ	to put things in order
预备	yùbèi	to prepare
偷懒	tōulǎn	be lazy; to loaf on the job
找借口	zhǎo jièkǒu	make an excuse for
不行	bùxíng	no way; doesn't work
偏	piān	deliberately; on purpose

对话三：情我领了
Dialogue III：Appreciate the Kindness

| 人 物
Characters | 甲：高年级学生
A：A senior student | 乙：新来的中国学生
B：A new Chinese student |

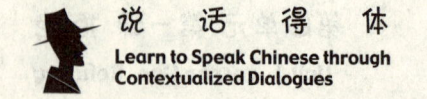

说 话 得 体
Learn to Speak Chinese through Contextualized Dialogues

关系 Relationship	在两位学生之间 Between two students
情景 Location	在学校 At the school

甲：我请你去吃西餐，赏不赏脸？
A： I invite you to have western style food. Will I have your honor?

乙：可是我吃不惯西餐，平时我都吃中餐。
B： But, I am not used to having western food. I usually eat Chinese food.

甲：没关系啦，交个朋友嘛。今天晚上怎么样？
A： It doesn't matter. We'll just get better acquainted with each other. How about this evening?

乙：很遗憾，今天晚上我已经跟别人约好了。
B： I am very sorry. I already have an appointment with someone else this evening.

甲：那明天中午呢？
A： How about lunch tomorrow?

乙：明天中午我也有事，我看还是免了吧，你的情我心领了。
B： I am also busy then. You don't have to do it. I appreciate your kindness.

词语表　New Words

西餐	xīcān	Western style food
赏脸	shǎngliǎn	do one the honor
平时	píngshí	in normal times; at ordinary times
交朋友	jiāo péngyou	to make friends with
约	yuē	to make an appointment
免了	miǎn le	excuse someone from something; exempt from
情	qíng	kindness
心领	xīnlǐng	to understand; to appreciate

Unit 4 Lesson One Refusing

对话四：销售代理
Dialogue IV：Becoming a Sales Representative

人 物 Characters	甲：代理商 A：An agent	乙：销售部经理 B：Sales manager
关 系 Relationship	在部门经理和代理商之间 Between the sales manager and the agent	
情 景 Location	在公司营销部门 In a company's sales department	

甲：我们是否可以成为贵公司产品在洛杉矶地区的独家销售代理呢？

A：We would like to be the sole agent for your company's products in the Los Angeles area?

乙：很高兴你们有推销我们产品的愿望。不过现在谈销售代理，恐怕为时过早，毕竟我们才接触，彼此还不够了解。

B：We are glad you wish to promote the sales of our products. However, I am afraid it is too early to discuss the possibility of being a sales agent. After all we just started to get in touch. We haven't gotten to know each other well.

甲：我可以向你们提供所需要的证明。请相信我们的信誉，凡是经我们手办理的业务，都能迅速完成，绝对错不了。

A：I can provide you with all of the required documents. Please trust our reputation. Any transactions through our processing will be accomplished rapidly, and trouble free.

乙：可是我们现在还不了解你们的经营能力、销售计划、每年可能周转的资金以及进口许可等情况，要我们马上考虑你的建议是有困难的。

B：But we still have no idea about your management competence, your sales plan, your possible annual capital turnover, and permission for importation. It is difficult to consider your suggestion right away.

甲：那我们先按拿佣金的办法做起来，等业务扩大了，相互有了更深的了解，再做进一步的关系改善，你觉得怎么样？

A：How about we start with commission. When the business expands, and we have a deep mutual understanding, then we make further improvements to our partnership. What do you think about that?

乙：你说的很有道理，我个人是赞成的。但是我还要请示总经理。

93

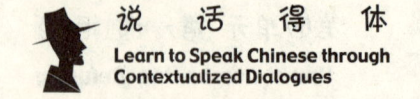

说话得体
Learn to Speak Chinese through Contextualized Dialogues

B：What you said is reasonable. I myself agree with you. But I have to request instructions from the general manager.

词语表 New Words

独家	dújiā	exclusive; sole
销售	xiāoshòu	to sell; marketing
代理	dàilǐ	agent; agency
推销	tuīxiāo	to promote sales
产品	chǎnpǐn	product
愿望	yuànwàng	wish
恐怕	kǒngpà	(I am) afraid
为时过早	wéi shí guò zǎo	it's not time yet; it's not ready
毕竟	bìjìng	after all
接触	jiēchù	get in touch
彼此	bǐcǐ	each other
了解	liǎojiě	to know; understand
提供	tígōng	to provide
需要	xūyào	in need
证明	zhèngmíng	certificate
信誉	xìnyù	honor
凡是	fánshì	any; all; every
经手	jīngshǒu	to handle; go through someone's hands
办理	bànlǐ	to process
业务	yèwù	business; transaction
迅速	xùnsù	rapidly
经营能力	jīngyíng nénglì	management competence
销售计划	xiāoshòu jìhuà	sales plan
周转	zhōuzhuǎn	turnover

Unit 4 Lesson One Refusing

资金	zījīn	capital; fund
进口	jìnkǒu	import
许可	xǔkě	permission
考虑	kǎolǜ	to consider
按(照)	àn(zhào)	according to
佣金	yòngjīn	commission
扩大	kuòdà	to expand
相互	xiānghù	mutually
改善	gǎishàn	to improve
有道理	yǒu dàolǐ	reasonable; to have sense
赞成	zànchéng	agree with
请示	qǐngshì	to request instructions
总经理	zǒngjīnglǐ	general manager

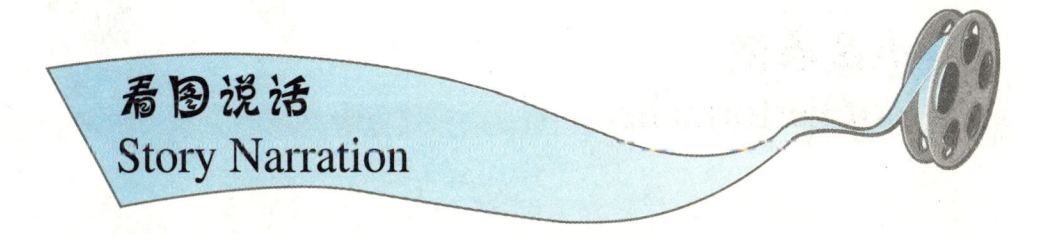

看图说话 Story Narration

按照以下图画顺序及各幅图画所提示的情景，叙述一个有始有终的完整故事。

Based on the order of the following pictures and the situations presented in each, narrate a story including a beginning and an end.

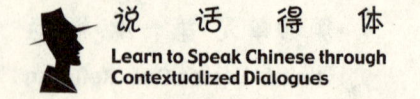

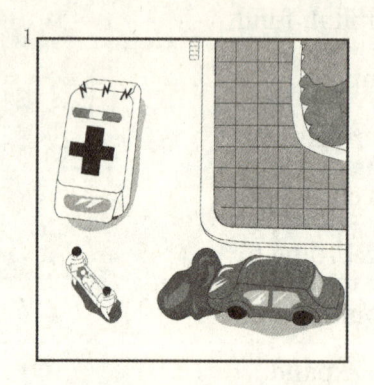

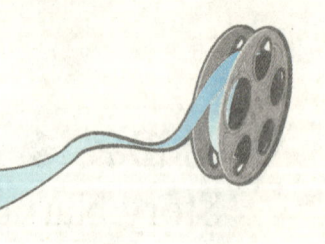

说 话 得 体
Learn to Speak Chinese through Contextualized Dialogues

小品表演
Skit Performance

学生创作对话小品时尽可能使用本单元列出的和学生学到的新词、新句。小品主题选择应该得到老师首肯，以免重复。

Create situational dialogues with topics approved by the teacher to avoid repetition. Use as many expressions listed/learned in this unit as possible.

对话地点（时间） Place (Time) of Dialogue	对话情景 Context	对话者之间的关系 Relation Between Speakers
1 在大学宿舍里 at the college dormitory	拒绝借新车让朋友去约会 declining to let a friend borrow one's new car for a date	在两位同屋之间 between two roommates

Unit 4 Lesson One Refusing

2	下课以后 after class	考试失败，婉言谢绝老师约请谈话 politely refusing to talk to the teacher after failing the test	在老师和学生之间 between a teacher and a student
3	在饭馆餐桌上 at the dinning table in a restaurant	拒绝共享桌子 refusing to share a table	在两位陌生人之间 between two strangers
4	在电话里 on the phone	婉拒看电影的邀请 politely turning down an invitation to a movie	在两位刚认识不久的朋友之间 between two new friends
5	考试时 during a test	不让同学借用你的课堂笔记 refusing to let a classmate borrow your notes	在两位同学之间 between two classmates
6	在街上 in the street	拒绝窝藏来路不明的包 refusing to hide a suspicious bag	在两位朋友之间 between two friends
7	在教室里 in the classroom	拒绝考试作弊 refusing to cheat during a testing	在两位同学之间 between two classmates
8	在美国华人家庭 at a Chinese-American family	拒绝学中文 refusing to study Chinese	在父母与子女之间 between parents and a kid
9	在旅馆 at a hotel	拒绝提供服务 refusing to provide a service	在旅馆老板与顾客之间 between a hotel owner and a customer
10	在警察局 at the police station	拒绝回答任何问题 refusing to answer any questions	在警察与犯罪嫌疑人之间 between a police officer and a suspect

练笔
Writing Exercise

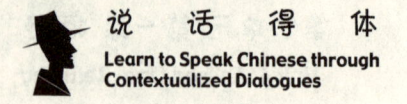

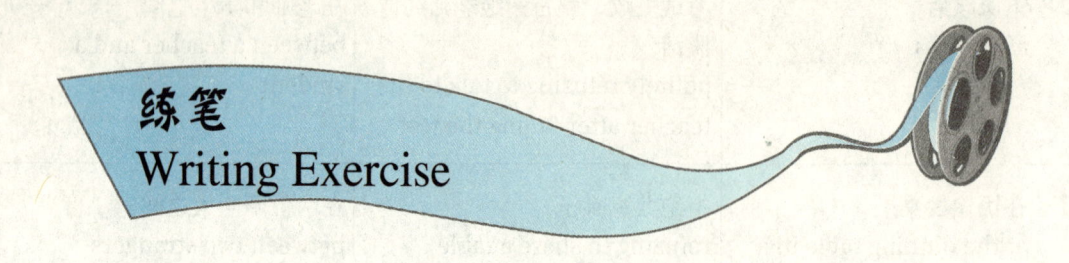

根据要求写一篇短文。尽可能用上本单元学到的词句。

Write a short passage on the given topic. Do your best to use words and expressions from the sentence patterns you have learned in this unit.

无法应邀看歌剧的回条 (Write a reply memo to decline an invitation to an opera.)

第二课 接受
Lesson Two   Accepting

常用词句
Common Expressions

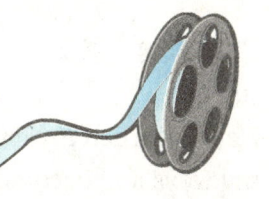

常用词句 Common Expressions	回应提示参考 Suggested Responses
1 谢谢你给我的生日礼物。 Thank you for the birthday present.	千里送鹅毛，礼轻情意重！我只是表表心意罢了。 It's nothing big, but it's from the heart. It's nothing but my best wishes.
2 行啊，我先拿去试试看。 It's very kind of you, and then I'll try it first.	不合适的话，回头再来找我。 If it is not suitable, you may come back to me afterwards.
3 你真是太客气了。 You are really too polite.	哪儿的话？你可不要见外。 What are you talking about? Don't treat me like a stranger.
4 我这是受之有愧啊。 I feel as though I don't deserve this award.	这是我们大家的心意，你就收下吧。 Please accept the gift. It comes from the heart.
5 感谢你的邀请，我一定准时出席。 Thank you for inviting me. I'll make sure to be there.	那我们会上再见。 Then we will meet each other at the conference.

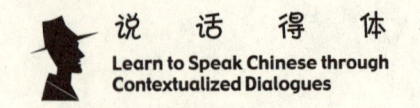

说 话 得 体
Learn to Speak Chinese through Contextualized Dialogues

常用词句 Common Expressions	回应提示参考 Suggested Responses
6 你的批评很中肯，我乐于接受。 Your criticism is very appropriate, so I am happy to consider it.	这也是我所希望听到的回应。 This is also the response that I expected to hear.
7 我愿意接受教训，痛改前非，重新做人。 I have learned my lesson. I'll change my ways and become a new person.	这才是你应有的态度。希望你不要辜负我们大家对你的期望。 This is the right attitude you should have. I hope you will not fail to live up to our expectations of you.
8 恭敬不如从命。 It's better to do what you want instead of being polite.	这就对了。 That's right.
9 我们会照你所建议的做进一步的修改。 We will make a further revision in accordance with your suggestion.	我很高兴你们能采纳我的意见。 I am pleased that you can accept my suggestion.
10 这次我就收下了，不过咱们下不为例。 I'll accept it this time, but please don't do it again.	好，好。记住了，没有下次了。 Fine. I will keep it in mind and will not do it again.
11 我决定接受贵公司的聘用，担任销售部主任。 I have decided to accept your company's offer and become the director of the Sales Department.	欢迎你成为我们公司的一员。 You're welcome to our company as a new employee.
12 我接受你的挑战，看谁能赢得这位小姐的芳心。 I accept your challenge. We'll see who will win this girl's heart.	等着瞧吧。鹿死谁手还不知道呢！ Just wait and see. It is not yet known who will emerge victorious.
13 这个价格我能承受。 I can live with this price.	可你要明白，我是作了多大的牺牲啊。 But you have to understand that I had sacrificed a lot.

Unit 4　Lesson Two　Accepting

常用词句 Common Expressions	回应提示参考 Suggested Responses
14　我已经把你的名字写下来了，你明天就可以来上课了。 I have written down your name, and you may come and attend class tomorrow.	谢谢老师！ Thank you, teacher.
15　这条收银线结束了，你是最后一个顾客。 This casher's counter is closed. You are the last customer.	我今天的运气还不错。 Today is my lucky day.
16　虽然我对媒体有点儿顾忌，但是我还是（愿意）接受你们的采访。 Although I have reservations about the media, I am willing to have the interview.	谢谢您对我们报社的支持。 I appreciate your support for our newspaper.
17　我代表公司虚心接受你的批评，马上对所有产品进行质量检验。 On behalf of the company, I cordially accept your criticism and we will immediately begin a quality examination of all our products.	我们乐见其成。 We will be looking forward to learning about the outcome.

情景对话
Contextualized Dialogues

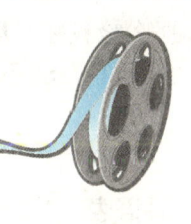

对话一：多买便宜
Dialogue I：The More, the Cheaper

人物 Characters	甲：小贩 A：A pedlar	乙：顾客 B：A customer

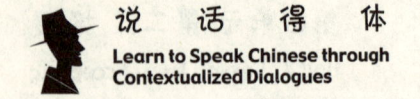

说 话 得 体
Learn to Speak Chinese through Contextualized Dialogues

关 系 Relationship	在小贩和顾客之间 Between a pedlar and a customer
情 景 Location	在菜市场 In a grocery market

甲：太太，您要买点什么?
A：What would you like to buy, Madam?

乙：这苹果多少钱一斤?
B：How much is it for one *jin* of apples?

甲：苹果两块五一斤。
A：Two fifty for one *jin* of apples.

乙：太贵了。能不能便宜一点?
B：Too expensive. Can it be a little bit cheaper?

甲：最多(一斤)便宜一毛钱。
A：Ten cents less for one *jin* is the best I can do.

乙：两块三一斤，行吗?要不我去别家买。
B：How about two thirty for one *jin*? Otherwise I will go to another store.

甲：多买可以。
A：Possibly, if you will buy more.

乙：那么给我称五斤。
B：Then I want five *jin*.

词语表　New Words

苹果	píngguǒ	apple
斤	jīn	a unit of weight (=1/2 kilogram)
贵	guì	expensive
便宜	piányi	inexpensive; let (sb) off (without punishment)
最多	zuìduō	at most; maximum
别家	biéjiā	others; other stores

Unit 4 Lesson Two Accepting

| 称 | chēng | to weigh |

对话二：祝贺生日
Dialogue II：Celebrating a Birthday

人物 Characters	甲：同事代表 A：Colleague representative	乙：过生日者 B：The one who is celebrating a birthday
关系 Relationship	在两位同事之间 Between two colleagues	
情景 Location	在同事家 At a colleague's home	

甲：祝你生日快乐！这是我们大家给你的生日礼物。
A：Happy birthday! This is the birthday gift we got for you.

乙：真不好意思，让你们破费了。
B：You don't have to buy me something.

甲：一点小意思，不成敬意，收下吧。
A：It's a small token of our friendship. It is not big, but it is a sign of our heartfelt respect.

乙：好，好！你们真是太客气了，谢谢啦！
B：Fine then. You are too polite. Thank you.

词语表 New Words

祝	zhù	express good wishes
生日	shēngrì	birthday
快乐	kuàilè	happy; cheerful
大家	dàjiā	everyone
礼物	lǐwù	gift; present
让	ràng	let; allow; make

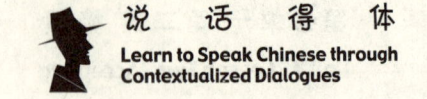

说 话 得 体
Learn to Speak Chinese through Contextualized Dialogues

破费	pòfèi	go to some expense
小意思	xiǎoyìsi	small gift; small token of kindly feelings
敬意	jìngyì	heartfelt respect
客气	kèqi	polite; courteous

对话三：接受任职
Dialogue III: Accepting a Job Offer

人 物 Characters	甲：人事部经理　　　　　　　　　　乙：新雇员 A: The manager of the personnel department　B: A new employee
关 系 Relationship	在人事部经理和新雇员之间 Between the manager of the personnel department and a new employee
情 景 Location	在公司办公室 In the office

甲：我代表太平洋电讯公司正式通知你，你的工作申请被接受了，即日起你就是本公司新产品研发部主任。恭喜你！

A: On behalf of the Pacific Ocean Electronic Communication Company, I officially inform you that your job application has been accepted. From now on you are the Director of the Department of Research and Development. Congratulations!

乙：谢谢！很荣幸成为贵公司一员，请多多关照。我会尽心尽责的。

B: Thank you very much! It is my great honor to be a member of the company. Please treat me favorably. Please accept me as a part of the team and I will fulfill my duty whole-heartedly.

甲：下个星期一早上八点王总经理在公司会议室为你举行欢迎会，希望届时出席。

A: Mr. Wang, our General Manager, will hold a welcome party for you in the conference room at eight o'clock next Monday morning.

乙：我一定准时出席。

B: I will certainly be there on time.

第四单元 第二课 接受
Unit 4　Lesson Two　Accepting

词语表　New Words

太平洋	Tàipíng Yáng	the Pacific Ocean
电讯	diànxùn	telecommunication
正式	zhèngshì	formally; officially
通知	tōngzhī	to inform; to notify; notice; circular; message
接受	jiēshòu	to accept
即日起	jírì qǐ	from today on
研发部	yánfābù	department of research and development
主任	zhǔrèn	director
关照	guānzhào	look after
尽心尽责	jìnxīn jìnzé	fulfill one's duty whole-heartedly
会议室	huìyìshì	conference room
举行	jǔxíng	to hold
欢迎会	huānyínghuì	a party (meeting) to welcome someone
届时	jièshí	at the appointed time; on the occasion
出席	chūxí	be present; to attend
准时	zhǔnshí	on time

对话四：接受建议
Dialogue IV: Taking a Suggestion

人物 Characters	甲：顾客　　　　　　　　乙：商店职员 A: A customer　　　　　　B: A store clerk
关系 Relationship	在商店职员和顾客之间 Between a store clerk and a customer
情景 Location	在商店顾客服务处 In the store's customer service department

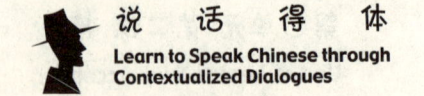

说 话 得 体
Learn to Speak Chinese through Contextualized Dialogues

甲：希望你们能认真考虑我们的意见和建议，并向有关厂商反映。

A: I wish you could seriously consider the criticism and suggestions we made, and pass them to the manufacturer concerned.

乙：您的意见很诚恳，想法很有建设性，我们乐于接受。我代表公司感谢客户对我们的厚爱。我们也会照您所建议的让有关厂商对所有的产品进行质量检查。

B: Your criticism is very earnest, and your suggestions are very productive. We are delighted to accept them. On behalf of our company, I extend our gratitude for your great kindness. We will also follow your suggestions, and let the manufacturer conduct a quality examination of all their products.

词语表　New Words

意见	yìjiàn	opinion; suggestion
建议	jiànyì	suggestion
有关	yǒuguān	to have relations with; concerned
反映	fǎnyìng	to reflect
诚恳	chéngkěn	sincere; earnest
建设性	jiànshèxìng	constructive
乐于	lèyú	be happy to; to take delight in
感谢	gǎnxiè	be grateful
客户	kèhù	customer; client; business connection
厚爱	hòu'ài	great kindness
进行	jìnxíng	to conduct; to carry on; to carry out
质量	zhìliàng	quality
检查	jiǎnchá	to examine; to check up

第四单元 第二课 接受
Unit 4 Lesson Two Accepting

看图说话
Story Narration

按照以下图画顺序及各幅图画所提示的情景，叙述一个有始有终的完整故事。

Based on the order of the following pictures and the situations presented in each, narrate a story including a beginning and an end.

107

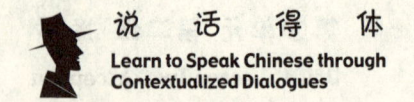

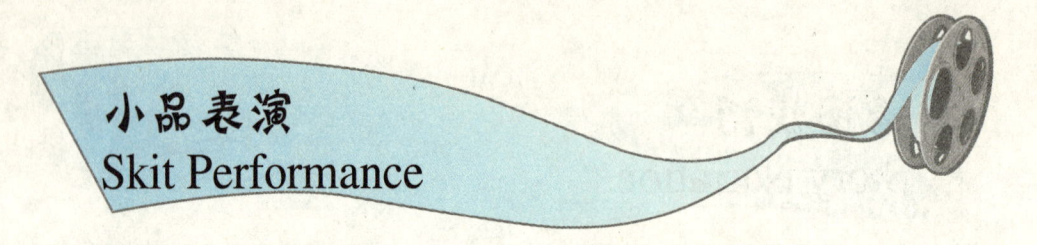

说 话 得 体
Learn to Speak Chinese through
Contextualized Dialogues

小品表演
Skit Performance

学生创作对话小品时尽可能使用本单元列出的和学生学到的新词、新句。小品主题选择应该得到老师首肯，以免重复。

Create situational dialogues with topics approved by the teacher to avoid repetition. Use as many expressions listed/learned in this unit as possible.

对话地点（时间） Place (Time) of Dialogue	对话情景 Context	对话者之间的关系 Relation Between Speakers
1　在家 　　at home	接受母亲节礼物 accepting a Mother's Day gift	在母亲与孩子之间 between a mother and her child
2　在教室里 　　in the classroom	接受学生的批评 accepting criticism from students	在老师与学生之间 between a teacher and a student
3　在办公室 　　at the office	接受对方的道歉 accepting an apology	在两位同事之间 between two colleagues
4　中国新年拜年时 　　when greeting at the Chinese New Year	接受新年红包 accepting the New Year red envelope	在长辈与晚辈之间 between an elder member and a younger member of a family
5　学期结束在老师的办公室 　　at the teacher's office when the semester is about to end	接受很差的成绩 accepting a bad grade	在老师与同学之间 between a teacher and a student
6　在某公司会客室 　　at the reception room of a company	接受聘用 accepting a job offer	在人事主管和工作申请者之间 between the manager of the human resources department and an applicant
7　在商店收银台 　　at the check-out	接受对方付款方式 accepting the method of payment	在收银员与顾客之间 between a cashier and a customer

Unit 4 Lesson Two Accepting

8	在商务洽谈时 during a business talk	接受对方提出的价格 accepting the price offer proposed by the other party	在推销员与客户之间 between a salesperson and a customer
9	法院宣判后 after hearing the verdict at the court	接受失败的现实 accepting the reality	在原告与被告之间 between the plaintiff and the defendant
10	在面谈时 during an interview	有条件地接受薪金调整 accepting to adjust pay rate with conditions	在老板与雇员之间 between an employer and an employee

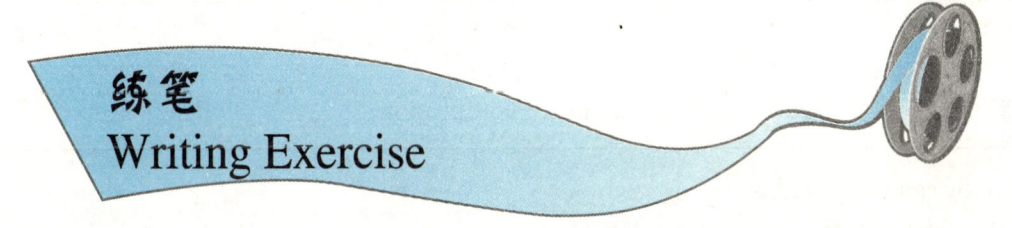

练笔 Writing Exercise

根据要求写一篇短文。尽可能用上本单元学到的词句。

Write a short passage on the given topic. Do your best to use words and expressions from the sentence patterns you have learned in this unit.

接受同学毕业舞会邀请的回条 (Write a reply memo to accept an invitation from your classmate to the senior prom.)

第四单元听力练习
Listening Comprehension Unit 4

听完以下各项听力练习的内容,先回答理解提示中的问题,再识别句子或语段的语境,然后尽可能使用本单元列出的和学到的新词、新句做适当的回应。

After listening to the sentences given, identify a proper context and response in each situation, using as many expressions listed/learned in this unit as possible.

	1. 理解提示 Comprehension	2. 情景识别 Context Identification	3. 学生回应 Student's Response
1	Why can't he go to the birthday party?		
2	Why can't he accept the gift?		
3	What is the second choice?		
4	Describe the relationship between the speaker and the listener.		
5	What will be taken into consideration?		
6	What was the consequence of the accident?		没关系,我这就去找别人。
7	What is being offered?		
8	What is being complimented?		
9	Is it a rejection or an approval? Why?		
10	Guess, what will happen next?		

第五单元 Unit 5

第一课 告诫
Lesson One   Cautioning

常用词句
Common Expressions

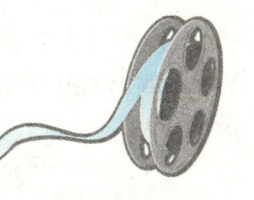

常用词句 Common Expressions	回应提示参考 Suggested Responses
1 下雪，路很滑，走慢点。 It's snowing. The road is slippery. Walk slowly.	谢谢你的提醒。 Thank you for your reminder.
2 你还是早点上路吧。 You'd better start your journey early.	好，我这就走。 Fine. Then I will leave right now.
3 要想身体好必须把烟戒掉。 You must quit smoking in order to stay healthy.	我知道你是为我好，我也早就想戒了。 I know that you are concerned about me. I have been thinking for a long time to give it up.
4 当心，路边有人骑自行车。 Watch out! Someone is riding a bicycle by the roadside.	谢谢！我会小心的。 Thank you. I will be careful.
5 留神，脚下有东西，别绊着。 Be careful! There is something underfoot. Watch your step!	真是的！是谁乱扔的垃圾？ Really? Who dumped the trash here?
6 注意！红灯！ Be careful! The traffic light is red.	幸亏你提醒。我光顾着说话，没注意交通信号灯。

113

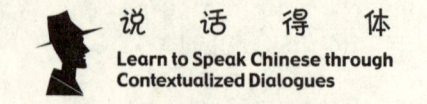

说 话 得 体
Learn to Speak Chinese through Contextualized Dialogues

常用词句 Common Expressions	回应提示参考 Suggested Responses
	I'm glad you told me. I kept talking and didn't notice the traffic light.
7 你们不能不注意产品质量。 You can't neglect the quality of your products.	你说得对。 You are right.
8 这是一笔大买卖，请谨慎为是。 You'd better be cautious about this big transaction.	谢谢你的提醒，我确实应该仔细一点。 Thank you for your reminder. I truly need to be more careful.
9 跟这种人打交道，还是小心一点好！ You should be careful with this kind of people.	你放心。我心里有数。 Please don't worry. I know that very well in my heart.
10 我奉劝你别去他那儿招惹麻烦了。 I think you should not go there and look for trouble.	是吗?他出什么事了? Really? What's wrong with him?
11 你再不交作业，那我就要对不住你了。 If you don't turn in your homework again, you will get into serious trouble.	好，好。我明天一定补齐。 Fine. I will make up everything tomorrow.
12 下星期一中文考试，别忘了! Don't forget there will be a Chinese test next Monday.	不会的。我已经记在脑子里了。 I won't forget.
13 别碰我，否则我就叫警察了。 Don't touch me, or I will call the police.	我不碰你，我走还不行吗? I won't touch you. Is it better that I leave?
14 我警告你，别骚扰我。 I warn you, don't harass me.	我哪儿骚扰你啊?你别太神经过敏了。 How did I harass you? You must be oversensitive.
15 危险!快走开! It's dangerous! Get away, quick!	亏得你提醒，要不真出事了。 Fortunately you reminded me, otherwise

第五单元 第一课 告诫
Unit 5　Lesson One　Cautioning

常用词句 Common Expressions	回应提示参考 Suggested Responses
	there really would have been an accident.
16 难道你不认为这儿的环境太糟了吗？ Don't you think the environmental situation here is too bad?	我也是这么认为的。可是我有什么办法？ I agree, but I am unable to find a solution.
17 眼下传染病流行，饮食起居可得注意。 The contagious disease is raging nowadays, so you have to pay special attention to diet and daily life.	谢谢！我一定会注意的。 Thank you. I will certainly pay attention.

情景对话
Contextualized Dialogues

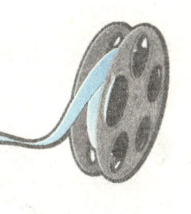

对话一：预防万一
Dialogue I: Prepare for the Worst

人物 Characters	甲：先生 A：A husband	乙：太太 B：A wife
关系 Relationship	在先生和太太之间 Between husband and wife	
情景 Location	在家中 At a residence	

甲：今天天气怎么样？
A：What is the weather like today?

115

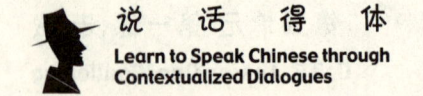

说 话 得 体
Learn to Speak Chinese through Contextualized Dialogues

乙：早上起来我忘了听天气预报，不知道下午会不会下雨。
B： I forgot to listen to the weather forecast when I got up this morning. I don't know if it will rain this afternoon.

甲：现在天气有点儿阴，但应该不会下雨吧？
A： It is a bit cloudy now, but it should not be rainy in the afternoon.

乙：难说，带把伞吧，预防万一。
B： You should bring an umbrella with you, just in case.

甲：我看没有必要，不会那么巧。
A： I don't see the need. I won't be so unlucky.

乙：还是小心一点的好。淋着雨，生了病，就不好玩儿了。
B： It's better to be prepared. In case you are caught in the rain and get sick. You will have no fun at all.

词语表 New Words

天气	tiānqì	weather
起来	qǐlái	to get up; to rise
忘了	wàng le	forgot
天气预报	tiānqì yùbào	weather forecast
下雨	xiàyǔ	to rain
阴	yīn	cloudy
伞	sǎn	umbrella
预防	yùfáng	to prevent; take precautions against
万一	wànyī	just in case; if by any chance
必要	bìyào	essential; necessary
巧	qiǎo	coincidental; as luck would have it
小心	xiǎoxīn	be careful; watch out
淋雨	línyǔ	be caught in the rain
生病	shēngbìng	fall ill
好玩儿	hǎowánr	to have fun; amusing; interesting

Unit 5 Lesson One Cautioning

对话二：第一次开车
Dialogue II: First Time Driving

人 物 Characters	甲：第一次开车的司机 A：A student driver	乙：有开车经验的教练 B：A driving school teacher
关 系 Relationship	在汽车教练和学员之间 Between a student driver and a driving school teacher	
情 景 Location	在汽车里 In the car	

甲：这是我第一次开车，实在没有把握。
A：This is my first time driving a car. I really don't have any confidence.

乙：别慌！握住方向盘，两眼注视前方，跟着前面的那辆车，保持距离，慢一点没有关系。
B：Don't be nervous! Hold the wheel, look forward attentively, follow the car in front of us, and keep your distance. It will be fine if you drive a little bit slower.

甲：我还是有点儿紧张。
A：I am still a bit nervous.

乙：留神！前面有行人过马路，让他先过去。
B：Watch out! There is a pedestrian crossing the street. Let him go first.

甲：现在是丁字路口，我该往哪儿转？
A：Now here is the T-shaped road junction. Which way should I turn?

乙：看清楚了，这是红灯，停车。
B：Pay attention. It is a red light. Stop!

甲：现在呢？
A：How about now?

乙：瞧！换绿灯了，还愣着干吗？快踩油门。
B：Look! It has changed to green. Why are you waiting for? Step on the gas.

说话得体 Learn to Speak Chinese through Contextualized Dialogues

词语表 New Words

开车	kāi chē	to drive (a vehicle)
实在	shízài	really; dependable; down to earth
把握	bǎwǒ	assurance; confidence
慌	huāng	flustered; confused
握	wǒ	to hold; grasp; to take by the hand
方向盘	fāngxiàngpán	steering wheel
注视	zhùshì	look attentively
前方	qiánfāng	front; the place ahead
辆	liàng	classifier (measure word) for vehicles
保持	bǎochí	to keep; to maintain
距离	jùlí	distance
紧张	jǐnzhāng	nervous; tense; intense
留神	liúshén	be careful; look sharp; lookout for
行人	xíngrén	pedestrian
过	guò	cross; pass
马路	mǎlù	street; road
丁字路口	dīngzì lùkǒu	T-shaped road junction
转	zhuǎn	to turn
清楚	qīngchu	clear; clearly
停车	tíngchē	to stop the car; to park
换	huàn	to change; to exchange
愣着	lèng zhe	absent-minded; distracted; blank
干吗	gànmá	what to do; why; whatever for
踩油门	cǎi yóumén	to step on the gas (accelerator)

118

第五单元 第一课 告诫
Unit 5 Lesson One Cautioning

对话三：别惹麻烦
Dialogue III：Don't Look for Trouble

人 物 Characters	甲：弱者 A：A weak person	乙：提醒者 B：A reminder
关 系 Relationship	在两位同学之间 Between two schoolmates	
情 景 Location	在校园里 On the campus	

甲：今天我去公园散步，小王又拦住我说要陪我一块儿走走。
A：When I took a walk in the park today, Xiao Wang blocked my way again and said he would like to accompany me for a walk.

乙：你已经吃过他的亏了，我奉劝你别去他那儿招惹麻烦。
B：You already had a bad experience with him. I advise you not to go near him and provoke trouble.

甲：可是我们都在一个班里，上课时总要碰面的。
A：But we are in the same class, and I can't avoid meeting him.

乙：跟这种人打交道，一定要小心。咱们害人之心不可有，防人之心不可无。
B：When you come into contact with such people, be careful. We can't think of harming others, but we should take precautions against dangerous people.

甲：好，我记住了。
A：Fine, I will keep that in mind.

词语表   New Words

公园	gōngyuán	park
散步	sànbù	to take a walk; go for a stroll
拦住	lánzhù	to block; hold back
陪	péi	accompany; escort
吃亏	chīkuī	suffer losses; in an unfavorable situation

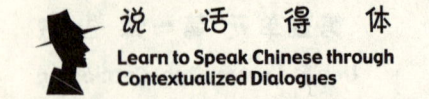

说 话 得 体
Learn to Speak Chinese through Contextualized Dialogues

奉劝	fèngquàn	to give a piece of advice
招惹	zhāorě	to provoke; stir up (trouble)
麻烦	máfan	trouble
碰面	pèngmiàn	to meet
咱们	zánmen	we; us (including the addressed)
害人	hài rén	to harm others
防人	fáng rén	to take precautions against (harmful) people

对话四：权衡得失
Dialogue IV: Weighing Gains and Losses

人物 Characters	甲：学生甲 　A：Student A	乙：学生乙 　B：Student B
关系 Relationship	在两位同学之间 Between two schoolmates	
情景 Location	在校园里 On the campus	

甲：明天数学考试，你复习了吗？
A：There is a math test tomorrow. Have you studied for the test?

乙：怎么，明天又有考试了？糟了，我整个星期都没有碰过数学书。
B：What? We have a test again tomorrow? That's bad. I haven't even touched the math book this whole week.

甲：你可不能开玩笑。抓紧时间把公式背一下，把做过的练习题再看一遍。要知道，刘教授的考试，事先不充分准备是很难通得过的呀。
A：You better be kidding. Make the best of your time and memorize all the formulas, and then go over all the exercises. Be aware that the tests given by Prof. Liu are very hard to pass if you don't prepare sufficiently.

乙：但是现在才开始复习，无论如何也来不及了。而且我已经跟朋友约好了今晚要去看一场棒球比赛。
B：But no matter what I do it is too late to start the review. Moreover, I already have an

120

Unit 5 Lesson One Cautioning

appointment with my friend to go and watch a baseball game.

甲：我要是你的话，就不去看棒球比赛了。今晚非熬夜下工夫不可。

A：If I were you, I would not go to the baseball game. I would do nothing but study late into the night.

乙：这怎么办呢？这场球赛是本季赛程中最关键的一场，我真不愿错过。不过……

B：What should I do now? This is the most important game of the season. I really don't want to miss it, but...

甲：听我一句话吧。为了看球赛，耽误了明天的考试，你会后悔的。

A：Just take my advice. You will regret it if you don't do well on the test because of watching the game.

乙：也许你是对的。让我再权衡一下。

B：Perhaps you are right. Let me think it over.

词语表　New Words

数学	shùxué	mathematics
复习	fùxí	review
糟	zāo	in a mess
开玩笑	kāi wánxiào	joke; to play a trick; to jest
抓紧	zhuājǐn	firmly grasp; make the best of (one's time)
公式	gōngshì	formula
背	bèi	to recite from memory; learn by heart
练习题	liànxítí	exercise
事先	shìxiān	before hand; in advance
充分	chōngfèn	sufficient; abundant
准备	zhǔnbèi	prepare
通得过	tōng de guò	able to pass (the test)
无论	wúlùn	no matter what (how); regardless of
如何	rúhé	how; what
来不及	láibují	there is not enough time
棒球	bàngqiú	baseball

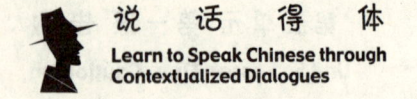

说话得体
Learn to Speak Chinese through Contextualized Dialogues

比赛	bǐsài	game; competition
非……不可	fēi...bùkě	must; have to (no other alternative)
熬夜	áoyè	stay up late; work until deep into the night
下工夫	xià gōngfu	devote time and energy; concentrate one's efforts
本季	běnjì	this season
赛程	sàichéng	schedule for the game
关键	guānjiàn	key; crux
错过	cuòguò	to miss; let slip
耽误	dānwu	to delay; to waste
后悔	hòuhuǐ	to regret
权衡	quánhéng	judge and weigh; to balance

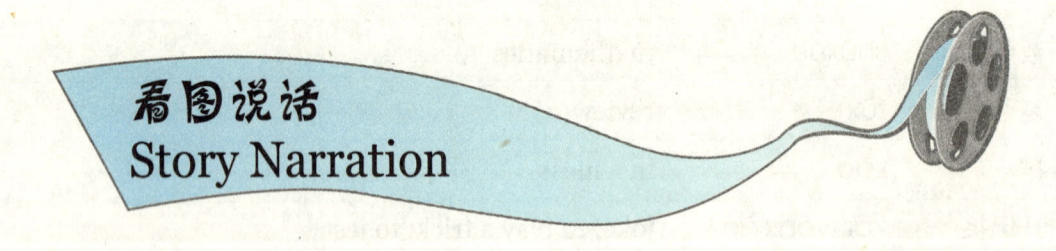

看图说话
Story Narration

按照以下图画顺序及各幅图画所提示的情景，叙述一个有始有终的完整故事。

Based on the order of the following pictures and the situations presented in each, narrate a story including a beginning and an end.

122

第五单元 第一课 告诫
Unit 5 Lesson One Cautioning

小品表演
Skit Performance

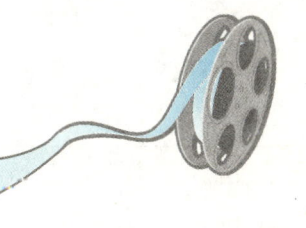

学生创作对话小品时尽可能使用本单元列出的和学生学到的新词、新句。小品主题选择应该得到老师首肯，以免重复。

Create situational dialogues with topics approved by the teacher to avoid repetition. Use as many expressions listed/learned in this unit as possible.

对话地点（时间） Place (Time) of Dialogue	对话情景 Context	对话者之间的关系 Relation Between Speakers
1　在家门口 　　at home gate	提醒别忘记出门时关门 reminding to close the door when leaving	在父母和孩子之间 between parents and a child

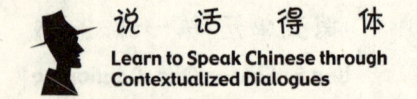

说 话 得 体
Learn to Speak Chinese through Contextualized Dialogues

2	在酒宴后 after a banquet	提醒酒后不要开车 reminding not to drive after drinking	在两个朋友之间 between two friends
3	在加油站 at a gas station	提醒慎用信用卡 warning to use the credit card carefully	在两个朋友之间 between two friends
4	在餐桌上 at the dining table	提醒交友、择友要小心 warning to be cautious when making friends	在父母与孩子之间 between parents and a child
5	晚会结束时 when an evening party is over	提醒夜路不好走 warning to be careful when walking at night	在两位同事之间 between two colleagues
6	在饭馆用餐时 dining at a restaurant	告诫菜肴的烫、辣、咸等 warning to be careful about a dish that is hot, spicy or heavily salted	在服务员和食客之间 between a waiter/waitress and a diner
7	放学以后 after school	告诫过马路小心 warning to be careful when crossing the street	在两个朋友之间 between two friends
8	在迪斯尼乐园门口 at the entrance of Disney World	告诫注意安全 warning to take safety measures at the entrance	在老师和同学之间 between a teacher and a student
9	在公园 at the park	告诫注意身体健康 cautioning to take care of one's health	在两个朋友之间 between two friends
10	在公车上 on the bus	警告不得骚扰 warning against harassment	在两位生人之间 between two strangers

练笔
Writing Exercise

根据要求写一篇短文。尽可能用上本单元学到的词句。

Write a short passage on the given topic. Do your best to use words and expressions from the sentence patterns you have learned in this unit.

给邻居写一张警告条,他家的宠物又咬人了 (Write a warning note to your neighbor that his/her pet had attacked people again.)

第二课 建议
Lesson Two Suggesting

常用词句
Common Expressions

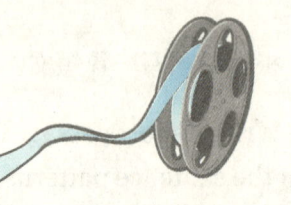

常用词句 Common Expressions	回应提示参考 Suggested Responses
1 我建议你马上去看医生。 I suggest that you see a doctor immediately.	好，我现在就去。 Fine. I will go right away.
2 你最好马上去图书馆学习。 You'd better go and study in the library.	有这个必要吗？ Do I have to?
3 她喜欢玫瑰花，你不妨给她送花。 Since she likes roses, you might as well give her roses.	对，这是一个好主意。 Right, this is a good idea.
4 （我觉得）游泳会很有意思。 I think swimming might be very interesting.	那我就试试。 Then I will try it.
5 你不吃鱼虾，可以尝尝鸡肉。 Since you don't eat seafood, you might try the chicken.	对，我对鸡肉不过敏。 Yes, I am not allergic to chicken.
6 你还是自己去跟他说吧。 You'd better go and talk to him yourself.	但愿他能听我的。 I hope he will listen to me.

Unit 5 Lesson Two Suggesting

常用词句 Common Expressions	回应提示参考 Suggested Responses
7 我说，你俩还是一块儿过吧。 I suggest that you two live together.	可是我不能一相情愿啊。 But that is just my own wishful thinking.
8 这事你能否跟你太太商量商量？ Can't you discuss this matter over with your wife?	当然要跟她商量，要不，什么事都干不了。 Of course I will discuss it with her, otherwise I could hardly do anything.
9 这么着吧，再给你一次机会。 How about I give you another chance?	我从心里感谢你，我绝不让你失望。 I thank you from the bottom of my heart, and I will absolutely not disappoint you.
10 你可以带你朋友去高级餐馆吃饭或者到市政厅艺术中心去。 You could take your friends to a first class restaurant or the city's art center.	你的主意都不错。让我再想想。 Yours is a good idea. Let me think about it.
11 今晚吃自助餐，怎么样？ We are eating at a buffet this evening. What do you think of that?	吃自助餐，不错。我们可以各取所需。 Buffet is pretty good. Each person can get what he wants.
12 既然人都来齐了，我们就开会吧。 Since everybody is present, let's start our meeting.	好，我们就开始吧。 Fine, let's begin.
13 希望你们先提供一个价格单。 I hope that you will first provide us with a price list.	我回去以后马上办，随后给你送来。 I will process it right after I get back, and send it to you immediately.
14 我想计算机会派上用处。 I think a computer will be useful.	我可以从你这儿借一台吗？ May I borrow one from you?
15 事情已经解决了，你何必再亲自跑一趟？	我不亲眼看到，总有些不放心。 If I don't see it with my own eyes,

127

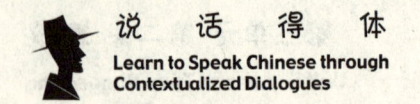

说 话 得 体
Learn to Speak Chinese through
Contextualized Dialogues

常用词句 Common Expressions	回应提示参考 Suggested Responses
Since this matter has already been resolved, why must you go there again?	I will feel somewhat uneasy.
16 如果我是你，就先工作几年再上大学。 If I were you, I would work for several years first, and then go to college.	你的想法我也会作为参考的。 I will take your suggestion into consideration.
17 别着急，慢慢养，既来之，则安之。 Don't worry too much. Build up your strength. It's better to just accept it and make the best of things.	谢谢你的关心。我会安心养病的。也请大家不必挂念。 Thank you for your concern. I will settle down so that I can recuperate. There is no need for you to worry about me.
18 学而不思则罔，思而不学则殆。 Learning without thought is labor lost; thought without learning is perilous.	圣人说得就是有道理。 What the sage said is absolutely true.

情景对话
Contextualized Dialogues

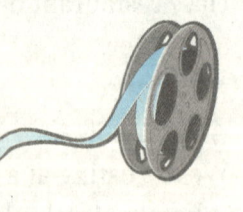

对话一：我感冒了
Dialogue I: I Have a Cold

人物 Characters	甲：一个生病的学生 A: A sick student	乙：一个健康的学生 B: A healthy student
关系 Relationship	在两个同学之间 Between two students	
情景 Location	在校园里 On the campus	

128

第五单元 第二课 建议
Unit 5　Lesson Two　Suggesting

甲：请你别靠近我，我感冒了，而且很严重。
A：Don't get any closer to me. I have a cold, and it is very bad.

乙：那你最好马上去看一下医生。
B：You'd better visit the doctor right now.

甲：早上已经看过医生了，也取了药。这一阵子感冒流行，你也少去公共场所为妙。
A：I went to the doctor this morning, and I also filled the prescription. These days, there is a flu epidemic. You'd better not go to public places frequently.

乙：好的。你要按时服药，多休息，多喝水，注意保暖。保重！
B：Good! You should take your medicine on time, get more rest, drink a lot of water, and keep warm. Take care.

甲：谢谢！
A：Thank you!

词语表　New Words

靠近	kàojìn	close to
感冒	gǎnmào	catch a cold; cold
严重	yánzhòng	serious
最好	zuìhǎo	best; had better
看医生	kàn yīshēng	visit a doctor
取药	qǔ yào	get medicine; fill the prescription
这阵子	zhèzhènzi	these days; a spell
流行	liúxíng	epidemic
公共场所	gōnggòng chǎngsuǒ	public place
妙	miào	excellent
按时	ànshí	on time; on schedule
服药	fúyào	take medicine
保暖	bǎonuǎn	keep warm

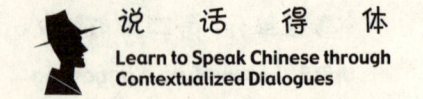

说　话　得　体
Learn to Speak Chinese through Contextualized Dialogues

对话二：去哪儿玩
Dialogue II: Where to Have Fun

人　物 Characters	甲：外地学生 　A: A nonlocal student	乙：本地学生 　B: A local student
关　系 Relationship	在外地学生和本地学生之间 Between a nonlocal student and a local student	
情　景 Location	在校园里 On the campus	

甲：我有个中国朋友今天下午从芝加哥到这儿来看我。你说今天晚上我带她到什么地方去玩儿呢？

A: I have a Chinese friend who will come to visit me from Chicago this afternoon. Where do you think I should take her for fun this evening?

乙：带她去艺术中心听音乐会，或者请几位朋友到这儿来聚聚。

B: Take her to the art center to entertain her with a concert, or you may invite several friends to have a gathering here.

甲：可是，她很怕应酬。

A: However she is afraid of socializing.

乙：那你不妨请她去饭馆吃顿饭，尝尝本地特有的海鲜菜肴。

B: How about treating her to a dinner at a restaurant to taste some of our local seafood?

甲：这个主意不错。

A: This is a good idea.

词语表　New Words

芝加哥	Zhījiāgē	Chicago
艺术中心	yìshù zhōngxīn	art center
音乐会	yīnyuèhuì	concert
怕	pà	afraid of

Unit 5 Lesson Two Suggesting

第五单元 第二课 建议

应酬	yìngchou	engage in social activities
顿	dùn	a measure word for meal
本地	běndì	local
海鲜	hǎixiān	sea food
菜肴	càiyáo	cooked dishes

对话三：温故而知新
Dialogue III：Review What has been Learned so as to Learn Something New

人 物 Characters	甲：学生 A：A student	乙：老师 B：A teacher
关 系 Relationship	在老师和学生之间 Between a teacher and a student	
情 景 Location	在老师办公室 At the teacher's office	

甲：朱老师，我们下个星期有一场英文大考，请问我该怎么复习最好？
A：Mr. Zhu, we are going to have a major English test next week. Will you please tell me how I should review for the test?

乙：我认为你应该去问问你们的英文老师。
B：I believe you should go and ask your English teacher.

甲：我刚去他办公室找过他，可是他人不在。
A：I just went to his office and looked for him, but he was not there.

乙：那依我看你先把课堂笔记仔细地看一遍，再温习一下课文后面的思考题。
B：Then from my point of view, you should first carefully examine your class notes, and then review the questions after the texts.

甲：好。课文前面的词汇会不会考呢？
A：Fine! Will he test us for the vocabulary listed before the texts?

乙：这也是免不了的。你最好每天都抽一点时间复习复习学过的东西。不能临时抱佛脚，对不对？
B：It is inevitable. You'd better find some time to review what you have learned every

131

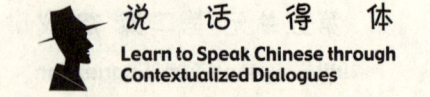

说话得体
Learn to Speak Chinese through Contextualized Dialogues

day. It is not good for you to take measures only at the last minute. Am I right?

甲：对。这就是你常常说的"温故而知新"嘛。老师，谢谢！

A: You are right. This is what you always said, "In order to learn something new, one should review what has been learned." Thank you, teacher.

乙：别客气！噢，对了，考试时千万不要紧张，审题最重要，得把考题看清楚了再答题。

B: You are welcome. Oh, yes. When you take the test, be sure not to get nervous. The most important step is to think about the questions. You have to make the questions clear before you start to answer.

词语表　New Words

大考	dàkǎo	final; important test
认为	rènwéi	to think; to believe
依我看	yī wǒ kàn	from my point of view
课堂笔记	kètáng bǐjì	notes taken during the class
仔细	zǐxì	careful; carefully
温习	wēnxí	review
词汇	cíhuì	vocabulary
免不了	miǎnbuliǎo	be bound to be; be unavoidable
抽时间	chōu shíjiān	to seize an opportunity; find time
临时抱佛脚	línshí bào fójiǎo	embrace Buddha's feet and pray for help in time of emergency; take measures only when in urgency
温故而知新	wēn gù ér zhī xīn	review what you have learned in order to learn sth. new
千万	qiānwàn	be sure to
审题	shěntí	to examine the questions (in a test)
答题	dátí	to answer questions; to solve problems

第五单元 第二课 建议
Unit 5 Lesson Two Suggesting

对话四：减肥要领
Dialogue IV: Key to Dieting

人　物 Characters	甲：减肥的学生 A: The student who is on a diet	乙：建议者 B: An advisor
关　系 Relationship	在两位朋友之间 Between two friends	
情　景 Location	在校园里 On the campus	

甲：我最近不知道是怎么回事，饭吃不下，夜里觉也睡不着。
A: I have no idea what has been wrong with me recently. I don't want to eat, and I can hardly fall asleep.

乙：我觉得你是太紧张了。是不是课业太重的缘故？功课太多，给你带来了很大的压力吧？
B: I think you are nervous. Is it because you have too much course work? Is it the amount of homework that is putting you under a lot of pressure?

甲：应该不会吧。这个学期我选的课都很轻松，老师布置的作业虽然多，可是并不难。哎，真是见鬼了！
A: It should not be the case. All the courses I selected this semester are easy. Although the teacher has assigned a lot of work for us, it is actually not difficult. It's absurd.

乙：那会是什么原因呢？你最近有没有服用了什么药物？
B: Then what can be the reason? Have you taken any medicine recently?

甲：药我倒是没吃，不过我在减肥，每天都喝减肥茶。
A: I haven't taken any medicine, but I am on a diet now, and I drink tea to reduce my weight.

乙：难怪你会不舒服，原来你在喝药减肥啊。其实像你这样的身材，没有必要减肥。就是要减肥，也应该先去医生那儿咨询一下，否则，反而会弄坏身体。
B: No wonder you feel uncomfortable. You are actually taking diet medicine. In fact, a person who has your figure doesn't need to be on a diet, and has no need to lose weight. If you want to lose weight, you should first go to your doctor for consultation, or you will ruin your health.

甲：我觉得我越来越胖，要是我不喝减肥茶，我能做什么呢？

133

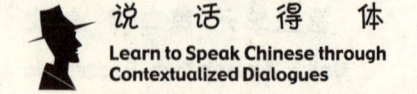

说 话 得 体
Learn to Speak Chinese through Contextualized Dialogues

A: I thought I was gaining weight. If I don't drink diet tea, what else should I do?

乙：你这完全是心理因素。我认为最好的方法是平时要坚持锻炼、多做运动。

B: What happened to you is entirely out of psychological factors. The best thing I can suggest is to do daily physical training, and do more exercises.

甲：对了，我家附近有一个健身房，刚开张。哪天抽空去看看。

A: That's right. There is a fitness center that has just opened. It is near my house. I should find a day to go and have a look there.

乙：越早越好！从健康考量，你得马上停止喝减肥茶。

B: The earlier, the better. For the benefit of your health, you should stop drinking the diet tea.

甲：好，听你的。

A: OK.

词语表　New Words

课业	kèyè	study; course work
缘故	yuángù	reason; cause; for the reason of
压力	yālì	pressure
轻松	qīngsōng	relaxed; light
布置	bùzhì	assign; make arrangements for
见鬼	jiànguǐ	see the ghost; absurd; fantastic
原因	yuányīn	cause
服用	fúyòng	take (medicine)
药物	yàowù	medicine; drug
减肥	jiǎnféi	on diet; reduce weight; weight-loss
难怪	nánguài	no wonder
舒服	shūfu	comfortable
身材	shēncái	stature; figure
咨询	zīxún	consult; seek advice from
否则	fǒuzé	otherwise

Unit 5 Lesson Two Suggesting

反而	fǎn'ér	on the contrary
心理	xīnlǐ	psychology; mentality
因素	yīnsù	factor; element
坚持	jiānchí	persist in; uphold; stick to
锻炼	duànliàn	to exercise; have physical training
运动	yùndòng	exercise; sports; athletics
健身房	jiànshēnfáng	gym; fitness center
开张	kāizhāng	open (for business)
健康	jiànkāng	health
考量	kǎoliáng	for the benefit of; consideration
停止	tíngzhǐ	to stop

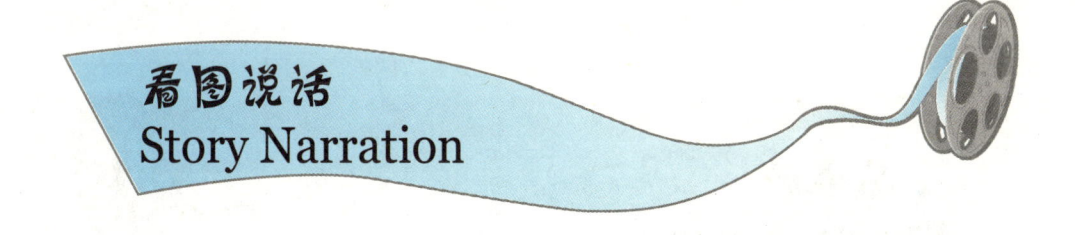

看图说话 Story Narration

按照以下图画顺序及各幅图画所提示的情景，叙述一个有始有终的完整故事。

Based on the order of the following pictures and the situations presented in each, narrate a story including a beginning and an end.

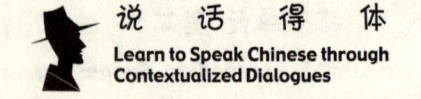

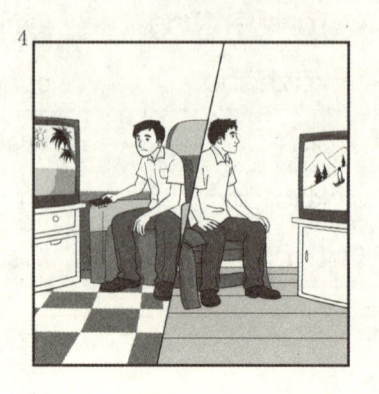

说 话 得 体
Learn to Speak Chinese through Contextualized Dialogues

小品表演
Skit Performance

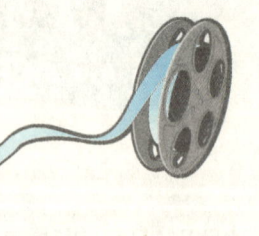

学生创作对话小品时尽可能使用本单元列出的和学生学到的新词、新句。小品主题选择应该得到老师首肯，以免重复。

Create situational dialogues with topics approved by the teacher to avoid repetition. Use as many expressions listed/learned in this unit as possible.

对话地点（时间） Place (Time) of Dialogue	对话情景 Context	对话者之间的关系 Relation Between Speakers
1　在电话里 　　on the phone	出主意买生日礼物 offering a suggestion on buying a birthday gift	在两位朋友之间 between two friends

136

第五单元 第二课 建议
Unit 5 Lesson Two Suggesting

2	在图书馆查阅资料时 when searching for materials at the library	出主意怎么选择好大学 suggesting how to select a good college to attend	在两位同学之间 between two classmates
3	在宿舍里 in the dormitory	出主意安排暑期生活 suggesting how to arrange the summer vacation	在两位同学之间 between two classmates
4	在旅行社里 at a travel agency	建议去中国旅游 making a suggestion to visit China	在旅行社职员和客人之间 between a travel agent and a customer
5	在学校里 in the school	出主意开个玩笑 suggesting to play a practical joke	在两位朋友之间 between two friends
6	在图书馆里 at the library	建议如何考美国历史 offering advice on studying for the exam of American History	在高年级学生和一年级学生之间 between a senior and a freshman
7	在讨论会上 at a discussion	建议改变教学方法 making suggestions to improve pedagogy	在学生和老师之间 between a student and a teacher
8	在计划课外活动时 when planning an extra curricular activity	建议参观一个博物馆 making a suggestion to visit a museum	在学生之间 between two students
9	在约会时 when dating with someone	建议去某家餐馆吃饭 suggesting to dine at a particular restaurant	在男女朋友之间 between a boyfriend and a girlfriend
10	在家里 at home	推荐一个值得看的地方 recommending a place worth seeing	在主人和来访客人之间 between a host/hostess and a visitor

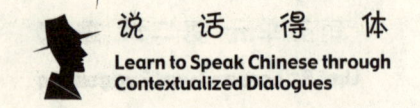

说 话 得 体
Learn to Speak Chinese through
Contextualized Dialogues

练笔
Writing Exercise

根据要求写一篇短文。尽可能用上本单元学到的词句。

Write a short passage on the given topic. Do your best to use words and expressions from the sentence patterns you have learned in this unit.

对有作弊习惯的同学提出建议 (Write a suggestion to your classmate who has a bad habit of cheating.)

第五单元听力练习
Listening Comprehension Unit 5

听完以下各项听力练习的内容，先回答理解提示中的问题，再识别句子或语段的语境，然后尽可能使用本单元列出的和学到的新词、新句做适当的回应。

After listening to the sentences given, identify a proper context and response in each situation, using as many expressions listed/learned in this unit as possible.

	1. 理解提示 Comprehension	2. 情景识别 Context Identification	3. 学生回应 Student's Response
1	What will the teacher receive for her birthday?		
2	What would the speaker do if he were the listener?		
3	What would the listener probably do after this conversation?		
4	What have they been doing?		
5	Who are the speaker and the listener?		
6	What if the listener does not take this advice?		
7	What happened to the listener?		我会的，谢谢你的关心。
8	What will the listener do tonight?		

139

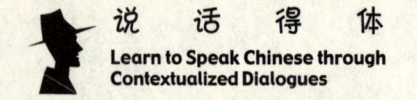

(续表)

	1. 理解提示 Comprehension	2. 情景识别 Context Identification	3. 学生回应 Student's Response
9	What do the policemen always do at this place?		
10	What should the listener bring? Why?		

第六单元
Unit 6

第一课 许诺
Lesson One   Promising

常用词句
Common Expressions

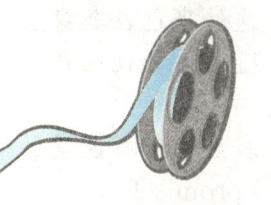

常用词句 Common Expressions	回应提示参考 Suggested Responses
1 我保证! I promise.	我怎么能相信你的保证? How can I believe your promise?
2 我肯定! I am sure.	你那么肯定?我倒有点儿怀疑了。 Are you so sure? On the contary, I am suspicious.
3 我答应你,明天我一定再来看你。 I promise I will come to see you tomorrow.	我等你。明天见! I will wait for you. See you tomorrow.
4 我对天发誓! I swear to God!	请你不要把话说绝了。 Don't be so sure.
5 我以我的名誉担保。 I swear by my honor.	好,我相信你。 Good, I trust you.
6 请你放心吧!下不为例。 Please feel assured that it won't happen again.	就这样吧。 That's fine.
7 请你相信我,我会以实际行动弥补我的过失。	只要认识错误,改正了就行了。

143

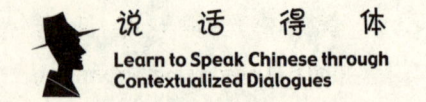

说 话 得 体
Learn to Speak Chinese through Contextualized Dialogues

常用词句 Common Expressions	回应提示参考 Suggested Responses
Trust me, I know I messed up, but I will fix it.	It is fine as long as you realize your mistake and correct it.
8 这件事包在我身上。 I'll take care of it.	有你负责，我也就放心了。 With you in charge, I feel at ease.
9 我敢为你打包票。 I promise!	你算老几?你说话算数吗? Who do you think you are? Do you live up to your word?
10 难道我会骗你吗?我敢跟你打赌。 Are you saying I'm lying to you? I promise you I'm not.	我才不跟你一般见识呢! I won't lower myself to the same level as you.
11 这是最后一次了，我再也不敢了。 This is the last time. It won't happen again.	我量你也不敢。 It better not.
12 我会努力让你满意的，你等着瞧吧。 I'll do my best to make you happy. You wait and see.	好。我等着你的好消息。 Good, I will wait for your good news.
13 我们是绝不会毁约的。 We will keep the contract.	行啊!我们有合同，一切都按合同行事。 Fine. We'll do everything in accordance with the contract.
14 这笔钱我一定按期如数还给你。 I swear to return your money on time.	我信得过你。 I trust you.
15 大丈夫一语既出，驷马难追。 What is said cannot be unsaid.	说的比唱的还好听。 It sounds better than it really is.
16 我吸取教训了。 I have learned a lesson.	但愿如此! I hope so.
17 一言为定。 It's settled.	好，一言为定。 Yes. It's settled.

第六单元 第一课 许诺
Unit 6　Lesson One　Promising

常用词句 Common Expressions	回应提示参考 Suggested Responses
18　我决不反悔。 I will never change my mind.	我要看你的实际行动。 Then I need to see your actions.

情景对话
Contextualized Dialogues

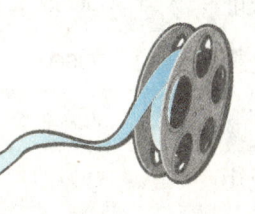

对话一：不再失信
Dialogue I：No More Breaking Promises

人　物 Characters	甲：学生 A：A student	乙：图书馆馆员 B：A library
关　系 Relationship	在图书馆馆员和同学之间 Between a librarian and a student	
情　景 Location	在图书馆里 In the library	

甲：我保证明天一定把书带来还给你。
A：I guarantee I will bring the book and return it to you tomorrow.

乙：我才不信呢。你这是第三次保证了。
B：I don't believe you. This is your third time promising.

甲：这回我发誓，真的不会再忘了。要不，我把学生证押在你这儿。
A：I swear I will this time. I really won't forget, or you may keep my student ID here.

乙：我们没有这种规矩。好吧，这次就算了。我再给你一次机会，你可不能老是这样。
B：We don't have such a rule. All right, never mind. I will give you another opportunity, but you can't act like this all the time.

甲：放心吧，我一定说到做到，不让你再失望。

145

说话得体
Learn to Speak Chinese through Contextualized Dialogues

A：You wait and see. Definitely, I will do as what I said, and you won't be disappointed.

词语表　New Words

保证	bǎozhèng	guarantee
发誓	fāshì	to swear
押	yā	give as security
规矩	guīju	established practice
算了	suànle	leave it at that, never mind

对话二：修理电脑
Dialogue II：Repairing a Computer

人　物 Characters	甲：技术员 A：A technician	乙：学生 B：A student
关　系 Relationship	在技术员和学生之间 Between a technician and a student	
情　景 Location	在电脑维修部门 At a computer repair shop	

甲：这台电脑没有什么大问题，留在这儿修吧，过一个星期来取。
A：There is no major problem with this computer. You may leave it here for repair, and come to pick it up in a week.

乙：要等到下个星期吗？我还得用它写实验报告，星期一就得交。师傅你能不能早一点为我修呢？
B：Do I have to wait for a week? I have to write a lab report on it, and it must be turned in next Monday. Sir, can you repair it for me earlier?

甲：既然你急着要用，那我马上就动手修，你明天下午来取吧。
A：Since you need it badly, I will start to repair it right away. You may come and pick it up tomorrow afternoon.

146

乙：太好了!明天肯定行吗?
B：That's wonderful! Are you sure about tomorrow?

甲：这还用说?我答应你了,你到时候来取就是了。
A：I'm sure. I promise. Just come to get it on time.

词语表　New Words

取	qǔ	to pick up
实验报告	shíyàn bàogào	lab report
交	jiāo	turn in; hand in
师傅	shīfu	master
既然	jìrán	since
急	jí	urgent; pressing; nervous; anxious
动手	dòngshǒu	start work; get to work
肯定	kěndìng	surely
行	xíng	fine; be all right
答应	dāying	assent; consent; to promise

对话三：额外加分
Dialogue III: Extra Credit

人物 Characters	甲：老师 A：A teacher	乙：学生 B：A student
关系 Relationship	在老师和学生之间 Between a teacher and a student	
情景 Location	在老师办公室 At teacher's office	

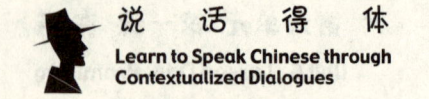

说 话 得 体
Learn to Speak Chinese through Contextualized Dialogues

甲：你答应上个星期补交作业，可是你食言了。
A： You promised to turn in your make-up homework last week, but you didn't keep your promise.

乙：对不起，老师。我不是故意的。再给我一个星期，我保证这个周末做完，星期一一早就放到您的桌子上。
B： I am sorry. Teacher, it was actually not on purpose. I will finish it this week. Please give me another chance, and I will place it on your desk early next Monday.

甲：只有这样了。我担心的是你这次考试，可千万别忘了准备。
A： That's fine for now. What concerns me is the test you will take this time. Be sure not to forget to be well prepared for it.

乙：保证忘不了。老师，要是我考试考得好，您能不能给我额外加分？
B： I promise I won't forget. Teacher, if I can do the test well, can you give me extra credit?

甲：那要看你自己了。平时作业不做，考试又怎么能考好呢？
A： It depends on you. You always fail to do homework. How can you do well on the test?

乙：老师，求求您了。这门课我一定得通过，否则下学期我要被列入试读名单了。
B： Teacher, I am begging you. I have to pass the test, or I will be on probation next semester.

甲：我不能保证，但是你如果考试成绩好，我会酌情处理的。加把劲吧！
A： I can't guarantee it, but if you have a good grade on the test, I will take the circumstance into consideration. Put forward your best effort.

乙：我会努力让您满意的。
B： I will work hard, and you will be satisfied.

词语表　New Words

补	bǔ	to make up
食言	shíyán	eat one's own words; break one's promise
并不是	bìng bù shì	actually not
故意	gùyì	on purpose; deliberately
一早	yīzǎo	early in the morning
担心	dānxīn	worry; feel anxious

第六单元 第一课 许诺
Unit 6　Lesson One　Promising

额外	éwài	extra; additional
加分	jiā fēn	to give extra credit
求	qiú	to beg
列入	lièrù	to be placed in
试读	shìdú	on probation; academic probation
名单	míngdān	name list
成绩	chéngjì	grade; achievement; progress
酌情	zhuóqíng	take the circumstance into consideration
处理	chǔlǐ	to handle; to settle
加把劲	jiā bǎ jìn	put on a spurt; put forth strength
努力	nǔlì	make great efforts; try hard; hard-working

对话四：促销期间
Dialogue IV: Sales Promotion

人物 Characters	甲：商店职员 A：A store clerk	乙：顾客 B：A customer
关系 Relationship	在商店职员和顾客之间 Between a store clerk and a customer	
情景 Location	在照相机商店 At a camera store	

甲：先生，您想买什么？
A：Sir, what would you like to buy?

乙：我想选购一架数码照相机，可是我不懂，你能不能帮我出出点子？
B：I'd like to buy a digital camera. But, I don't know anything about cameras. Do you have any suggestions?

甲：没问题。我给您当参谋，您会满意的。
A：No problem. I will give you some advice to meet your needs.

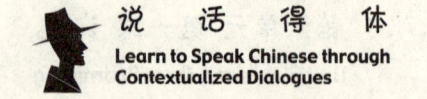

说 话 得 体
Learn to Speak Chinese through Contextualized Dialogues

乙：这架相机怎么样？
B：What do you think of this one?

甲：这架相机外观很漂亮，可是有些过时了，功能不够多，我不敢保证您会喜欢。
A：Its appearance is good, but it is a little bit out of date, and it does not have many functions. I can't guarantee that you will like it.

乙：那个呢？
B：How about that one?

甲：这种相机应该算是不错的。价格虽然贵了点儿，可是功能齐全，操作也比较简单，质量我敢打包票。
A：This camera is pretty good. Although it is expensive, it has complete functions, and it is easy to operate. As for the quality, I can guarantee it.

乙：听你这么一说，我确实有点动心了。可是这么贵的商品，万一坏了怎么办呢？
B：Having heard what you have said, I am indeed considering buying it. But since it is so expensive, what if it does not work?

甲：这家公司的产品除了货真价实以外，还有保修期长、售后服务好的特点。心动不如行动，趁现在正值促销的机会，花这笔钱还是值得的。买了，您绝对不会后悔的，我以本店的声誉担保。
A：The products of this company are genuine goods at a fair price. In addition to that it has a special long-term warranty and good after-sales service. Don't hesitate, but take action. Take advantage of the sales promotion right at this moment. It is worth spending this amount of money. You will absolutely not regret it. I can vouch for it with the reputation of this store.

词语表　New Words

选购	xuǎngòu	pick out and buy; selective purchasing
数码	shùmǎ	digital
照相机	zhàoxiàngjī	camera
出点子	chū diǎnzi	make suggestions
参谋	cānmóu	give advice
外观	wàiguān	appearance; exterior
过时	guòshí	out of date; out of fashion

Unit 6 Lesson One Promising

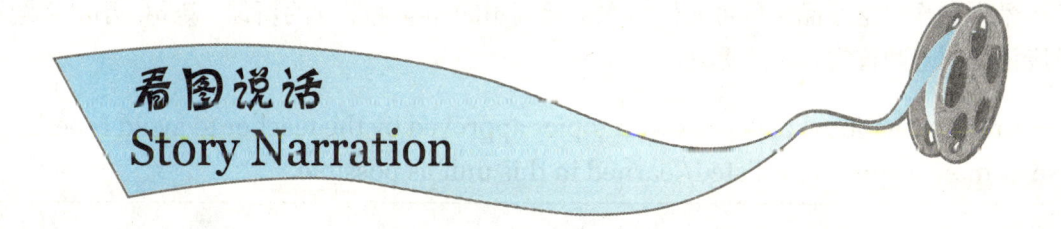

功能	gōngnéng	function
价格	jiàgé	price
齐全	qíquán	complete; all in readiness
打包票	dǎ bāopiào	guarantee; vouch for
确实	quèshí	in deed
动心	dòngxīn	touched; moved
商品	shāngpǐn	product
货真价实	huò zhēn jià shí	genuine goods at a fair price
售后服务	shòuhòu fúwù	after sale service
心动	xīndòng	touched; moved
行动	xíngdòng	take action
趁	chèn	take advantage of
正值	zhèngzhí	right at the time of
促销	cùxiāo	sales promotion
期间	qījiān	during; period; time
声誉	shēngyù	reputation; fame
担保	dānbǎo	warrant; guarantee

看图说话 Story Narration

按照以下图画顺序及各幅图画所提示的情景，叙述一个有始有终的完整故事。

Based on the order of the following pictures and the situations presented in each, narrate a story including a beginning and an end.

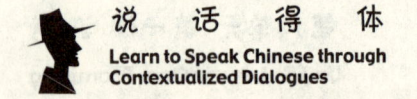

说 话 得 体
Learn to Speak Chinese through Contextualized Dialogues

小品表演
Skit Performance

学生创作对话小品时尽可能使用本单元列出的和学生学到的新词、新句。小品主题选择应该得到老师首肯，以免重复。

Create situational dialogues with topics approved by the teacher to avoid repetition. Use as many expressions listed/learned in this unit as possible.

对话地点（时间） Place (Time) of Dialogue	对话情景 Context	对话者之间的关系 Relation Between Speakers
1 在电话里 on the phone	答应保守秘密 agreeing to keep a secret	在两位朋友之间 between two friends
2 在电梯里 in the elevator	答应帮忙 agreeing to offer help	在两位邻居之间 between two neighbors

152

第六单元 第一课 许诺
Unit 6 Lesson One Promising

3	课后 after class	答应给同学看课堂笔记 agreeing to lend class notes to a classmate	在两位同学之间 between two classmates
4	准备明天的会议 when preparing tomorrow's meeting	答应在会前把文件准备好 agreeing to get documents prepared before the meeting	在公司主管和秘书之间 between a manager and a secretary
5	在电话里 on the phone	答应去看医生 agreeing to visit the doctor	在两位亲戚之间 between two relatives
6	在校长办公室里 at the principal's office	保证改正，不再犯了 promising not to commit the wrong doing again	在校长和学生之间 between a principal and a student
7	在学校停车场 at the school's parking lot	保证赔偿损失 promising to pay for the damage	在两位同学之间 between two classmates
8	在教室里 in the classroom	保证按时归还 promising to return on time	在两位同学之间 between two classmates
9	在电话里 on the phone	保证准时出席 promising to attend a meeting	在邀请者和被邀请者之间 between an inviter and the invited
10	在商务洽谈时 during a business talk	保证按合约办事 promising to follow the contract	在推销员和客户之间 between a salesperson and his/her client

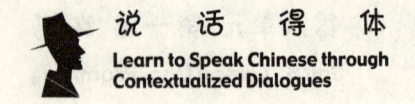

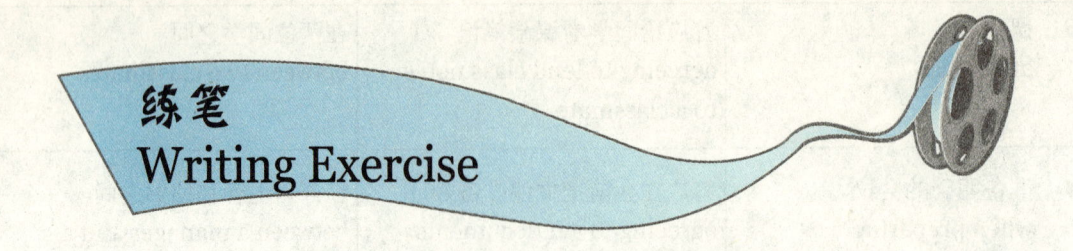

说 话 得 体
Learn to Speak Chinese through Contextualized Dialogues

练笔
Writing Exercise

根据要求写一篇短文。尽可能用上本单元学到的词句。

Write a short passage on the given topic. Do your best to use words and expressions from the sentence patterns you have learned in this unit.

写信给老师保证不再旷课 (Write a letter to the teacher promising to no longer cut class.)

第二课 致歉
Lesson Two Apologizing

常用词句
Common Expressions

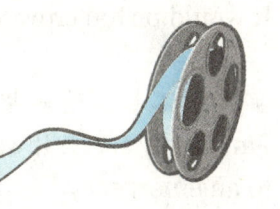

常用词句 Common Expressions	回应提示参考 Suggested Responses
1　对不起！请原谅！ I am sorry! Please forgive me.	行了，不必再说了。 It's okay. You don't have to say anything.
2　抱歉，抱歉。请多多包涵！ I am sorry. Please excuse any mistakes.	没有关系啦。把这件事忘了吧。 It doesn't matter. Just forget it.
3　我很后悔做了这件事。都是我不对。 I regret having done it. It's my fault.	知错就改，还是好样的。 You are still a great man by correcting your mistake once you recognized it.
4　来晚了，来晚了，让你们久等了，真不好意思。 I feel really embarrassed that I came late and made you wait for a long time.	那你看吧，你应该为我们做些什么来弥补？ So how will you fix it for us?
5　我先走一步，失陪了！ I have to leave early. Excuse me for my absence.	你走好！不送了。 Walk carefully. I will not see you off any further.
6　我真不知道您会来。有失远迎。 I didn't expect you to come. Sorry for not greeting you.	我是临时决定的。谁也没告诉。 I made the decision unexpectedly, and I didn't tell anybody about the trip.

155

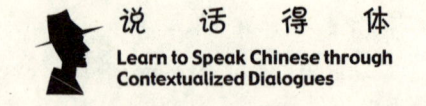

说 话 得 体
Learn to Speak Chinese through Contextualized Dialogues

常用词句 Common Expressions	回应提示参考 Suggested Responses
7 真对不住你。我的车太小，你坐进来也许会太挤了。 I am really sorry. My car is too small. It would be too crowded if I took you.	你总有办法拒绝我。 You always find excuses to refuse me.
8 实在对不起，这是临时决定改变的。 I am really sorry. It was changed due to an emergency.	没关系，我已经习惯了。 It doesn't matter. I am used to it.
9 我失信了，可是我并不是故意的。 I broke the promise, but it was not on purpose.	记住了，下不为例。 Don't forget that, you can't do it again.
10 请你别太认真。 Please don't take it too seriously.	我哪儿认真了?是你自己太敏感了吧。 Do I take it seriously? Is it you who is too sensitive about it?
11 这不是我的本意，你就高抬贵手吧。 I didn't mean it. Will you please forgive me?	你走吧! You may leave.
12 我承认这是我的过错。我在这儿向你道歉。 This is my mistake. My apologies!	算了，下不为例。 OK. Just this once.
13 这是我的失职，我愿意接受任何处罚。 This is my fault, and I am willing to accept any punishment.	这我做不了主，由人事部门处理。 I can't make the final decision. It is up to the Division of Human Resources to process.
14 我听了一面之词，错怪你了，请你原谅。 Please forgive me for only listening to the one-sided story and unjustly blaming you.	我原谅你了。你也别把它当成一回事儿。 I will forgive you. Don't take it seriously.
15 是我失礼了，请你千万别在意，大人不计小人过。	看你说的。你把我当什么人了? What are you talking about? Who do

156

Unit 6 Lesson Two Apologizing

常用词句 Common Expressions	回应提示参考 Suggested Responses
It's my impoliteness. Don't take it seriously. Please be generous and forgiving.	you think I am?
16 我知道错了，请再给我一个机会吧。 I know I made it wrong. Please give me another chance.	好，我就再给你一次将功补过的机会。 Fine. I will give you another chance to make it up.
17 是我不小心闯的祸，一切损失由我来赔偿。 It's an accident caused by my carelessness. I'll pay for all the damages.	不必了。以后小心点儿就行了。 It is not necessary. It will be fine if you are careful next time.
18 我真该死！我怎么会这样呢？ Oh, no. How can I be like this?	你不必那么自责了。谁能不犯一点儿错？ Don't be so hard to yourself. Everyone makes mistakes.
19 昨天我说的话都收回，咱们和解吧。 I take back what I said yesterday. Let us make up.	对对对！和为贵嘛。我们和解了。 You are absolutely right. It is important to be harmonious. We have made up with each other.
20 我倒没什么，可是却让您操（费）心了。 It's fine with me, but it has caused you too much trouble.	我只是做了我应该做的事。 I only did what I should do.

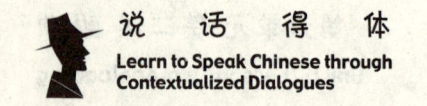

说 话 得 体
Learn to Speak Chinese through Contextualized Dialogues

情景对话
Contextualized Dialogues

对话一：隐私权
Dialogue I：Right to Privacy

人 物 Characters	甲：室友甲 　A：Roommate A	乙：室友乙 　B：Roommate B
关 系 Relationship	在两位同屋之间 Between two roommates	
情 景 Location	在学生宿舍里 At the student dormitory	

甲：真对不起，我也不知道是怎么回事，看了你的日记。
A：I am sorry. I didn't know what was wrong with me when I read your diary.

乙：你怎么可以私自翻看我的东西？
B：How can you look through my stuff without my permission?

甲：我真不知道我是怎么了。我该死!请你原谅!
A：I really don't know what was wrong with me. "I deserve to die." Please forgive me.

乙：你也真是的。日记是我个人隐私，是随便让人看的吗?这次我可以原谅你，可是，记住没有下回了。
B：You are really something. My diary is private. Is it for people to read at their whim? I may forgive you this time, but keep in mind that you don't have a second chance.

第六单元 第二课 致歉
Unit 6　Lesson Two Apologizing

词语表　New Words

怎么回事	zěnme huíshì	what's the matter?
日记	rìjì	diary; journal
私自	sīzì	without permission
翻	fān	to search
该死	gāisǐ	deserve death
原谅	yuánliàng	to excuse
真是的	zhēnshi de	(used in a complaint or an apology) indeed; really
个人隐私	gèrén yǐnsī	privacy
记住	jìzhù	to keep in mind
下回(次)	xiàhuí(cì)	next time

对话二：坏记性
Dialogue II：A Poor Memory

人物 Characters	甲：女朋友 A：The girlfriend	乙：男朋友 B：The boyfriend
关系 Relationship	在一对恋人之间 Between two lovers	
情景 Location	在学校 At the school	

甲：昨天晚上你是怎么回事?

A：What happened yesterday evening?

乙：我怎么啦?

B：Did I do anything wrong?

甲：我们不是说得好好的，一块儿去看林老师，你还让我买了鲜花在图书馆门口等你呢!

A：Didn't we make an appointment to visit Mr. Lin? You made me buy flowers and wait for you at the library entrance.

159

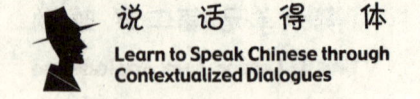

说 话 得 体
Learn to Speak Chinese through Contextualized Dialogues

乙：啊呀!瞧我这记性。我把这件事忘得一干二净。昨天丁新来看我，我俩一块儿去市内看电影了。

B：Oh, my! Look at my poor memory. I had completely forgotten about it. Ding Xin came to see me yesterday, and we went together to see a movie downtown.

甲：你怎么这么不负责任?让我一个人捧着花在图书馆门口傻等了四十五分钟。

A：Why were you so irresponsible? I stupidly waited alone at the library entrance, holding the flowers, for 45 minutes.

乙：我不是故意的。我一定接受这次教训，保证不再犯了。你宽宏大量就原谅我这一次吧。

B：I didn't do it deliberately. I have learned a lesson from it, and I promise I will not do it again. You are kind and generous. Forgive me this time.

甲：看你这次是初犯，我就饶了你，下不为例，听清楚了没有?

A：Since this is your first time, I forgive you, but not next time. Have you clearly heard what I said?

词语表　New Words

怎么啦	zěnme la	What's wrong?
鲜花	xiānhuā	fresh flower
记性	jìxing	memory
一干二净	yī gān èr jìng	clean out completely; cleared up without reminder
俩	liǎ	two
市内	shì nèi	in the city; downtown
捧	pěng	hold or carry in both hands
傻	shǎ	stupid; silly
教训	jiàoxun	lesson
犯	fàn	to do; to offend; to commit a wrong doing
宽宏大量	kuānhóng dàliàng	kind and generous
初犯	chūfàn	first offense
饶	ráo	to forgive
下不为例	xià bù wéi lì	not to be repeated

Unit 6 Lesson Two Apologizing

对话三：又迟到了
Dialogue III: Being Late Again

人 物 Characters	甲：同事甲 A: Colleague A	乙：同事乙 B: Colleague B
关 系 Relationship	在老同事之间 Between two old colleagues	
情 景 Location	在餐桌上 At the dinner table	

甲：你(老兄)怎么又姗姗来迟?这回又是怎么啦?
A：You, old friend, arrived late again. What happened this time?

乙：不好意思，临时有点儿事耽搁了，来晚了，让诸位久等。请多多原谅。
B：I am sorry. I was delayed by something unexpected. Please excuse me for being late and making you wait so long.

甲：一声"请原谅"就行了吗?这回是绝不会再便宜你了。
A：Is saying, "excuse me", going to make everything fine? We will not let you get away with it so easily.

乙：那你们说我该为你们做些什么来弥补过错?今天晚上吃饭，我请各位了，怎么样?
B：Then what should I do for you to make up for my mistake? I will treat you and pay for the meal this evening. What do you think about that?

甲：这还不够，还要罚酒三杯，大家说好不好?
A：It's not enough. I will make you drink as punishment. Is that okay?

乙：对对对!你说得完全对!我该罚，该罚。我今天吸取点儿教训，保证下次不敢再迟到了。
B：It's okay! You are perfectly right. I deserve the punishment, and I will draw a lesson from it. I promise I won't be late again.

词语表 New Words

姗姗来迟	shānshān lái chí	be long (slow) in coming; arrive late
临时	línshí	at the time when sth. happens

161

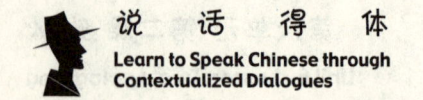

说话得体
Learn to Speak Chinese through Contextualized Dialogues

诸位	zhūwèi	everybody; all of you
久等	jiǔděng	wait for long time
弥补	míbǔ	to make up; to smooth over
过错	guòcuò	fault
罚酒	fájiǔ	be made to drink as punishment
吸取	xīqǔ	to draw a lesson
迟到	chídào	be late; arrive late; tardy

对话四：收回所说的话
Dialogue IV: Taking Back What was Said

人 物 Characters	甲：男朋友 A: The boyfriend	乙：女朋友 B: The girlfriend
关 系 Relationship	在一对恋人之间 Between two lovers	
情 景 Location	在街上 In the street	

甲：玛丽，请等一下，我想我们俩应该找个时间好好谈谈。
A: Mary, please wait a minute. I think we two should find some time to sit down and have a good talk.

乙：事情已经这样了，没什么好谈的了。
B: It happened already, and I don't have anything to say.

甲：昨天是我不好，我听了别人的一面之词，错怪了你，还说了重话。现在我知道错了，我把我说的话全收回，该行了吧？
A: It was my bad last night. I listened to a one-sided statement and blamed you wrongly. Moreover, I used harsh words. Now I realize it was my fault, and I take back my words. Is that okay with you?

乙：没门儿！我已经说过了，我再也不想见到你了。
B: No way! I have already said that I don't want to see you any more.

162

Unit 6 Lesson Two Apologizing

甲：玛丽，别这样。我是真心向你忏悔，向你道歉。我们和解吧，我会像以前那样待你。
A：Mary, don't be like that. I sincerely apologize. Let's become reconciled. I promise I will be nice to you just like before.

乙：我不相信你会回心转意。
B：I don't believe that you will change your mind.

甲：亲爱的，请想想我以前对你的种种好，就再给我一个机会吧。我说的都是心里话。难道你要我把心掏出来给你看吗？
A：My dear, think of my good deeds of all kinds in the past, and give me another chance. All my words are from the bottom of my heart. Do you really want me to take out my heart for you to examine?

乙：这倒也没有必要。只要你真的认识到自己的错误，不再重犯，我也会很快把这件不愉快的事忘掉。
B：No, it is not necessary. As long as you have truly realized your mistake, and are determined not to repeat it, I will forget this unpleasant event.

甲：太好了！那我现在请你去喝咖啡，怎么样？
A：Wonderful! I will treat you to coffee now, how about that?

乙：好吧，走吧。遇到你这样的朋友，我真不知道该怎么做才好。
B：Fine. Let's go. I really don't know what to do with a friend like you.

词语表 New Words

别人	biéren	other people, others
一面之词	yī miàn zhī cí	one-sided story; one-sided statement
错怪	cuòguài	to blame wrongly or unjustly
重话	zhònghuà	harsh words
收回	shōuhuí	take back
没门儿	méiménr	have no access; have no means
真心	zhēnxīn	heartfelt; sincere; true intention
忏悔	chànhuǐ	repent; confess (one's sin)
道歉	dàoqiàn	to apologize; make an apology
和解	héjiě	become reconciled

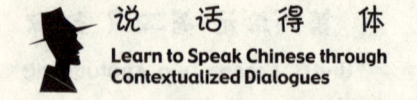

说话得体
Learn to Speak Chinese through Contextualized Dialogues

待	dāi	to treat
回心转意	huí xīn zhuǎn yì	turn back one's heart and change one's mind
种种好	zhǒngzhǒng hǎo	good deeds of all kinds
心里话	xīnlihuà	words from the bottom of the heart
掏	tāo	speak (from the bottom of the heart); take out
重犯	chóngfàn	repeat (an error or offense)
愉快	yúkuài	happy; pleasant
遇到	yùdào	to encounter; to come across

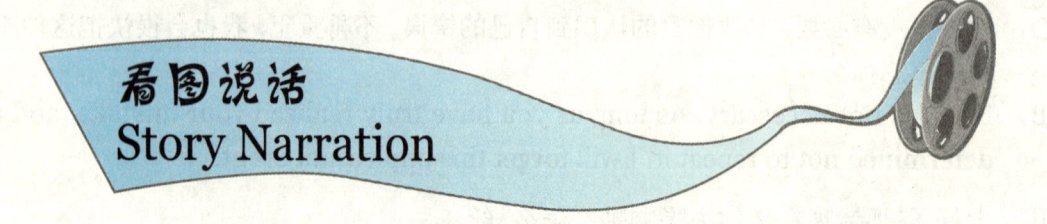

看图说话
Story Narration

按照以下图画顺序及各幅图画所提示的情景，叙述一个有始有终的完整故事。

Based on the order of the following pictures and the situations presented in each, narrate a story including a beginning and an end.

Unit 6 Lesson Two Apologizing

小品表演
Skit Performance

学生创作对话小品时尽可能使用本单元列出的和学生学到的新词、新句。小品主题选择应该得到老师首肯，以免重复。

Create situational dialogues with topics approved by the teacher to avoid repetition. Use as many expressions listed/learned in this unit as possible.

对话地点（时间） Place (Time) of Dialogue	对话情景 Context	对话者之间的关系 Relation Between Speakers
1 在学校门口 at the school gate	失约了 failing to keep an appointment	在男女朋友之间 between a boyfriend and a girlfriend
2 在电话里 on the phone	对朋友动了粗 having resorted to force with a friend	在两个好朋友之间 between two good friends
3 在马路上 in the street	看错了人 having recognized a person incorrectly	在两位路人之间 between two pedestrians
4 在办公室里 at the office	错怪了人 blaming a person wrongly	在单位主管和员工之间 between a department manager and a junior clerk
5 在办公室里 at the office	误了事 causing delay in work	在单位主管和员工之间 between a department manager and a junior clerk
6 在教室里 in the classroom	忘了事 forgetting something	在两个同学之间 between two students
7 在居住区 at the residential area	帮不了忙 beyond one's capacity	在两个朋友之间 between two friends

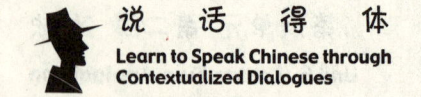

8	在家里 at home	做错了事 committing a wrong doing	在父母和孩子之间 between parents and a child
9	在教室里 in the classroom	完不了事 being unable to finish a task	在老师和学生之间 between a teacher and a student
10	在宿舍里 in the dormitory	说了谎话 having told a lie	在两个同学之间 between two classmates

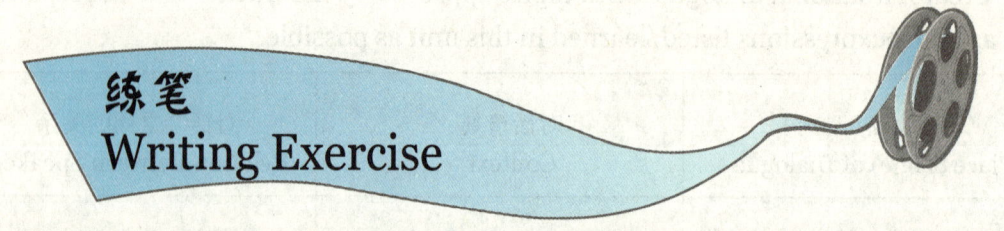

练笔
Writing Exercise

根据要求写一篇短文。尽可能用上本单元学到的词句。

Write a short passage on the given topic. Do your best to use words and expressions from the sentence patterns you have learned in this unit.

错怪了同屋，写信致歉 (Write a letter apologizing for having blamed a roommate wrongly.)

第六单元听力练习
Listening Comprehension Unit 6

听完以下各项听力练习的内容，先回答理解提示中的问题，再识别句子或语段的语境，然后尽可能使用本单元列出的和学到的新词、新句做适当的回应。

After listening to the sentences given, identify a proper context and response in each situation, using as many expressions listed/learned in this unit as possible.

	1. 理解提示 Comprehension	2. 情景识别 Context Identification	3. 学生回应 Student's Response
1	What did the speaker do wrong?		
2	Why was the speaker sorry?		
3	What did the speaker promise?		这才像话嘛。
4	When will it be ready for pick-up?		
5	What did the speaker do yesterday?		
6	What will the speaker do after the conversation?		
7	What did the listener do?		
8	What will the speaker receive?		
9	What did the speaker promise?		
10	What is the speaker trying to say?		

第七单元
Unit 7

第一课 同情
Lesson One   Showing Sympathy

常用词句
Common Expressions

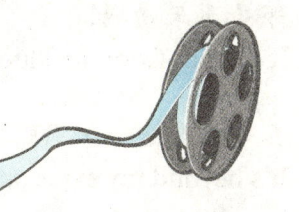

常用词句 Common Expressions	回应提示参考 Suggested Responses
1　我知道他失去了这份工作很难受，我也有过这种遭遇。 I know he feels upset over losing his job, I had a similar experience.	除了遗憾，我也无能为力。 I can't help but feel regret.
2　你没获胜，真(替你)可惜！ What a pity that you didn't win.	没关系。比赛嘛，总会有输赢的。我会总结经验教训的。 It's fine. Regarding competitions, there is always winning or losing. I will learn from the experience.
3　知道你输了，我深表同情。 I felt really sorry when I heard you had lost.	胜败乃兵家常事，不必想得太多。 Winning or losing a battle is a common military occurrence. You needn't think too much about it.
4　真想不到会出这样的事。 I really never thought it would happen like this.	我也是没有料到。真是"天有不测风云"啊。 I didn't expect it either. It is true that the unexpected always happens.
5　我简直不敢相信(我的眼睛/耳朵)。 I can't believe my eyes (ears).	谢谢你的关心。 Thank you for your concern.

171

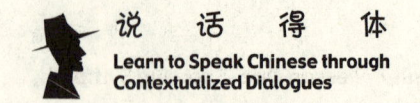

说 话 得 体
Learn to Speak Chinese through Contextualized Dialogues

常用词句 Common Expressions	回应提示参考 Suggested Responses
6 实在是不走运。 How unfortunate!	出点儿小岔，没关系。 It's only a small matter, and nothing serious.
7 那是飞来横祸! It's a blot from the blue.	只能怪我自己不小心。 I could only blame myself for my carelessness.
8 真是出人意料，不可思议。 It's beyond my expectation. It's incredible.	没关系，谁都会有马失前蹄的时候。 It doesn't matter. Anyone could encounter the situation of "falling on one's knees".
9 那样的事谁都无可奈何。 That's something no one can help with.	是啊。我现在想明白了。 You are right. I understand now.
10 你现在这个样子，让我很不安心。 I feel uncomfortable looking at your current state.	请放心，我会慢慢儿地好起来的。 Please feel at ease. I will be getting better gradually.
11 我为你感到非常惋惜。 I feel very sorry for you.	不必担心啦!我们去喝杯咖啡，把烦恼忘掉就没事了。 Don't worry about it. Let's go and have a cup of coffee so as to forget this unhappiness.
12 听到这个消息我很难受。 I felt bad when I heard the news.	大家都一样。事情很快就会过去的。一切都会好起来的。 Everyone feels this way. The problem will blow over, and everything will be fine.
13 我知道这是什么感受。 I know that feeling.	谢谢你的同情。 Thank you for your sympathy.
14 我能理解你此时此刻的心情。 I know how you're feeling at this moment.	只有你能理解我。真谢谢你。 Only you can understand me. I really thank you.
15 这真是一件不幸的事。 It is really unfortunate.	谁说不是呢? Who says it is not?
16 请允许我向你们表示最深切的同情。 Please allow me to express my deepest sympathies and condolences.	您这么忙,还来看我们,让我怎么担当得起? Although you are very busy, you came to see me. I don't think I am worthy of such a visit.

Unit 7　Lesson One　Showing Sympathy

常用词句 Common Expressions	回应提示参考 Suggested Responses
17 请接受我们最诚挚的慰问。 Please accept our sincerest condolences.	我从心底里感谢大家。 I thank every one of you from the bottom of my heart.
18 可怜！她现在一定很不好受。 What a pity! She must feel really bad now.	我们能为她做点儿什么吗？ Shall we do something for her?
19 我能为你做点什么吗？ Can I do anything for you?	不必了，谢谢！你们来我已经很感激了。 It is not necessary, but thank you. I already appreciated your coming.
20 愿你尽快恢复到最佳状态。 I hope you return to your peak condition soon.	谢谢！我会努力的。 Thank you! I will do my best.

情景对话
Contextualized Dialogues

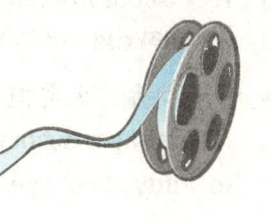

对话一：谈学业
Dialogue I：Talking about College Study

人物 Characters	甲：高中生 A：A high school student	乙：大学生 B：A college student
关系 Relationship	在大学生和高中生之间 Between a college student and a high school student	
情景 Location	在大学里 At the college	

甲：你答应过我，今天陪我去打网球的。
A：You had promised to play tennis with me today.

乙：今天不行了，明天我有一个物理实验报告要交。
B：I can't do it today. I have a lab report to turn in tomorrow.

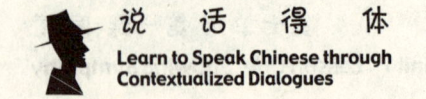

说话得体
Learn to Speak Chinese through Contextualized Dialogues

甲：真可惜。那后天星期六，怎么样？
A：What a pity! Then how about Saturday, the day after tomorrow?

乙：后天也不行，我们历史课有一个小组讨论，不知道什么时候才能结束。
B：It won't do either. We will have a group study for our history class. I have no idea when it will be over.

甲：真糟糕透了！那星期天，你该有空了吧。
A：That's terrible! Then how about Sunday? You must be free on Sunday.

乙：星期天更不行了，下星期是期末考试，星期一就有两个考试，我得认真复习。
B：Sunday would be the least possible. It will be our finals week next week. I have two tests on Monday, therefore I have to study seriously for the tests.

甲：你啊，真可怜！不就是上学念书吗？怎么会有那么多的事？
A：I feel sorry for you. You are always studying at college. How do you have so much work to do?

乙：你不知道。等你上了大学，你也会尝到这种滋味的。
B：You have no idea. When you attend college, you will have to experience it too.

甲：这样拼命，太可怕了。我为你们难过。我宁可不上大学。
A：To put up a desperate fight is very frightening. I feel bad for you. I prefer not to go to study at college.

词语表　New Words

网球	wǎngqiú	tennis
物理	wùlǐ	physics
可惜	kěxī	It's a pity; unfortunately
历史	lìshǐ	history
小组讨论	xiǎozǔ tǎolūn	group discussion
结束	jiéshù	to end
糟糕	zāogāo	What a mess! What bad luck!
透	tōu	fully; extremely
期末考试	qīmō kǎoshì	finals; final examination
可怜	kělián	pitiful; to have pity on

Unit 7 Lesson One Showing Sympathy

滋味	zīwèi	flavor; taste
拼命	pīnmìng	to risk one's life; put up a desperate fight
可怕	kěpà	fearful; frightening; horrible
难过	nánguò	have a hard time; upset
宁可	nìngkě	would rather

对话二：探望受伤者
Dialogue II: Visiting the Injured

人物 Characters	甲：学生甲 A：Student A	乙：学生乙 B：Student B
关系 Relationship	在两位毕业班学生之间 Between two seniors	
情景 Location	在医院 At the hospital	

甲：听说你出车祸了，我们大家都不敢相信，很为你担心哪！这不，派我赶来医院慰问你。
A: When we heard that you had a traffic accident, all of us could hardly believe it. We are worried about you. That's why I was sent to the hospital to extend our sympathy and best wishes.

乙：我已经好多了，谢谢你们的关心。
B: I am getting better now. Thank you for your concern.

甲：见到你现在平安无事，我感到很欣慰，心里的一块石头总算是落了地。
A: Having seen that you are safe and sound now, I feel delighted and pleased. We are now fully relieved.

乙：可是因为住院，前天通用公司的面试，我没能去成。
B: Because I was staying at the hospital, I was not able to make it for the interview with the General Electrics.

甲：是啊，出了车祸，连申请工作的面试机会也失去了，真可惜。
A: It is true that you had the car accident, and even lost the opportunity for the job interview. It really is a shame.

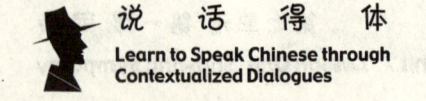

说 话 得 体
Learn to Speak Chinese through Contextualized Dialogues

乙：祸不单行，我也实在是太不走运了。
B: Bad events rarely come one at a time. It was really not my moment.

甲：别泄气，"留得青山在，不怕没柴烧"，只要身体康复了，一切都会好的。
A: Don't be discouraged. "As long as the green hills are there, one need not worry about firewood." When you are restored to health, everything will turn for the better.

词语表　New Words

听说	tīngshuō	it is said that
车祸	chēhuò	car accident
这不	zhè bù	that is why
派	pài	send
慰问	wèiwèn	to express sympathy and solicitude for; to console
关心	guānxīn	be concerned with; show solicitude for
感到	gǎndào	feel; to sense
欣慰	xīnwèi	feel delighted and pleased; pleasure
石头落地	shítou luòdì	lift (take) a weight off one's mind; fully relieved
面试	miànshì	interview
祸不单行	huò bù dān xíng	mishaps always come in battalions; misfortunes never come singly
走运	zǒuyùn	have one's moment; be lucky
留得青山在，	liú dé qīng shān zài,	As long as the green hills are there,
不怕没柴烧	bù pà méi chái shāo	one need not worry about firewood.
康复	kāngfù	recovery; restored to health

对话三：等待大学入学通知
Dialogue III: Waiting for College Admission

| 人物
Characters | 甲：学生甲
A: Student A | 乙：学生乙
B: Student B |

176

Unit 7 Lesson One Showing Sympathy

关 系 Relationship	在两位同学之间 Between two students
情 景 Location	在高中校园里 At the high school

甲：你还在等大学入学通知吗?
A：Are you still waiting for the college admission notice?

乙：是啊!我还在等东部几个大学的消息。加州大学也许是没有希望了。
B：Yes. I am waiting for the news from the universities in the east. It seems that I can't expect anything from the University of California.

甲：怎么啦?加州大学没有录取你?那太不幸了。
A：What was wrong that the University of California would not accept you? That is very unfortunate.

乙：我也不知道是出了什么问题，到现在还没有得到回音。
B：I don't know what was wrong. There hasn't been any information until now.

甲：真是出人意料，不可思议。不过，你不必过分烦恼，车到山前必有路，再说离截止日期还有一段日子，也许有更好的大学在向你招手呢!
A：This is really unexpected. It's incredible. But you don't have to be worried. Things will eventually sort themselves out. There are still quite a few days before the deadline. Probably a better university will admit you.

乙：真是这样，那就谢天谢地了。
B：Hopefully it is true. Thank goodness!

甲：你也可以打电话去问问，尽量朝好的方面想。
A：You may also make a telephone call and inquire about it. Do your best and keep thinking positively.

乙：我想向加州大学提出请求，希望他们复查我的档案，重新考虑。
B：I think I will turn in my petition, and ask them to reexamine my application and give a second consideration.

甲：对，应该试试，否则，太遗憾了。
A：Right. You should try or you will regret it.

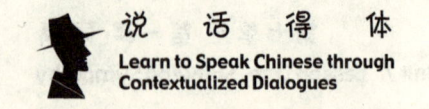

说话得体
Learn to Speak Chinese through Contextualized Dialogues

词语表　New Words

入学	rùxué	enter a school
东部	dōng bù	eastern part; in the east
加州	Jiāzhōu	California
录取	lùqǔ	enrollment; to recruit; admit to
不幸	bùxìng	unfortunately
回音	huíyīn	reply; response; echo
出人意料	chū rén yì liào	exceeding all expectations
不可思议	bù kě sī yì	inconceivable; unthinkable; beyond comprehension
烦恼	fánnǎo	be worried
车到山前必有路	chē dào shān qián bì yǒu lù　things will eventually sort themselves out	
截止日期	jiézhǐ rìqī	deadline
招手	zhāoshǒu	wave; welcome
谢天谢地	xiè tiān xiè dì	Thank goodness!
尽量	jǐnliàng	do all one can; to the best of one's ability
请求	qǐngqiú	request
复查	fùchá	check; double-check; reexamine
档案	dàng'àn	files; archives; record
重新	chóngxīn	again; anew; afresh
遗憾	yíhàn	regretful; sorry

对话四：最需要的关心
Dialogue IV：The Most Needed Care

人物 Characters	甲：街坊甲 A：Neighbor A	乙：街坊乙 B：Neighbor B

178

Unit 7　Lesson One　Showing Sympathy

关 系 Relationship	在两位街坊之间 Between two neighbors
情 景 Location	在社区里 In the community

甲：李太太的先生因病去世了。这几天李太太一直闭门不出。
A：Mrs. Li's husband just died of an illness. She has confined herself to the house these days.

乙：可怜的人啊！她现在一定很不好受。
B：Poor woman! She must find herself beset with all sorts of difficulties.

甲：他们俩身边没有子女，相依为伴这么多年了，今后李太太的日子该怎么过呢？
A：They have no kids, and have been depending on each other's company for so many years. It is hard to imagine how she will spend her days in the future.

乙：我能理解这是什么感受。
B：I can understand the overwhelming feeling she has.

甲：眼前她最需要的是大家的关心。
A：At this moment, what she needs most is our care.

乙：你看，我们能为她做点什么事吗？
B：Let's see, what can we do for her?

甲：我先去探望一下，看看她生活上缺少什么，回头我们再商量商量。
A：I will first pay a visit to her to see if she needs anything for daily life. After that we may have a discussion.

乙：请向她转达我诚挚的问候，请她节哀。
B：Please convey my sincere regards to her, and ask her not to feel so sad.

甲：好的，我会的。
A：Fine, I will.

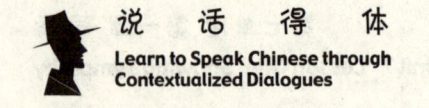

说话得体
Learn to Speak Chinese through Contextualized Dialogues

词语表 New Words

因病故世	yīn bìng gùshì	die of an illness
闭门不出	bì mén bù chū	be confined to the house
不好受	bù hǎoshòu	find oneself beset (with difficulties)
相依为伴	xiāng yī wéi bàn	depend on each other's company
理解	lǐjiě	to understand
感受	gǎnshòu	to feel; feelings; experience
探望	tànwàng	to visit
生活	shēnghuó	life; living
缺少	quēshǎo	lack; be short of
商量	shāngliang	consult; discuss
转达	zhuǎndá	pass on
诚挚	chéngzhì	sincere
问候	wènhòu	send one's regards (respects) to; extend greetings to
节哀	jié'āi	restrain one's grief

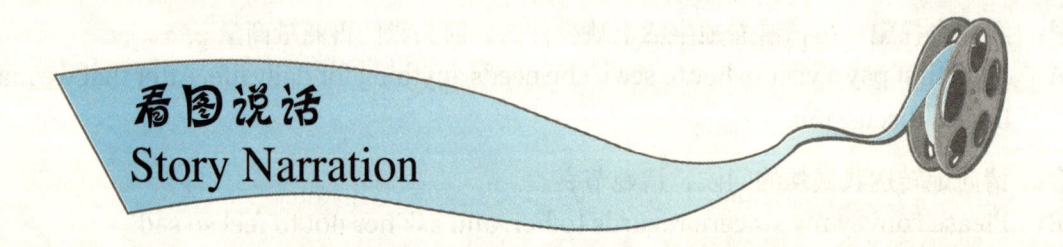

看图说话 Story Narration

按照以下图画顺序及各幅图画所提示的情景，叙述一个有始有终的完整故事。

Based on the order of the following pictures and the situations presented in each, narrate a story including a beginning and an end.

Unit 7 Lesson One Showing Sympathy

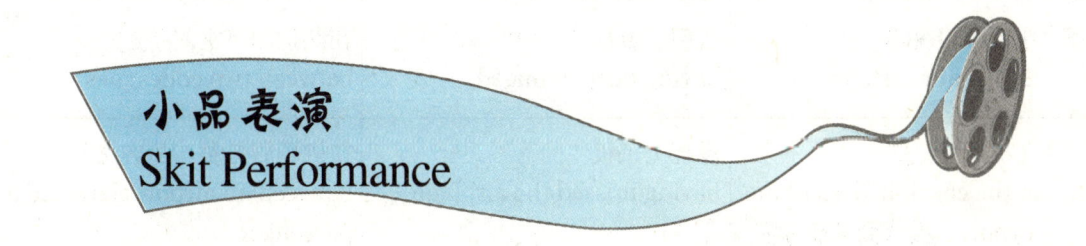

小品表演
Skit Performance

学生创作对话小品时尽可能使用本单元列出的和学生学到的新词、新句。小品主题选择应该得到老师首肯，以免重复。

Create situational dialogues with topics approved by the teacher to avoid repetition. Use as many expressions listed/learned in this unit as possible.

对话地点（时间） Place (Time) of Dialogue	对话情景 Context	对话者之间的关系 Relation Between Speakers
1　在电话里 　　on the phone	朋友的父（母）亲故世了 a friend's parent having passed away	在两位朋友之间 between two friends

181

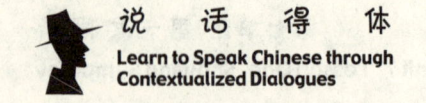

2	在宿舍里 in the dormitory	室友丢失了钱 roommate having lost money	在两位室友之间 between two roommates
3	在学校里 inside the school	同学家失窃了 classmate's house having been broken into	在两位同学之间 between two classmates
4	在社区内 inside the community	邻居出了车祸 a neighbor having had a car accident	在两位邻居之间 between two neighbors
5	最后一天课 last day of school	老师被校方解雇了 the teacher having been laid off	在老师与学生之间 between a teacher and a student
6	在考场外 outside of a testing center	考试没及格 having failed the test	在两位学生之间 between two students
7	在赛场外 outside of a stadium	球赛输了 having lost the game	在运动员与他的朋友之间 between an athlete and his friend
8	在停车场 at the parking lot	吃了一张交通罚单 having gotten a ticket	在两位老同学之间 between two former classmates
9	在餐厅用餐时 dining at a restaurant	受到了冤枉 having been wronged	在两位同事之间 between two colleagues
10	在机场登记处 at the check-in desk of the airport	没赶上班机 having missed the airplane	在机场服务员与旅客之间 between an airport clerk and a passenger

Unit 7　Lesson One　Showing Sympathy

Writing Exercise

根据要求写一篇短文。尽可能用上本单元学到的词句。

Write a short passage on the given topic. Do your best to use words and expressions from the sentence patterns you have learned in this unit.

老师被校方解雇了，写信表示同情 (Write a letter to your teacher who has been laid off by the school.)

第二课 安慰
Lesson Two　Giving Comfort and Reassurance

常用词句
Common Expressions

常用词句 Common Expressions	回应提示参考 Suggested Responses
1　别想不开！ 　　Don't take things too seriously.	我真不知道该怎么去面对将来？ I really don't know how to confront the future.
2　如果我是你，我就不会如此担心。 　　If I were you, I would not worry too much.	可我不是你啊。 But I'm not you.
3　别再难过了，一切都会好的。 　　Don't be upset. Everything will be fine.	谢谢你！ Thank you.
4　我确信事情最终会变好的。 　　I surely believe things will eventually get better.	我也是这么想的，可是我要等多久呢？ I think so too. But how long should I wait?
5　胜败乃兵家常事，输球也是难免的。 　　Winning or losing a battle is a common military occurrence, just as in a ball game.	你说得完全对。我们应该总结输球的原因，再接再厉。 What you said is perfectly right. We must learn from experience and continue to exert ourselves.

第七单元 第二课 安慰

Unit 7 Lesson Two Giving Comfort and Reassurance

常用词句 Common Expressions	回应提示参考 Suggested Responses
6 算了吧，感情的事是很难勉强的。你又何必吊死在一棵树上呢？ Leave it at that. These emotional feelings cannot be forced. Why must you keep a one-track mind?	谢谢你，可是我就是不明白，他为什么要这么对待我？ Thank you for your kindness. But I still don't understand why he treated me this way.
7 这不是你的错，你不必再为此不安了。 This is not your fault. You needn't feel bad at it.	不管怎么样，我也牵在里面，总感到有些内疚。 No matter what is going on, I have been involved in it. I somehow keep feeling guilty.
8 倒霉的不会是你一个人，我也有过这种麻烦，别难过了。 It's not only you that suffers from misfortune, I have experienced this trouble before too. Don't be upset.	我知道你这是在安慰我。 I know you are giving me words of comfort.
9 放心吧，事情还不至于那么糟。 You may rest assured, things are not that bad.	我也希望会出现转机。 I am also expecting a welcome change.
10 我保证你下次考试会及格的。 I guarantee that you will pass the next test.	有你这句话，我就有信心了。 With your words, I now have confidence.
11 天有不测风云，人有旦夕祸福。 Fortunes are as unpredictable as the weather.	你说得对极了。好在这种日子很快就会过去。 What you said is extremely correct. It is fortunate that the bad days will be over before long.
12 谁也不可能事事都如意的，你要尽量往好的方面看。 No one can expect everything to turn out as one wish. Do your best to look on the	我也同样有这种感觉。虽然，没能如愿，但是我们尽了最大的努力，可以为此感到欣慰了。 I feel the same way. We have done our

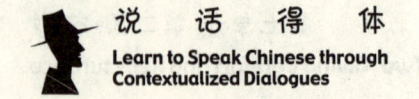

常用词句 Common Expressions	回应提示参考 Suggested Responses
bright side.	best, though we did not realize what we had expected. We should be grateful for the result.
13 道路是曲折的，前途是光明的。 The road is tortuous; the future is bright.	对,我们都应该把目光放远一点,向前看。 Right. We should look longterm and face forward.
14 千万别泄气，还有机会。 Never feel discouraged. There is a way out.	谢谢你的鼓励! Thank you for your encouragement.
15 别再过度忧伤了，过去的事情就让它过去吧。Don't be too upset. Let bygones be bygones.	是啊!是到该振作起来的时候了。 You are right. It's high time that we pull ourselves together.
16 不要再为这件事烦恼了。 Don't be upset by little things.	好，我听你的就是了。 Fine. I will just listen to you.
17 破财消灾!只要人没事就好。 Suffering unexpected financial losses removes bad luck. It is fine when nothing harmful happens to the person.	你说得对!东西没了可以再置。要是没了人还谈什么东西? That's ture. Things can be bought again. But what if lives are lost?
18 大难不死，必有后福!一切都会好起来的。 One who survives a great disaster is destined to have good fortune forever afterwards. Everything will be OK.	是啊，顺其自然吧。 Let it be.

第七单元 第二课 安慰
Unit 7　Lesson Two　Giving Comfort and Reassurance

情景对话
Contextualized Dialogues

对话一：违规受罚
Dialogue I：Fine for Traffic Violation

人 物 Characters	甲：街坊甲 A：Neighbor A	乙：街坊乙 B：Neighbor B
关 系 Relationship	在两位街坊之间 Between two neighbors	
情 景 Location	在社区里 In the neighborhood	

甲：今天我真倒霉，一出门就被警察拦住了，说我超速，给了我一张罚单。
A：It was not my day today. The police officer stopped me right after I left my house. He said I was speeding, and gave me a ticket.

乙：人不可能事事都如意。吃一张罚单，让你接受一次教训，有点警觉，学乖一点，这总比出车祸伤人要好得多。
B：You can't have everything as you wish it. Getting a ticket will teach you a lesson, gain some vigilance and learn to behave. It is much better than having an accident and hurting someone.

甲：可你知道吗？我要交两百多块钱的罚款，还要去交通学校上课呢。
A：But, do you know I have to attend traffic school in addition to paying more than two hundred yuan?

乙：你也不必太在乎这件事。挨罚的不是只有你一个人，谁都会遇到这种麻烦的，破财消灾嘛。
B：You don't have to worry too much about it. You are not the only one who gets tickets. Anyone could have ran into such trouble. It is said that suffering unexpected personal

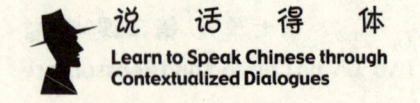

说话得体
Learn to Speak Chinese through Contextualized Dialogues

financial losses removes bad luck.

词语表   New Words

倒霉	dǎoméi	have bad luck; fall on hard time
出门	chūmén	get out; leave home
警察	jǐngchá	police officer
超速	chāosù	speeding
罚单	fádān	ticket (notice) for penalty
如意	rúyì	as one wishes
警觉	jǐngjué	(to arouse) vigilance
学乖	xué guāi	learn to be well-behaved
伤人	shāng rén	to hurt other people
罚款	fákuǎn	fine; penalty
交通	jiāotōng	traffic
在乎	zàihu	care about
破财消灾	pòcái xiāozāi	suffer unexpected personal financial losses to remove ill fortune

对话二：发挥正常
Dialogue II：Performing Normally

人物 Characters	甲：考生甲 A：Candidate A	乙：考生乙 B：Candidate B
关系 Relationship	在两位考生之间 Between two medical college candidates for an entrance examination	
情景 Location	在考场外 At the entrance of a testing center	

188

Unit 7　Lesson Two　Giving Comfort and Reassurance

甲：今天的考试是我的最后一次机会，考不好，我就进不了医学院。

A：Today's test is my last chance. If I fail, I will not be able to get into the medical college.

乙：我看你的担心是多余的，凭你的聪明天赋和平时的勤奋努力，只要发挥正常，你应该能通过这场考试。

B：It seems to me that your concern is unnecessary. With your gifted intelligence and hardwork during normal times, you should pass the test as long as you perform normally.

甲：可是我上次就没考好，现在心里一点儿把握都没有。

A：But I didn't do well on the last test. Now I don't have any confidence.

乙：上次没考好是事出有因，别再为那件事烦恼了。这回你没有后顾之忧，加上有了上次考试的经验，你没有理由为此再担忧了。

B：You did not do well last time because of your situation. This time you don't have any worries, plus with your experience last time, you don't have any reason to worry.

甲：你说得轻巧，可我还是有很大的压力。

A：It is easy for you to say. But I still have a lot of pressure.

乙：每个参加考试的人都会有压力。你只要有必胜的信念，用平常心去对待。我相信这次考试你会顺利通过的。

B：Every test taker has this kind of pressure. As long as you have confidence in your success and treat it with your normal state of mind, I believe you will successfully pass the test.

词语表　New Words

医学院	yīxuéyuàn	medical school
多余	duōyú	more than what is due; unnecessary
凭	píng	to go by; to depend on
聪明	cōngmíng	intelligent; clever; bright
天赋	tiānfù	inborn; innate; endowed by nature
努力	nǔlì	make great efforts; try hard; hard-working
发挥	fāhuī	bring into play
正常	zhèngcháng	normal
事出有因	shì chū yǒu yīn	it is by no means accidental; there is no smoke without fire

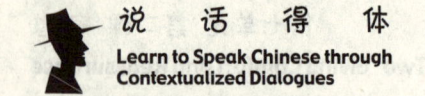

说话得体
Learn to Speak Chinese through Contextualized Dialogues

后顾之忧	hòu gù zhī yōu	fear of disturbance in the rear; trouble back at home
经验	jīngyàn	experience
理由	lǐyóu	reason
担忧	dānyōu	to worry; be concerned
轻巧	qīngqiǎo	easy; light
必胜	bìshèng	will most certainly win; be sure to win
信念	xìnniàn	faith; belief; conviction
平常心	píngchángxīn	normal state of mind
顺利	shùnlì	smoothly; successfully

对话三：你们尽力了
Dialogue III：You Did All You Could

人物 Characters	甲：运动员 A：An athlete	乙：运动员的朋友 B：His friend
关系 Relationship	在一位运动员和她朋友之间 Between an athlete and his friend	
情景 Location	在赛场外 Out of a stadium	

甲：这次比赛，我们又输了。我真恨我们自己不争气。
A：We lost this game as well. I really hate us for not living up to the expectations.

乙：你们没能获胜，我替你们可惜，可是这也不能完全怨你们自己，对方占了主场的天时地利，裁判又明显偏护他们。我觉得你们已经尽了最大的努力了。
B：I'm sorry that you didn't win the game. But you can't entirely blame it on yourselves. Your rival held the home ground, which provided them with a favorable climate and geographical conditions. It was also very obvious that the referee had a bias towards them. I think you did great with your efforts.

甲：我们已经输了两场了，我（似乎）是没有信心了。
A：We already lost two games. I seem to have no confidence.

190

Unit 7　Lesson Two　Giving Comfort and Reassurance

乙：你可千万别泄气。常言说得好，"胜败乃兵家常事"，"失败是成功之母"，只要认真总结经验教训，坚定信心，继续努力，坚持到底，你们是一定会赢的。

B：Be sure not to be discouraged. It is often said that "victory and defeat are both common in battle", and "failure is the mother of success". As long as you earnestly learn from your experiences, have the confidence, and hold on to the end, you are bound to ultimately win in the end.

甲：谢谢你的鼓励。

A：Thank you for your encouragement.

乙：要记住：道路是曲折的，前途是光明的。

B：In a word, while the prospects are bright, the road has twists and turns.

词语表　New Words

输	shū	to lose
恨	hèn	to hate; regret
不争气	bù zhēngqì	fail to live up to expectations
获胜	huòshèng	to win victory
怨	yuàn	to complain; to blame
对方	duìfāng	opponent; the other side
占	zhàn	to occupy; to own; to hold
主场	zhǔchǎng	host; home ground (court)
天时	tiānshí	favorable climate (situation)
地利	dìlì	favorable geographical conditions
裁判	cáipàn	referee
明显	míngxiǎn	obvious; evident
偏护	piānhù	have a bias towards; show partiality
场	chǎng	quantifier (measure word) for sports games
泄气	xièqì	be discouraged; to lose heart
常言	chángyán	common saying; as the saying goes
胜败乃兵家常事	shēngbài nǎi bīngjiā chángshì	
		victory and defeat are both common in battle

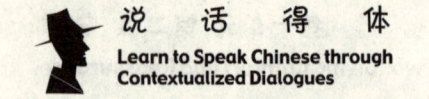

说话得体
Learn to Speak Chinese through Contextualized Dialogues

失败是成功之母	shībài shì chénggōng zhī mǔ	failure is the mother of success
总结经验	zǒngjié jīngyàn	sum up the experience
坚定	jiāndìng	firm; steadfast
继续	jìxù	to continue; to go on
坚持到底	jiānchí dàodǐ	hold on straight to the end
鼓励	gǔlì	to encourage
道路	dàolù	road; the way
前途	qiántú	prospect; future
光明	guāngmíng	bright

对话四：振作起来
Dialogue IV：Pull Yourself Together

人 物 Characters	甲：女士甲 A：Lady A	乙：女士乙 B：Lady B
关 系 Relationship	在两位女士之间 Between two ladies	
情 景 Location	在朋友家 At a friend's home	

甲：小李跟我分手了，我真想……
A：Xiao Li and I have broken up. I really want to ...

乙：你们的事，我是刚听说的。事情已经过去了，你要保持冷静，别再让这件事折磨你自己了。
B：I just heard about the thing between you two. Everything is over now. Keep calm and don't let it bother you any more.

甲：我们上个礼拜还见过面，分别时还是好好的。他昨天突然来电话说要跟我吹。我一点思想准备都没有。

192

第七单元 第二课 安慰
Unit 7　Lesson Two　Giving Comfort and Reassurance

A：We met last week. It was fine when we parted. He called me yesterday and told me he wanted to break up. I didn't have any mental preparation.

乙：也许他有什么事难以启齿。你不要为这事过于悲伤，尽量朝好的方面想。

B：Perhaps he has something too embarrassing to say. Don't feel too sad. Do your best to think of good things.

甲：我们已经交往三年了，亲戚朋友都知道，这往后叫我怎么见人啊？

A：We have been dating for three years. All my relatives and friends know about our relationship. How shall I face these people?

乙：要是我处在你的地位，我也会有你这样的感受。

B：If I were in your situation, I would have thought this way, too.

甲：谢谢你的安慰。你说得都对，可是我就是想不明白他为什么这样对待我。

A：Thank you for your sympathy. What you said is right, but I just don't understand why he treated me this way.

乙：感情的事是很难勉强的。其实天下好男人多得很，你又何必吊死在一棵树上呢？把这件事忘了吧，重新振作起来！

B：Emotional things cannot be forced. In fact, there are a lot of good men in the world. Why hang yourself on one tree? Leave it behind and pull yourself together.

词语表　New Words

分手	fēnshǒu	part (company); say goodbye; break up
冷静	lěngjìng	calm; to keep calm
折磨	zhémó	cause physical or mental suffering
思想准备	sīxiǎng zhǔnbèi	mental preparation
难以启齿	nányǐ qǐchǐ	too embarrassing to say
过于	guòyú	excessive
悲伤	bēishāng	painfully sad
亲戚	qīnqi	relative
往后	wǎnghòu	from now on; in the future
处在	chǔzài	be in a certain situation
安慰	ānwèi	condolence; to comfort; to console
明白	míngbai	to understand

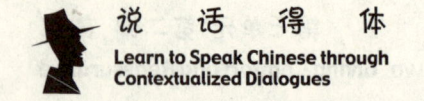

说话得体
Learn to Speak Chinese through Contextualized Dialogues

对待	duìdài	to treat; to deal with
勉强	miǎnqiǎng	be forced; to do with difficulty
何必	hébì	why must
吊死	diàosǐ	to hang oneself; to hang by the neck (committing suicide)
振作	zhènzuò	pull oneself together; bestir oneself; display vigour

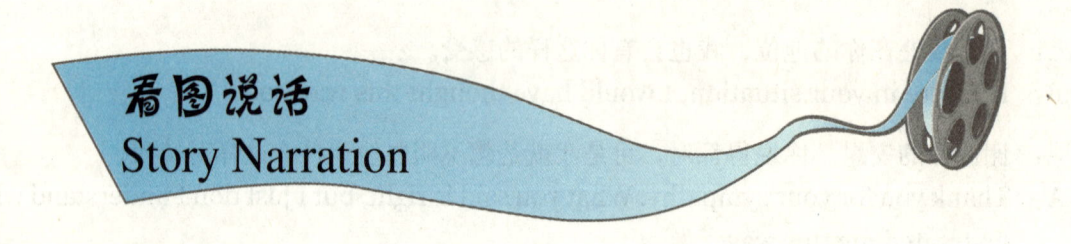

看图说话
Story Narration

按照以下图画顺序及各幅图画所提示的情景，叙述一个有始有终的完整故事。

Based on the order of the following pictures and the situations presented in each, narrate a story including a beginning and an end.

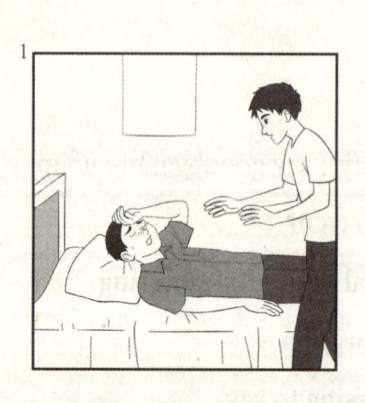

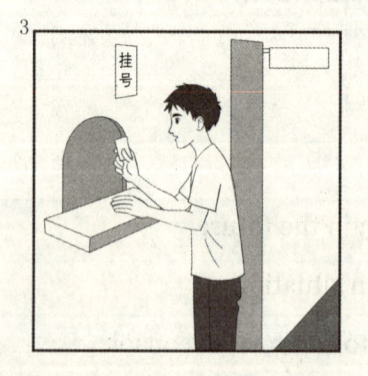

194

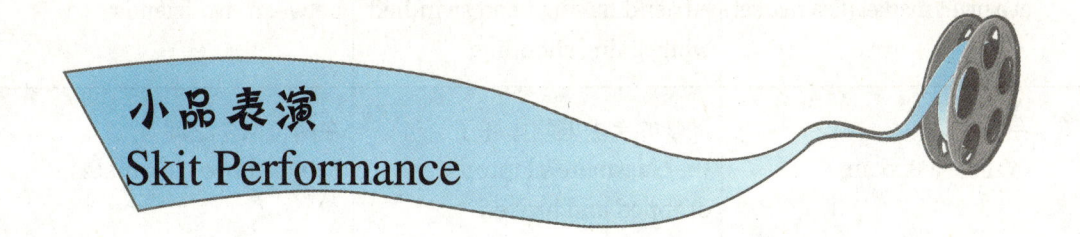

Unit 7 Lesson Two Giving Comfort and Reassurance

小品表演
Skit Performance

学生创作对话小品时尽可能使用本单元列出的和学生学到的新词、新句。小品主题选择应该得到老师首肯，以免重复。

Create situational dialogues with topics approved by the teacher to avoid repetition. Use as many expressions listed/learned in this unit as possible.

对话地点（时间） Place (Time) of Dialogue	对话情景 Context	对话者之间的关系 Relation Between Speakers
1 在咖啡馆里 at a coffee shop	朋友丢了工作，生活困难 a friend having lost his/her job and life becomes tough	在两位朋友之间 between two friends
2 在医院里 at the hospital	亲人生病等候手术 a sick relative is expecting surgery	在两位亲人之间 between two relatives
3 在某公共场合 at a public place	与男（女）朋友分手了 having broken up with a boy (girl) friend	在两位朋友之间 between two friends
4 在外国旅行时 traveling abroad	找不到护照，无法回国 can't find the passport, then can't go back to the home country	在导游与游客之间 between a tour guide and a tourist
5 在学校里 inside school	申请大学被拒绝了 application having been rejected by a university	在同学与指导老师之间 between a student and his/her counselor
6 在灾区 at a devastated area	自然灾害（地震、疾风） describing a natural disaster (earthquake or hurricane)	在两位落难者之间 between two victims

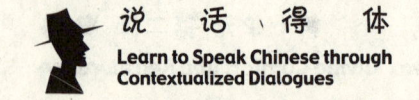

7	在夜市(跳蚤市场) at a night market (flea market)	朋友买东西上当受了骗 a friend having been swindled while going shopping	在两位朋友之间 between two friends
8	在教室里 in the classroom	同学的手提电脑摔坏了 the classmate's laptop was dropped and broken	在两位同学之间 between two classmates
9	在家里 at home	信用卡被盗又被使用了 having lost the credit card and it having been used	在父母与孩子之间 between parents and a child
10	在同学家里 at a classmate's home	跟父母吵架以后 after quarreling with parents	在两位同学之间 between two classmates

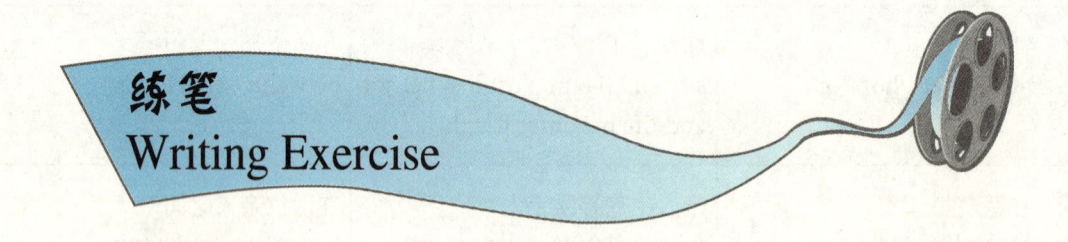

练笔 Writing Exercise

根据要求写一篇短文。尽可能用上本单元学到的词句。

Write a short passage on the given topic. Do your best to use words and expressions from the sentence patterns you have learned in this unit.

同学出车祸住医院，写慰问信 (Write a note to express your consolation to a classmate who had a car accident.)

第七单元听力练习
Listening Comprehension Unit 7

听完以下各项听力练习的内容，先回答理解提示中的问题，再识别句子或语段的语境，然后尽可能使用本单元列出的和学到的新词、新句做适当的回应。

After listening to the sentences given, identify a proper context and response in each situation, using as many expressions listed/learned in this unit as possible.

	1. 理解提示 Comprehension	2. 情景识别 Context Identification	3. 学生回应 Student's Response
1	What is fortunate?		
2	What is the speaker sure about?		
3	What can't people resist?		
4	What happened yesterday?		我们能为她做点什么吗?
5	What is the hope mentioned?		
6	Does the speaker consider it a serious mistake?		
7	If you were him, what would you do?		
8	How can people be successful?		
9	Why didn't they win?		
10	What is the wish?		

第八单元
Unit 8

Complimenting

Complaining

第一课 恭维
Lesson One   Complimenting

常用词句
Common Expressions

常用词句 Common Expressions	回应提示参考 Suggested Responses
1 你今天真漂亮！ You are beautiful today!	谢谢！ Thank you!
2 你今天的气色特别好。 You look great today.	真的吗？谢谢！ Really? Thank you!
3 我真喜欢你衣服的颜色。 I really like the color of your clothes.	是吗？我觉得这种颜色很适合我们学生穿。 Really? I think this color is suitable for us students.
4 你今天戴上这条领带，看起来很潇洒。 Today you look elegant and sophisticated wearing this tie.	谢谢，您过奖了！ Thank you! You flatter me.
5 我从来没有吃过这么可口的菜。 I have never had such delicious food.	这不算什么，我最拿手的菜还没有上呢！ It's nothing. I haven't served my best dish.
6 你真有眼力，选择了这块风水宝地。 You are a man of excellent judgment and have selected a good location.	过奖了，这是因为我找到了一个有经验的房产经纪。 You flatter me. This is because I found an experienced real estate agent.

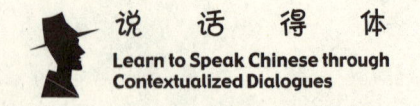

说 话 得 体
Learn to Speak Chinese through Contextualized Dialogues

常用词句 Common Expressions	回应提示参考 Suggested Responses
7 我欣赏你的演讲，深入浅出，很有说服力。 I appreciate your speech. You explained the profound in simple terms, and it was very convincing.	哪里，哪里！这应该感谢我的指导教师。 Oh, it's nothing. I should express my heart-felt thanks to my mentor.
8 没想到你还有这一手。是从哪儿（什么时候）学的？ I didn't expect you to have such a remarkable skill. Where (when) did you learn it?	你不知道的东西还多着呢！ There are a lot more things that you don't know yet.
9 你房间的装饰真是别具一格。 The decoration of your room is unique in style.	这是室内装潢设计师设计的。 It's a creation by an interior designer.
10 像你这样的人才真是百里挑一啊。 You are one in a hundred.	你就别拿我开心了，我哪是什么人才啊？ Am I really so good? Are you making fun of me?
11 你很有气质，我就欣赏你这样的人。 You have great temperament! I admire those who have your qualities.	惭愧，惭愧。 You're embarrassing me.
12 你老兄的为人，侠肝义胆，兄弟我佩服得五体投地。 I admire you with great respect because you have such a chivalrous frame of mind.	过奖，过奖！ You flatter me.
13 你是怎么赢得她的芳心的？ How did you win her love?	我可是下了不少工夫哦！ I did put in a lot of efforts.
14 你的棋艺我领教了，甘拜下风。 After experiencing your great talent with chess, I admit defeat.	不，不，不！我这是侥幸的，你是在让我。 Oh, no. I won by a fluke. It was you that conceded.

Unit 8 Lesson One Complimenting

常用词句 Common Expressions	回应提示参考 Suggested Responses
15 你那么有天赋，难道说你自己没有感觉到吗？ You have such a great natural gift. Do you mean to say that you didn't know?	瞧你说的！我要是真有天赋，我今天就不在这儿了。 What are you talking about? If I were really gifted, I would not be staying here.
16 你俩真是男才女貌，天生的一对。 You two are born to be an ideal couple: the man is talented and the woman is beautiful.	你可真会说话。 You really know how to flatter people.
17 你的眼睛好像会说话。 Your eyes are very expressive.	真的吗？我怎么不知道？ For real? How come I don't know?
18 我早就知道你一定会成功的。 I knew you would be successful.	连我自己都不能预测，你又是怎么知道的呢？你这是在奉承我。 Even I myself can hardly predict such things. How do you know? You are flattering me.

情景对话
Contextualized Dialogues

对话一：托你的福
Dialogue I: Thanks to You

人物 Characters	甲：王妈妈 A: Mother Wang	乙：李小姐 B: Miss Li
关系 Relationship	在两位老邻居之间 Between two old neighbors	
情景 Location	在超市里 At a supermarket	

说 话 得 体
Learn to Speak Chinese through Contextualized Dialogues

甲：这不是李小姐吗？

A： Aren't you Miss Li?

乙：是啊。你是王志贤的妈妈。您好，伯母！两年不见了，您还是老样子，一点儿都没变，还是那么精神。

B： Oh, yes. You are Wang Zhixian's mother. How are you, Mrs. Wang? I haven't seen you for two years. You are still the same, no change at all, and full of energy.

甲：哪儿啊？老了，不行了，特别是眼睛不好使了，跟你们年轻人是没法子比了。

A： It's very kind of you. I am old. I am not able to do many things. Particularly my eyes are not functioning well. I can no longer compare with you young people.

乙：瞧您说的。您的气色特别好，走路还像一阵风似的，一点儿都不显老。

B： Look at what you said. You look especially good. Your walk is like a gust of wind. You haven't shown any sign of old age.

甲：李小姐，你可真会说话，说得老太太我真高兴。那就托你的福了。

A： Ms. Li, you are really good at speaking with nice words, and have made me happy. Thank you.

乙：伯母，我说的可是真话。

B： I really mean what I said.

词语表　New Words

伯母	bómǔ	aunt
老样子	lǎoyàngzi	the same appearance (manner, air)
变	biàn	change
精神	jīngshen	spirit and energy
不好使	bù hǎo shǐ	be inconvenient to use; do not work well
年轻人	niánqīngrén	young people
一阵风	yīzhènfēng	a gust of wind
显（得）老	xiǎn(de)lǎo	look older (than one's real age)
托福	tuōfú	thanks to you

Unit 8　Lesson One　Complimenting

对话二：找舞伴
Dialogue II：Looking for a Prom Date

人　物 Characters	甲：男学生 A：A boy student	乙：女学生 B：A girl student
关　系 Relationship	在两位朋友之间 Between two friends	
情　景 Location	在教室外 Outside the classroom	

甲：你今天穿的衣服的式样很别致，与众不同，你有没有注意到过往的人都朝你看呢？
A：The fashion of the clothes you are wearing today is unique, different from others'. Have you noticed that everyone is looking at you?

乙：是吗？我怎么一点儿也没有感觉到？倒是你今天戴着这条红领带，人显得格外精神。
B：Really? How did I not realize that? Actually you look energetic with the tie you are wearing today.

甲：谢谢！你的项链很漂亮，跟这件衣服很配，你很有品味的嘛，什么时候开始戴项链的？我都没发现。
A：Thank you. This necklace is beautiful. It matches well with your clothes. You really have good taste. By the way, when did you start to wear the necklace? I have never noticed it before.

乙：衣服和项链我都是上个礼拜刚买的，就是为了参加这个周末的毕业舞会！
B：I bought these clothes and the necklace last week. They are for the senior prom this weekend.

甲：我很佩服你的眼力。对了，你找到舞伴了吗？
A：I admire your good taste. By the way, have you found a prom date?

乙：我来就是为了请你当我的舞伴。不知道你愿不愿意？
B：I came especially to invite you to be my dance partner. I wonder if you will accept my invitation.

甲：太好了！我就等着你来邀请我。我早就知道你有好眼力，会选择我，哈哈。
A：That's wonderful. I was waiting for you to invite me. I knew for a long time that you have good taste, and you would choose me. Haha.

205

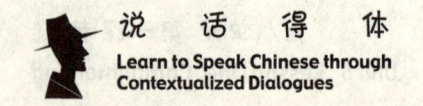

说 话 得 体
Learn to Speak Chinese through Contextualized Dialogues

词语表   New Words

式样	shìyàng	fashion; style
别致	biézhì	unique
与众不同	yǔ zhòng bù tóng	different from others
朝	cháo	towards
领带	lǐngdài	tie
格外	géwài	exceptionally; especially
项链	xiàngliàn	necklace
配	pèi	to match
有品味	yǒu pǐnwèi	have good taste (savour)
毕业舞会	bìyè wǔhuì	graduation prom; graduation dancing party
佩服	pèifú	admire; have admiration (respect) for
选择	xuǎnzé	to select; to choose
眼力	yǎnlì	have good taste and judgement
舞伴	wǔbàn	dancing partner
邀请	yāoqǐng	to invite

对话三：乔迁之喜
Dialogue III: Congratulations on Moving to a New Home

人 物 Characters	甲：房主 A：The landlady	乙：访客 B：A visitor
关 系 Relationship	在两位女士之间 Between two ladies	
情 景 Location	在朋友家 At a friend's home	

206

Unit 8 Lesson One Complimenting

甲：很高兴你来祝贺我搬新家。来，进屋看看房子吧。

A：I am so glad that you came to congratulate me on moving to a new house. Come in and have a look at this house.

乙：你是怎么找到这所又宽敞、光线又充足的房子的？真羡慕啊。

B：How did you find this house? It is both spacious and bright. I truly envy you.

甲：我有一个做房产经纪的朋友，他帮了很大的忙。

A：I found a friend who is in the real estate business. He helped me vastly.

乙：客厅的布局非常合理，装饰别具一格，家具和墙的颜色也很协调，整体的格调品味都很高。

B：The arrangement of your living room is very reasonable. The interior decoration has a distinctive style. The colors of the furniture and the wall are well harmonized. The style as a whole is in good taste.

甲：那是因为我请了一位高级室内装潢设计师，一切都出自他的高手。

A：That is because I hired an expert interior designer. Everything is this master's creation.

乙：我也喜欢这窗外的景色，周围的环境很幽雅。但愿我也能拥有这么一套豪宅。

B：I also like the scenery from the window. The surrounding environment is quiet and tastefully laid out. I wish I had such a splendid house.

甲：谢谢你的夸奖，你这么一说，我更喜欢我的新家了。

A：Thank you for your compliment. Having heard what you said, I like my new residence even more.

词语表　New Words

乔迁之喜	qiāoqiān zhī xǐ	best wishes for moving to a new residence
祝贺	zhùhè	congratulation
宽敞	kuānchang	spacious; capacious
光线	guāngxiàn	light; ray of light
羡慕	xiànmù	to admire; to envy
房产经济	fángchǎn jīngjì	real estate agent
功劳	gōngláo	contribution; meritorious service (deed)
布局	bùjú	arrangement; layout
合理	hélǐ	reasonable; rational
装饰	zhuāngshì	(interior) decoration

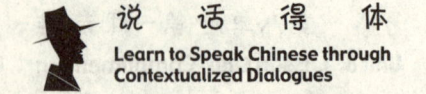

说话得体
Learn to Speak Chinese through Contextualized Dialogues

别具一格	bié jù yī gé	have a style of one's own; having a distinctive style
颜色	yánsè	color
协调	xiétiáo	harmonize; integrate; cohere with
整体	zhěngtǐ	whole; entirety; overall
格调	gédiào	(literary or artistic) style
室内装潢	shìnèi zhuānghuáng	interior designing and decoration; upholster
设计师	shèjìshī	designer; creator
高手	gāoshǒu	master-hand
景色	jǐngsè	scenery; view; landscape
周围	zhōuwéi	around; vicinity
环境	huánjìng	environment
幽雅	yōuyǎ	(of a place) quiet and tastefully laid out
但愿	dànyuàn	if only; wish
拥有	yōngyǒu	possess
豪宅	háozhái	splendid house
夸奖	kuājiǎng	praise; compliment
新居	xīnjū	new residence; new home

对话四：名师出高徒
Dialogue IV: A Great Master Brings Up Brilliant Disciples.

人物 Characters	甲：林教授 A：Professor Lin	乙：张教授 B：Professor Zhang
关系 Relationship	在两位教授之间 Between two professors	
情景 Location	在演讲会后 After a speech contest	

Unit 8 Lesson One Complimenting
第八单元 第一课 恭维

甲：张教授，祝贺您的学生获奖。他的演说太精彩了。培养出这么优秀的学生，只有您张教授能做到。名师出高徒啊。

A：Congratulations, Professor Zhang. Your student won the prize. He presented an exciting speech. It is only you that can train such a brilliant student. This is what people always say, "an accomplished disciple owes his accomplishments to his great teacher".

乙：林教授，您过奖了。您的学生表现也同样出色。

B：Professor Lin, you flatter me. Your student was the same, demonstrating an outstanding performance.

甲：不不不。是真的。您学生今天的演讲深入浅出，又有大量的个案说明，加上旁征博引，说服力很强，有您做学问的风格。

A：Not really. Your student presented the speech by explaining the profound using simple terms. He gave explanations supported by ample individual cases. He quoted and cited extensively by way of corroboration. His speech was very persuasive. He has your scholastic style.

乙：哪里，哪里，过奖了。

B：You are exaggerating. It's very kind of you to say so.

甲：我说的是实话，他的基本功很扎实，知识面很广，反应敏捷，答题机智，跟您多年来的辛勤培养是分不开的。这个孩子真幸运。

A：What I say is true. He has a good grasp of essential techniques, a wide range of knowledge, quick-witted sensitivity, and is full of resources. All are not separate from your hard work in training. He is fortunate to have you as his teacher.

乙：您过奖了。常言说得好，"师傅领进门，修行在个人"，他的成功是他自己努力的结果。

B：You flatter me. It is well said that the master teaches the trade, but the apprentice's skill is self-made. His success is the outcome of his hard work.

甲：您还是像以前那样谦虚谨慎。佩服，佩服！

A：You are still the same as you were before, modest and prudent. I admire you a lot.

词语表 New Words

获奖	huòjiǎng	win an award
演说	yǎnshuō	speech
精彩	jīngcǎi	exciting
培养	péiyǎng	to train; to cultivate

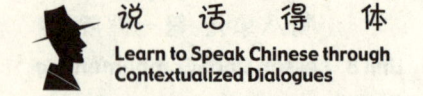

说话得体
Learn to Speak Chinese through Contextualized Dialogues

优秀	yōuxiù	brilliant; excellent
名师出高徒	míngshī chū gāotú	an accomplished disciple owes his accomplishment to his great teacher
同样	tóngyàng	the same
表现	biǎoxiàn	performance; presentation
出色	chūsè	outstanding; remarkable
深入浅出	shēn rù qiǎn chū	explain the profound using simple terms
大量	dàliàng	a great quantity; abundant; enormous
个案	gè'àn	individual case
说明	shuōmíng	explanation; illustration
旁征博引	páng zhēng bó yǐn	well-provided with extensive supporting materials
说服力	shuōfúlì	persuasion
强	qiáng	strong
学问	xuéwen	scholarship; knowledge
风格	fēnggé	style; manner (attitude)
哪里，哪里	nǎlǐ, nǎlǐ	a polite expression responding a compliment
过奖	guòjiǎng	over praise; "You flatter me."
基本功	jīběngōng	basic training; essential technique
扎实	zhāshi	solid; have a good grasp of
知识面	zhīshimiàn	range of knowledge
广	guǎng	wide; broad
反应	fǎnyìng	reaction; reflection
敏捷	mǐnjié	quick-witted
机智	jīzhì	resourceful; quick-witted
辛勤	xīnqín	diligently; hard working
分不开	fēn bù kāi	can not be separated
师傅领进门，	shīfu lǐng jìn mén,	the master teaches the trade,
修行在个人	xiūxíng zài gèrén	but the apprentice's skill is self-made
成功	chénggōng	success

Unit 8　Lesson One　Complimenting

结果	jiéguǒ	result
谦虚谨慎	qiānxū jǐnshèn	be modest and prudent; humble and cautious
佩服，佩服	pèifú, pèifú	a polite way to express admiration

看图说话　Story Narration

按照以下图画顺序及各幅图画所提示的情景，叙述一个有始有终的完整故事。

Based on the order of the following pictures and the situations presented in each, narrate a story including a beginning and an end.

211

小品表演
Skit Performance

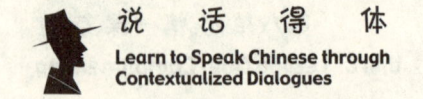

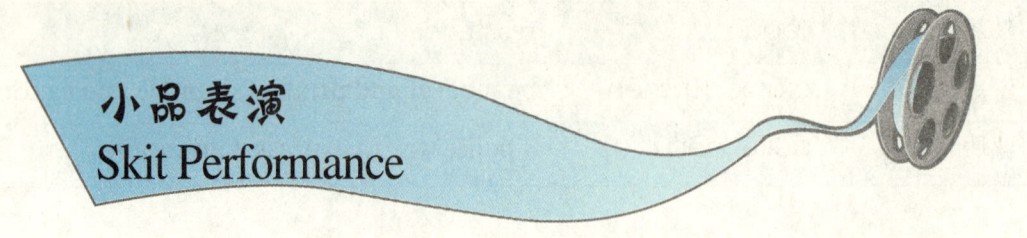

学生创作对话小品时尽可能使用本单元列出的和学生学到的新词、新句。小品主题选择应该得到老师首肯，以免重复。

Create situational dialogues with topics approved by the teacher to avoid repetition. Use as many expressions listed/learned in this unit as possible.

对话地点（时间） Place (Time) of Dialogue	对话情景 Context	对话者之间的关系 Relation Between Speakers
1 在婚礼宴会上 at wedding banquet	赞美一对新婚夫妇 complimenting the newlyweds	在新婚夫妇与前来祝贺者之间 between the newlyweds and a well-wisher
2 在家宴时 during a feast at home	赞美烹调手艺 complimenting cooking ability	在老朋友之间 between two old friends
3 参观艺术馆时 when visiting an art museum	赞美一件艺术品 complementing a piece of art	在两位参观者之间 between two visitors
4 在同学的书房里 at a classmate's study	赞美一台新电脑 complimenting a new computer	在两位同学之间 between two classmates
5 观看一个新设计时 observing a new design	赞美某人的品味 complimenting one's taste	在两位同事之间 between two colleagues
6 在旅游路途中 on the road of a guided tour	赞美某个旅游景观 complimenting a scenic spot	在导游与游客之间 between a tour guide and a tourist
7 在竞赛场外 outside of a competition arena	称赞某人的比赛成绩 praising an achievement during a competition	在两位同学之间 between two classmates

Unit 8　Lesson One　Complimenting

8 在阅览室里 in the reading room	称赞一篇报刊文章 praising a newspaper article	在图书馆馆员和读者之间 between a librarian and a reader
9 在会议室里 in the meeting room	称赞某人工作的责任心 praising one's sense of responsibility toward his/her work	在上级与下级之间 between a superior and a subordinate
10 在街上 in the street	称赞助人为乐的行为 praising a conduct of helping others with pleasure	在两位路人之间 between two pedestrians

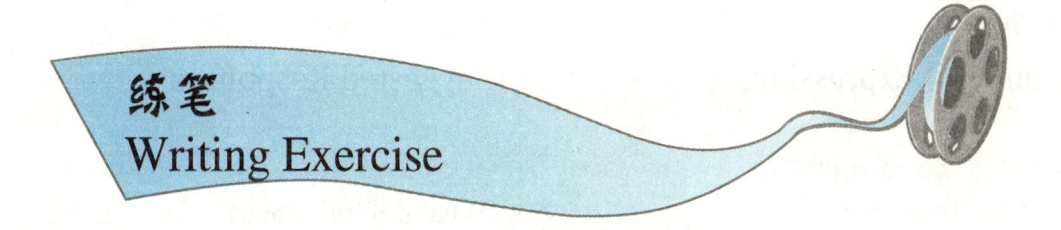

练笔 Writing Exercise

根据要求写一篇短文。尽可能用上本单元学到的词句。

Write a short passage on the given topic. Do your best to use words and expressions from the sentence patterns you have learned in this unit.

祝贺朋友上大学 (Write a letter to congratulate your friend who is going to college.)

第二课 抱怨
Lesson Two Complaining

常用词句
Common Expressions

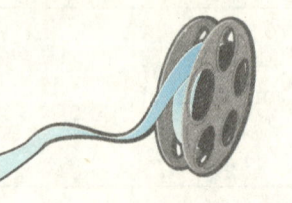

常用词句 Common Expressions	回应提示参考 Suggested Responses
1 都怨你，都是你不对。 It's all your fault.	又怎么啦？ What's all this about?
2 看！你把事情全弄糟了。 Look! You have messed everything up.	我真不知道我是怎么把事情弄糟的。请你告诉我。 I really didn't know. Please tell me how I messed everything up?
3 这样糟糕的作品，恐怕没有人会欣赏。 I am afraid that no one would want to read (appreciate) such a poor work.	你批评得对。我也不欣赏。 Your criticism is right. I don't enjoy it, either.
4 喂！这是怎么回事？ Hey! What's the matter?	有什么不对劲吗？ Is there something wrong?
5 请你们不要吵了，别再来烦我，好吗？ Please don't argue anymore. Don't bother me again.	行，行！我们走吧。 Fine. Let's leave.
6 你应该先跟我说一声再开我的车嘛。 You should have told me before you drove my car.	我以后一定注意。 I will certainly keep that in mind.

Unit 8 Lesson Two Complaining

常用词句 Common Expressions	回应提示参考 Suggested Responses
7 希望你把音响声音开得小一点儿。 I wish you would lower the volume of your hi-fi.	真对不起!我们没注意到您在休息。 I am really sorry. We didn't notice you were resting.
8 他总是这样神秘兮兮的，让人捉摸不透。 He is a mysterious person, and no one can figure out what he is doing.	这样的朋友不如不交。 It's better not to make friends with such a person.
9 你对我太不公平，太残忍了! You treated me unfairly. It's cruel.	我觉得我一碗水端平了。 I think it was perfectly fair to both sides.
10 谁知道他下一步会闯出什么祸来? Who knows what trouble he will get into next?	由他去吧! Let fate take its course.
11 我才不会相信你的谎言呢。 I will never believe the lies you tell.	我说的是真的，一点儿也没有骗你。不信你去问老师。 What I said is true. I was not lying at all. You may go and ask the teacher if you don't trust me.
12 这是哪儿跟哪儿啊?这种事真是闻所未闻! What are you talking about? I have never heard of it.	你这是少见多怪! It is simply because you have not seen it before.
13 你就不能节省一点儿吗? Can't you cut down on your expenses?	好，好，好!你真啰唆! Okay! Fine then. You are really annoying.
14 我觉得你有点不太慎重。 I don't think you are cautious enough.	事后我也意识到了，可是已经来不及了。 I was aware of it afterwards, but it was too late.
15 他的所作所为令人无法容忍，没有人受得了。	可是你拿他有什么办法呢?"有其父必有其子。"

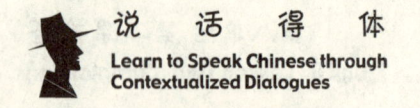

说 话 得 体
Learn to Speak Chinese through Contextualized Dialogues

常用词句 Common Expressions	回应提示参考 Suggested Responses
No one is able to endure and tolerate what he does.	But "like father, like son". What are you going to do with him?
16 你怎么不先给我打个电话就上门来了? Why didn't you make a phone call before coming over to my house?	对不起，我没有时间，身边又没带手机。 I am sorry. I didn't have time, and I didn't have my cell phone with me.
17 我从来没见过你这样不讲礼貌的人。 I have never seen such a rude person as you.	我就是要让你见识见识。 Now you have!
18 如果你继续不来上课，不做功课，你会后悔的。 If you continue to miss class, and fail to turn in your homework, you will regret it.	你说得对!我马上把功课补齐，天天都来上课。 You are right. I will immediately make up all missing work and come to class everyday.
19 要是不是误会，那就是你的无知。 If it is not a misunderstanding, it is your ignorance.	你说得对，是我无知。你满意了吧? What you said is true. It was my ignorance. Are you happy now?
20 "己所不欲，勿施于人。"这种道理再简单不过了。 It is for the simple reason: "Treat others the way you want to be treated."	没错，没错!我绝不强加于人。 I am quite sure. I will certainly not force anyone to do what he is unwilling to do.

Unit 8 Lesson Two Complaining

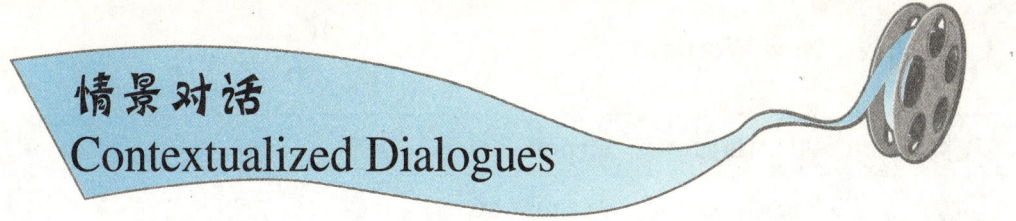

情景对话
CONTEXTUALIZED Dialogues

对话一：不能随便
Dialogue I：Can't Do as You Wish

人 物 Characters	甲：室友甲 A：Roommate A	乙：室友乙 B：Roommate B
关 系 Relationship	在两位室友之间 Between two roommates	
情 景 Location	在宿舍里 At the dormitory	

甲：小江，你是什么时候把我的车开走的？
A：Xiao Jiang, when did you drive my car?

乙：你去餐厅吃饭时我接到一个电话，要我马上去飞机场接一个朋友。
B：It was the time when you went to the cafeteria for lunch. I received a telephone call, and I had to pick up a friend at the airport.

甲：你应该先跟我说一声，得到我的同意再开车嘛。我还以为车子被盗了呢，急得我都想报警了。
A：You should have told me first, and gotten my permission before you drove the car. I thought it was stolen. I was so nervous that I was about to report it to the police.

乙：对不起，我不是有意这么做的，实在是来不及找你商量了。
B：I am sorry. I wasn't on purpose. I really didn't have enough time to inform you.

甲：不管怎么样，借车不是一件小事，不能随随便便，何况那是一辆新车。
A：No matter what you say, I just want to tell you it is no minor thing to borrow a car. You can't drive it at will. On top of everything, it is a new car.

乙：请你原谅，这是最后一次。
B：Please forgive me. This is the last time that I will do this.

217

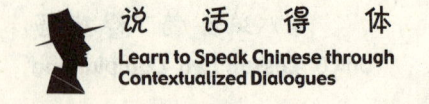

说话得体
Learn to Speak Chinese through Contextualized Dialogues

词语表　New Words

飞机场	fēijīchǎng	airport
同意	tóngyì	permission
被盗	bèi dào	be stolen
报警	bàojǐng	call (report to) the police
有意	yǒuyì	intentionally; on purpose
不管	bùguǎn	no matter how (what)
何况	hékuàng	much less; let alone

对话二：怎么回事
Dialogue II：What's the matter?

人物 Characters	甲：顾客 A：The customer	乙：服务员 B：The waiter
关系 Relationship	在服务员和顾客之间 Between a waiter and a customer	
情景 Location	在饭馆 At a Chinese restaurant	

甲：喂! 服务员，这是怎么回事?
A：Excuse me, Waiter, I think there is something wrong with this.

乙：先生，有什么不对劲吗?
B：Sir, is there anything wrong?

甲：这碗汤是凉的。
A：The soup is cold.

乙：对不起，我马上给你端一碗热的来。
B：I am sorry I will bring you a warm one.

Unit 8 Lesson Two Complaining

甲：还有，这道菜太咸了，难道你们的盐不用花钱买吗？
A：And this dish is too salty. Is it that the salt is costless?

乙：先生，这话是怎么讲的？好，我把菜端回去，让厨师给你重做。
B：Sir, I don't get why you said this. Fine, I will take it back and ask the chef to make another one for you.

甲：为了这顿饭，我已经等了半个多钟头了。你还要我等多长时间？
A：I have already been waiting for half an hour for the meal. How long do you expect me to wait?

乙：真不好意思让你久等了。其实街对面有一家麦当劳快餐店。先生，你去那儿吃饭，保证不用等。
B：I am sorry to keep you waiting so long. Actually there is a McDonalds fast food restaurant across the street. If you go there to dine, Sir, I guarantee you that you don't have to wait.

甲：你这是什么意思？哪有你这样说话的？你们的汤太凉，菜太咸，等菜的时间又这么久，服务员说话还这么刻薄。我从来没有见过你们这样差的服务质量。你去把你们的经理找来。
A：What do you mean by this? How can you speak to me that way? Your soup is cold, your dish is too salty, the service takes so long, and the waiter is so mean. I have never encountered such bad service. Go and get your manager.

乙：请再稍等片刻。（自言自语）我今天可碰到世界上最挑剔的顾客了。
B：Please wait a minute. (to himself) I have met the pickiest customer in the world today.

词语表　New Words

服务员	fúwùyuán	waiter (waitress); attendant
不对劲	búduìjìn	(feeling) awkward; inappropriate
凉	liáng	cool
端	duān	hold something level with both hands
热	rè	warm; hot
道	dào	course (of cooked dishes)
咸	xián	salty
盐	yán	salt

219

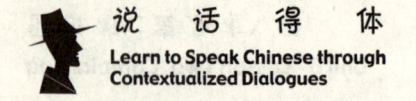

说话得体
Learn to Speak Chinese through Contextualized Dialogues

厨师	chúshī	chef; cook
重做	chóng zuò	cook again
街对面	jiē duìmiàn	cross the street
麦当劳快餐店	Màidāngláo kuàicāndiàn	McDonalds fast food restaurant
刻薄	kèbó	mean; harsh
差	chà	poor; not up to standard
服务质量	fúwù zhìliàng	service quality
片刻	piànkè	a short while
自言自语	zì yán zì yǔ	talk (murmur) to oneself
挑剔	tiāotī	picky; find fault with
顾客	gùkè	customer

对话三：人影都没有
Dialogue III: Can't Find Him

人物 Characters	甲：学生甲 A：Student A	乙：学生乙 B：Student B
关系 Relationship	在两位学生之间 Between two students	
情景 Location	在实验室 At a laboratory	

甲：小李说他一会儿就回来，可是他去了那么长时间，快二十分钟了，怎么还不见他回来呢？

A：Xiao Li said he would be back in a while, but he has been gone for so long. It has been about 20 minutes. Why hasn't he come back?

乙：我拿他一点儿办法都没有。小李就是那样的人，做事总是神秘兮兮的，让人捉摸不透。

B：I can't get along with him. He is that kind of person, doing things mysteriously, and being unpredictable.

甲：那你为什么还跟他合作一块儿做课题呢？

第八单元 第二课 抱怨
Unit 8　Lesson Two　Complaining

A：Then why do you have to work with him for the project?

乙：我有什么办法呢?老师硬把他放在我们小组里。
B：Do I have a choice? It was the teacher that insisted and assigned him to our group.

甲：既然你不喜欢他，为什么不去找老师，要求换一个人呢?
A：Since you don't like him, why didn't you ask your teacher and demand a change?

乙：别提了。你还不知道钱老师的脾气吗?我是不会到他那儿去自讨没趣的。
B：Forget it. Don't you know our teacher's personality? I will not go to him and look for trouble for myself.

甲：你说得对。我吃过亏。他的确是从来都不听学生意见的。
A：You are right. I did have a bad time with him. Indeed he never takes students' advice.

乙：再说，钱老师喜欢小李，老是袒护他，很不公平。
B：Moreover, he likes Xiao Li, and always favors him. It's not fair.

甲：看来，你们只好自认倒霉了。
A：It seems that you have no alternative, but to accept the bad luck without any complaints.

乙：瞧，半个钟头过去了，连个人影都没有。真糟糕!
B：See, half an hour has gone. We don't have any sign of him. What an awful nuisance!

词语表　New Words

神秘兮兮	shénmì xīxī	kind of mysterious
捉摸不透	zhuōmō bù tòu	unpredictable; difficult to ascertain
合作	hézuò	cooperation
课题	kètí	project; a question for study or discussion
硬	yìng	insist
脾气	píqi	temperament; characteristics
自讨没趣	zì tǎo méiqù	look for trouble
从来不（没）	cónglái bù(méi)	never
袒护	tǎnhù	give biased favor to
公平	gōngpíng	fair; justice
自认倒霉	zì rèn dǎoméi	accept bad luck without complaint

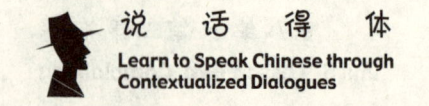

说话得体
Learn to Speak Chinese through Contextualized Dialogues

对话四：习惯了就行
Dialogue IV：You Will Get Used to It

人物 Characters	甲：同学甲 A：Student A	乙：同学乙 B：Student B
关系 Relationship	在两位老同学之间 Between two old schoolmates	
情景 Location	在大街上 in the street	

甲：小凤，毕业以后一直没见到你，你现在做什么呢？
A：Xiao Feng, I haven't seen you since graduation. What are you doing now?

乙：我去北加州了，在一所中学教物理。
B：I have gone to Northern California, to teach physics in a middle school.

甲：怎么？你当老师了？做老师整天和孩子打交道，我觉得当孩子头真没意思，换一个带有挑战性的工作吧。
A：How come you became a teacher? Being a teacher, you have to deal with kids every day. You can't accomplish anything being the king of children. How about changing for a more challenging job?

乙：我也是没有办法。现在经济不景气，工作难找，加上我学的是物理，不是热门学科，市场就更小了。能在学校找到一份工作也就算不错了。
B：I have no way out because the economic situation is depressing. It is difficult to find a job; moreover I studied physics, not a subject in applied science. The job market is even more limited. It can be considered pretty good to get a job in a school.

甲：你说的是实话，也很实在。想过转行吗？
A：You are right and practical. Have you considered changing your job?

乙：目前还没有。你呢？你一定找到了一份称心如意的工作吧？
B：Not yet. How about you? You must have found a job which keeps you content.

甲：也就将就了吧。我在一家电脑公司当会计。
A：I am making the best of it, working as an accountant in a computer firm.

乙：当会计好哇！有很高的薪金。
B：That must be good. You should be earning a nice salary.

甲：收入是不错，可是每天都是数字进数字出的，太枯燥了。尤其是现在还是试用期，做

第八单元 第二课 抱怨
Unit 8 Lesson Two Complaining

什么事都得看别人的脸色。我最讨厌看人脸色行事,自己一点儿自由都没有。

A：I have a good salary, but it is too boring dealing with figures. Especially since I am still on the probation period. I have to please others. I don't have any freedom at all.

乙：这是刚开始,做一段时间,习惯了就好了。

B：You are just beginning to work. You will get used to it after working for a period of time.

词语表　New Words

北加州	Běi Jiāzhōu	Northern California
孩子头	háizitóu	king of children
没意思	méiyìsi	not promising; good for nothing
经济	jīngjì	cconomy; economic situation
不景气	bù jǐngqì	depressing
学科	xuékē	subjects
实话	shíhuà	truth
转行	zhuǎnháng	change professions
将就	jiāngjiu	to make the best of it
薪金	xīnjīn	salary
收入	shōurù	income; gain
枯燥	kūzào	boring; uninteresting
尤其	yóuqí	especially; particularly
试用期	shìyòngqī	probationary period; trial stage
脸色	liǎnsè	face; look
讨厌	tǎoyàn	nuisance; to loathe
行事	xíngshì	to handle matters; to act
自由	zìyóu	freedom
习惯	xíguàn	be accustomed to; habit; custom

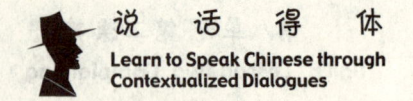

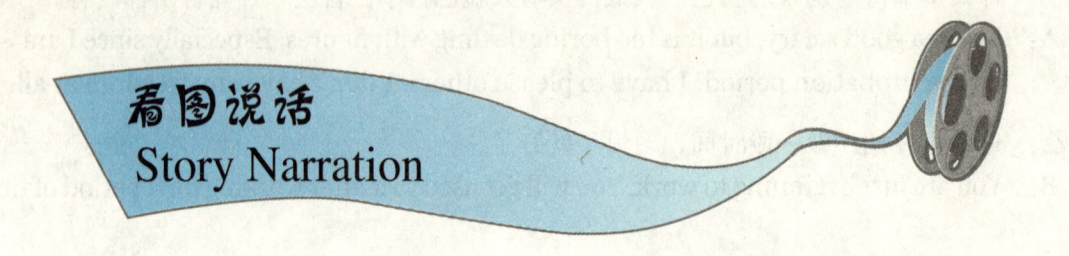

说话得体
Learn to Speak Chinese through Contextualized Dialogues

看图说话
Story Narration

按照以下图画顺序及各幅图画所提示的情景，叙述一个有始有终的完整故事。

Based on the order of the following pictures and the situations presented in each, narrate a story including a beginning and an end.

1.

2. 每天都有做不完的作业，要是……

3.

4.

224

Unit 8 Lesson Two Complaining

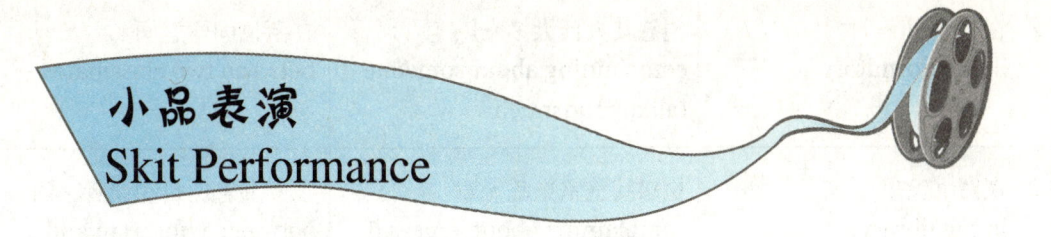

小品表演
Skit Performance

学生创作对话小品时尽可能使用本单元列出的和学生学到的新词、新句。小品主题选择应该得到老师首肯，以免重复。

Create situational dialogues with topics approved by the teacher to avoid repetition. Use as many expressions listed/learned in this unit as possible.

对话地点（时间） Place (Time) of Dialogue	对话情景 Context	对话者之间的关系 Relation Between Speakers
1 在公交车站 at a bus stop	抱怨班车又误点了 complaining about bus being late again	在两位乘客之间 between two passengers
2 在手提电话里 on a cell phone	抱怨高速公路堵车 complaining about traffic jam on the highway	在司机和家人之间 between a driver and his/her family
3 在家里 at home	抱怨连续下了三天雨 complaining about having rained for three days	在兄弟姐妹之间 between two siblings
4 在加油站 at a gas station	抱怨油价又上涨了 complaining about gas prices having gone up again	在两位顾客之间 between two customers
5 在校园里 on the campus	抱怨自动售货机收了钱不工作 complaining about the vending machine being broken down	在两位同学之间 between two students
6 在咖啡馆里 at a coffee shop	抱怨咖啡没有味道 complaining about coffee being weak	在服务员和顾客之间 between a server and a customer

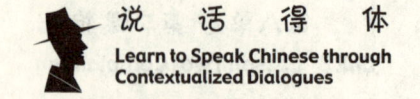

说话得体
Learn to Speak Chinese through Contextualized Dialogues

7 在宿舍里 in the dormitory	抱怨某人话太多 complaining about someone talking too much	在两位同学之间 between two classmates
8 在图书馆里 in the library	抱怨阅览室杂乱无章 complaining about a mess in the reading room	在图书管理员和读者之间 between a librarian and a reader
9 在教学楼走廊里 at the hall way of a teaching building	抱怨老师布置的作业太多 complaining about the teacher having given too much assignments	在两位同学之间 between two classmates
10 在大学招生办公室 at the admission office of a college	抱怨大学录取新生不公平 complaining about bias when accepting new students	在大学招生办公室职员和学生家长之间 between a college admission officer and a parent

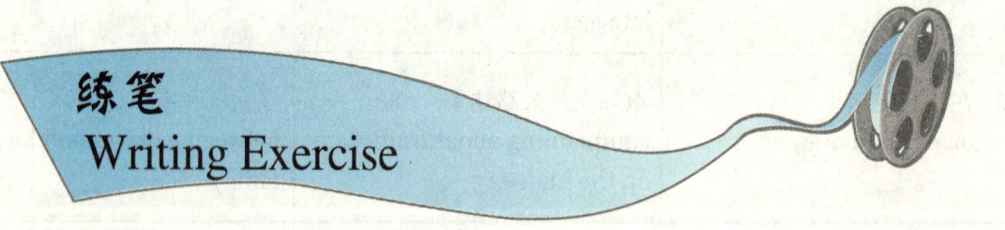

练笔
Writing Exercise

根据要求写一篇短文。尽可能用上本单元学到的词句。

Write a short passage on the given topic. Do your best to use words and expressions from the sentence patterns you have learned in this unit.

写一篇日记抱怨生不逢时 (Write a diary entry complaining that everything is going against your wishes.)

第八单元听力练习
Listening Comprehension Unit 8

听完以下各项听力练习的内容，先回答理解提示中的问题，再识别句子或语段的语境，然后尽可能使用本单元列出的和学到的新词、新句做适当的回应。

After listening to the sentences given, identify a proper context and response in each situation, using as many expressions listed/learned in this unit as possible.

	1. 理解提示 Comprehension	2. 情景识别 Context Identification	3. 学生回应 Student's Response
1	What is the competition?		我参与了，尽力了，我不后悔！
2	What's wrong with the telephone?		
3	What did the speaker request?		
4	What didn't the speaker do?		
5	What is the good news?		
6	What are the listeners doing?		
7	What is complimented?		
8	Why is the shawl good for the listener?		
9	Please list six advantages of the SUV.		
10	Why does the speaker like the listener?		

227

学生生活中常用的120句话
120 Popular Expressions in Daily Life Among Students

中文表达 Chinese	英文对照 English
1. Wǒ dǒng le. 我懂了。	I see.
2. Wǒ bù gàn le. 我不干了。	I quit.
3. Fàngshǒu (fàngkāi wǒ / fàng le wǒ)! 放手 (放开我 / 放了我)!	Let go! (Release me!)
4. Wǒ yě shì / yīyàng. 我也是 / 一样。	Me too.
5. Tiān na! 天哪!	Oh, god!
6. Bù xíng! (méiménr!) 不行! (没门儿!)	No way!
7. Gǎnkuài! (zhuā jǐn shíjiān!) 赶快! (抓紧时间!)	Quickly! (Don't waste time!)
8. Děng yī děng. (Děng yī xià.) 等一等。(等一下。)	Wait.

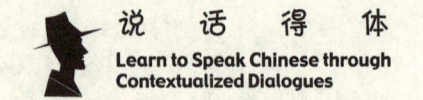

说 话 得 体
Learn to Speak Chinese through Contextualized Dialogues

中文表达 Chinese	英文对照 English
9. Wǒ tóngyì. 我同意。	I agree.
10. Hái bùcuò / hái hǎo. 还不错 / 还好。	Pretty good.
11. Tǎoyàn! 讨厌！	Annoying!
12. Qù nǐ de! 去你的！	Get out of here!
13. Bìzuǐ! 闭嘴！	Shut up!
14. Nǐ shì zài kāi wánxiào ba? 你是在开玩笑吧？	You've got to be kidding.
15. Wèi shénme bù ne? 为什么不呢？	Why not?
16. Dāngrán. 当然。	Of course.
17. Ānjìng! (Bié shuōhuà le!) 安静！（别说话了！）	Hush! (Stop talking!)
18. Zhènzuò yīdiǎnr! 振作一点儿！	Pull yourself together!
19. Zuò de hǎo (duì)! 做得好（对）！	Well done!
20. Wán de kāixīn / hǎo! 玩得开心 / 好！	Have fun!
21. (yào/ mài) Duōshǎo qián? （要 / 卖）多少钱？	How much (does it cost)?
22. Wǒ chī bǎo (hǎo/wán) le. 我吃饱（好 / 完）了。	I'm full (satisfied / finished).

230

120 Popular Expressions in Daily Life Among Students

中文表达 Chinese	英文对照 English
23. Wǒ yào huí jiā le. 我要回家了。	I want to go home.
24. Wǒ nòng hútu le. 我弄糊涂了。	I got lost.
25. Wǒ qǐngkè (wǒ qǐng nǐ…). 我请客(我请你……)。	It's my treat (I'll treat you to…).
26. Hébì ne? 何必呢?	Why must …?
27. Gǔn! 滚!	Beat it!
28. Nǐ chī cuò shénme yào le? 你吃错什么药了?	What's your problem?
29. Kù! (Zhēn bàng!) 酷!(真棒!)	That's hot (cool)!
30. Suànle ba! 算了吧!	Never mind!
31. Xiūxiǎng! 休想!	Don't even think about it!
32. Zhù nǐ hǎoyùn! 祝你好运!	Good luck!
33. Nǐ zǒuyùn le! 你走运了!	You lucky dog!
34. Wánwan éryǐ! 玩玩而已!	Just for fun.
35. Wúliáo de hěn! 无聊得很!	I am bored.
36. Màn yīdiǎnr! 慢一点儿!	Slow down!

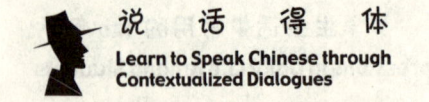

中文表达 Chinese	英文对照 English
37. Bǎozhòng! 保重!	Take care!
38. Xiǎoyìsi. (Jǔ shǒu zhī láo.) 小意思。(举手之劳。)	It's a piece of cake.
39. Zài shìshi (kàn)! 再试试(看)!	Try again!
40. Xiǎoxīn! (zhùyì!) 小心!(注意!)	Be careful! (Watch out!)
41. Zuìjìn zěnmeyàng? 最近怎么样?	What's up?
42. Xiànshí yīdiǎnr! 现实一点儿!	Get real!
43. Zhēnde ma? 真的吗?	Really?
44. Bùxǔ dòng! 不许动!	Don't move!
45. Cāicai kàn! 猜猜看!	Guess!
46. Wǒ huáiyí. (Wǒ bùxìn.) 我怀疑。(我不信。)	I doubt it. (I'm suspicious.)
47. Bié zhuāng shǎ le! 别装傻了!	Don't be a fool!
48. Dāngzhēn? 当真?	Are you serious?
49. Jiānchí xiàqù! 坚持下去!	Stick to it! (Persevere!)
50. Nǐ fāfēng le! 你发疯了!	You've got to be out of your mind.

120 Popular Expressions in Daily Life Among Students

中文表达 Chinese	英文对照 English
51. Bù yàojǐn! (méi wèntí!) 不要紧！(没问题！)	No problem!
52. Bù yào tài guòfèn le. 不要太过分了。	Don't cross the line.
53. Jiù zhèyàng ba. 就这样吧。	Keep it that way.
54. Shíjiān kuài dào le. 时间快到了。	Time is running out.
55. Zhè shì gěi nǐ de. 这是给你的。	This is for you.
56. Suàn wǒ yī gè. 算我一个。	Count me in.
57. Bié dānxīn. 别担心。	Don't worry.
58. Hǎo diǎnr le ma? 好点儿了吗？	Are you feeling any better?
59. Bié lǐ tā. 别理她。	Leave her alone.
60. Wǒ shì tā de yǐngmí. 我是他的影迷。	I am his fan.
61. Zhè bùguān wǒ de shì. 这不关我的事。	This does not concern me.
62. Hǎo (miào) jí le! 好（妙）极了！	Wonderful!
63. Nǐ gǎn kěndìng ma? 你敢肯定吗？	Are you sure?
64. Wǒ fēi zuò bù kě ma? 我非做不可吗？	Do I have to?

233

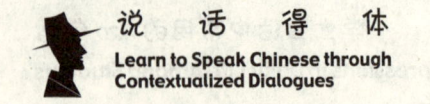

说 话 得 体
Learn to Speak Chinese through Contextualized Dialogues

中文表达 Chinese	英文对照 English
65. Wǒ cónglái bù … 我从来不……	I've never...
66. Tài kuāzhāng le ba. 太夸张了吧。	It's exaggerated.
67. Bù zhīdào / xiǎode. 不知道／晓得。	I don't know.
68. Fàng (qīng) sōng diǎnr. 放（轻）松点儿。	Just relax.
69. Tài yíhàn le. 太遗憾了。	I'm very sorry.
70. Hái yǒu qítā xuǎnzé ma? 还有其他选择吗？	What are the other choices?
71. Yídìng yào / qiānwàn bié … 一定要／千万别……	Be sure to (not to)...
72. Bāngbang máng, hǎo ma? 帮帮忙，好吗？	Can you help me out?
73. Bié kè qi! 别客气！	You're welcome!
74. Wǒ zhèng mángzhe ne! 我正忙着呢！	I am busy now.
75. Bǎochí liánxì! 保持联系！	Keep in touch!
76. Shíjiān jiùshì jīnqián. 时间就是金钱。	Time is money.
77. Shì nǎ yī wèi? 是哪一位？	Who is it?
78. Wǒ wú lù kě zǒu le. 我无路可走了。	I'm desperate.

学生生活中常用的 120 句话
120 Popular Expressions in Daily Life Among Students

中文表达 Chinese	英文对照 English
79. Wǒ shàng nǐ dàng le! 我上你当了!	You set me up!
80. Yào bāngmáng ma? 要帮忙吗?	Need help?
81. Zuò nǐ de báirìmèng! 做你的白日梦!	In your dreams!
82. Nǐ yíng le. 你赢了。	You win.
83. Wǒ zuòdào / chénggōng le! 我做到/成功了!	I made it!
84. Jìnxíng de zěnmeyàng le? 进行得怎么样了?	How's it coming along?
85. Tiān xiǎode. 天晓得。	Heaven knows.
86. Wǒ bù zàihu. 我不在乎。	I don't care.
87. Wǒ huì zhùyì / liúyì de. 我会注意/留意的。	I will pay attention.
88. Wǒ gǎn shíjiān. 我赶时间。	I'm in a hurry.
89. Nà shì tā de běnháng. 那是她的本行。	That's her specialty.
90. Yóu nǐ lái juédìng ba. 由你来决定吧。	It's up to you.
91. Lái ba, kuài! 来吧,快!	Oh, come on!
92. Guǎn hǎo nǐ zìjǐ jiù xíng le. 管好你自己就行了。	Mind your own business.

235

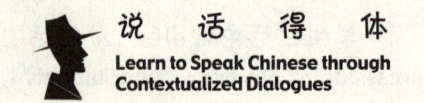

说 话 得 体
Learn to Speak Chinese through Contextualized Dialogues

中文表达 Chinese	英文对照 English
93. Nǐ qiàn wǒ yī gè (rén) qíng. 你欠我一个（人）情。	You owe me one.
94. Zánliǎ chěpíng le. 咱俩扯平了。	We (two) are even.
95. Shénme shíhou dōu xíng. 什么时候都行。	Any time is fine.
96. Nǐ méi dǎnliàng! 你没胆量！	You don't have the guts!
97. Wǒ shì rěn bù zhù / qíng bù zì jìn. 我是忍不住 / 情不自禁。	I can't help it.
98. Wǒ bù shì gùyì de. 我不是故意的。	I didn't mean to.
99. Kàn wǒ zěnme xiūlǐ nǐ! 看我怎么修理你！	I'll teach you a lesson!
100. Hǎo jiǔ bū jiàn. 好久不见。	Long time no see.
101. (dàodǐ shì) Shénme yuányīn? （到底是）什么原因？	Oh what?
102. Bié fán wǒ! 别烦我！	Don't bother me!
103. Nǐ kě shū cǎn le. 你可输惨了。	You are bitterly defeated.
104. Nǐ hěn yǒu tiānfù. 你很有天赋。	You are really talented.
105. Nǐ de Zhōngwén zhème hǎo, zhēn bù gǎn xiǎngxiàng. 你的中文这么好，真不敢想象。	Your Chinese is incredible.
106. Jīntiān wǒ nǎr dōu bù duìjìn. 今天我哪儿都不对劲。	Today is not my day.

学生生活中常用的 120 句话
120 Popular Expressions in Daily Life Among Students

中文表达 Chinese	英文对照 English
107. Bié gēn wǒ guòbuqù. 别跟我过不去。	Don't give me hard time.
108. Nǐ kàn shàngqù hěn jīngshen! 你看上去很精神！	You are looking sharp!
109. Bié wàngle gěi wǒ dǎ diànhuà. 别忘了给我打电话。	Don't forget to call me.
110. Wǒ shénme dōu bù zhīdào. 我什么都不知道。	I don't know anything.
111. Nǐ gǎnjué hǎo diǎnr le ma? 你感觉好点儿了吗？	Are you feeling better?
112. Zhù nǐ jīntiān guò de yúkuài! 祝你今天过得愉快！	Have a nice day!
113. Nǐ zài sāhuǎng. 你在撒谎。	You are lying.
114. Nǐ ràng wǒ chīle yī jīng. 你让我吃了一惊。	You surprised me.
115. Nǐ kàn shàngqù hěn lèi. 你看上去很累。	You look tired.
116. Gòu le! 够了！	That's enough.
117. Wǒ wèi nǐ jiāo'ào. 我为你骄傲。	I am proud of you.
118. Nǐ zhēn yōumò. 你真幽默。	You have a sense of humor.
119. Wǒ huì xiǎng nǐ de. 我会想你的。	I'll miss you.
120. Ràng wǒ xiǎng yī xiǎng. 让我想一想。	Let me think.

237

附录一　Appendix I

外语学习阶段准则(简介)
The Language Learning Continuum

美国加利福尼亚教育委员会2003年通过的《加利福尼亚州公立学校外语学习准则》[①]，其中"外语学习阶段准则"介绍了在第二语言学习过程中学生在不同学习阶段应该达到的程度，同时也介绍了第二语言习得过程中各进阶阶段的典例。《说话得体》中的四个基本用法是按照《加州公立学校外语学习准则》的"外语学习五个阶段"的前四个准则编排的。下表就是外语学习阶段准则的简要说明，仅供参考。

外语学习阶段准则
The Language Learning Continuum

外语学习 第一阶段 (结构性学习) **Stage I** **(Formulaic)**	· 学生领会并使用结构型语言(记忆词、词组、句子，有时是段落)。 Learners comprehend and produce formulaic language (memorized words, phrases, sentences, and in some cases paragraphs). · 学生应对可预知的普通生活场景中的各种日常生活细节。 Learners deal with discrete elements of daily life in highly predictable common daily settings. · 在听与读的过程中，当学生反复操练过记忆内容，而且与说话者或写作者之间具有一定的默契时，学生能够理解听读的内容。 When listening or reading, learners comprehend when memorized content is well rehearsed and when speakers or writers are highly sympathetic. · 在说与写的过程中，除非记忆的内容经过充分操练，否则，即使是与学生具有一定默契的听者或读者也不能理解学生的表述。 When speaking or writing, learners are unintelligible even to highly sympathetic listeners or readers unless the memorized content is well rehearsed.

---

① Reprinted, by permission, from the California Department of Education, CDE Press, 1430 N Street 3207, Sacramento, CA 95814.

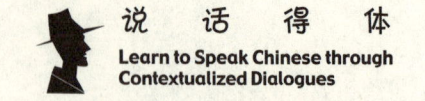

说 话 得 体
Learn to Speak Chinese through Contextualized Dialogues

外语学习 第二阶段 （自创性学习） **Stage II (Created)**	· 学生领会并使用自创性语言（句子以及连贯的句子）。 Learners comprehend and produce created language (sentences and strings of sentences). · 学生应付与个人相关的日常礼节要求和话题，以及某些非正式的和社交互动时的即时话题。 Learners deal with everyday courtesy requirements and topics related to self and the immediate environment in some informal and transactional settings. · 在听与读的过程中，学生理解与他们有默契的说话者或写作者所使用的自创性语言。 When listening or reading, learners comprehend sympathetic speakers or writers using created language. · 在说与写的过程中，与学生有默契感的听者或读者能理解学生所使用的自创性语言。 When speaking or writing, learners are intelligible to sympathetic listeners or readers when using created language.
外语学习 第三阶段 （规划性学习） **Stage III (Planned)**	· 学生领会和使用规划性语言（段落以及连贯的段落）。 Learners comprehend and produce planned language (paragraphs and strings paragraphs). · 学生应对（课堂以外）多数非正式和某些正式场合中能引起公众兴趣的、具体而真实的话题。 Learners deal with concrete and factual topics of public interest (the external environment) in most informal and some formal settings. · 在听与读的过程中，学生理解普通说话者或文字作者使用的规划性语言。 When listening or reading, learners comprehend non-sympathetic speakers or writers using planned language. · 在说与写的过程中，普通的听者和读者能理解学生所使用的规划性语言。 When speaking or writing, learners are intelligible to non-sympathetic listeners or readers when using planned language.
外语学习 第四阶段 （拓展性学习） **Stage IV (Extended)**	· 学生领会和使用拓展语言（口头表达和书面文章）。 Learners comprehend and produce extended language (oral and written essays). · 学生应对多数正式和非正式场合中不熟悉的、抽象的、实用的、社会性的和专业性的话题。

附录一 外语学习阶段准则(简介)
Appendix I The Language Learning Continuum

	Learners deal with unfamiliar, abstract, practical, social, and professional topics in most formal and informal settings. · 在听与读的过程中，学生理解普通说话者或写作者使用的正式的拓展语言。 When listening or reading, learners comprehend non-sympathetic speakers or writers using formal extended language. · 在说与写的过程中，普通的听者或读者能理解学生所使用的正式的拓展语言。 When speaking or writing, learners are intelligible to non-sympathetic listeners or readers when using formal, extended language.
外语学习 第五阶段 (特设性学习) **Stage V** **(Tailored)**	· 学生领会和使用在所学语言国家文化架构内，适合各种对象的拓展语言的多种文体和风格。 Learners comprehend and produce most forms and style of extended language tailored to various audiences from within the target-culture framework. · 学生应对各种话题以及适应各种相关专业的需求。 Learners deal with all topics and in all settings pertinent to professional needs. · 在听与读的过程中，学生理解普通说话者或写作者使用的这种特别设计的拓展语言。 When listening or reading, learners comprehend non-sympathetic speakers or writers using tailored, extended language. · 在说与写的过程中，普通的听者和读者都能理解处于这一阶段的学生所使用的特别设计的拓展语言。 When speaking or writing, learners functioning within this stage are intelligible to non-sympathetic listeners or readers when using tailored, extended language.

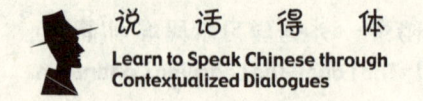

外语学习阶段准则要素
Continuum Components

阶段准则要素 Continuum Component	定义诠释 Definitions
功能 Function	**功能**就是使用语言正常完成的某特别任务，比如获取信息，表达好恶，描述以及给出建议。 **Functions** are specific tasks that are normally performed using a language, such as obtaining information, expressing likes or dislikes, describing, and giving advice.
情景 Context	**情景**指的是特定语言功能所使用的场合以及环境，比如面对面社交场合的问候或告别。情景提供交流系统，回答诸如"在哪儿"、"什么时候"以及"和谁一起"等问题。 **Context** refers to the situations or setting in which a particular function takes place, such as greetings or leave-taking that may occur in face-to-face social interaction. The context provides a delivery system, answering questions, "where", "when", and "with whom".
形式 Text Type	**形式**指的是书面语或口语的结构，从单词、词组到句子，再到段落。这些组成部分表明学生在各个阶段正常使用语言形式的范围。 **Text Type** refers to the structure of the written or spoken language, progressing from words and phrases to sentences and paragraphs. This component describes the range of text types normally used by students at the various stages.
内容 Content	**内容**指学生理解或表达信息的相对复杂性——学生能够理解、谈论及写出什么讨论的话题。范围除了涉及熟悉的学校及家庭生活以外，还包括时事、历史、艺术和文学等高层次专题。内容必须提供交际素材。 **Content** refers to the relative complexity of the information understood or conveyed by studnets — what topics of discussion students are able to understand, talk about, and write about. Examples include familiar topics such as school and family, as well as more advanced topics such as current events, history, art, and literature. The content provides the substance of the communication.

附录一 外语学习阶段准则(简介)
Appendix I The Language Learning Continuum

阶段准则要素 Continuum Component	定义诠释 Definitions
准确度 Accuracy	**准确度**指的是学生使用语言时表现语言结构性的正确程度，以及学生的举止在文化上的符合程度。社会语言学因素、词汇、句法、发音及流利表达都在准确度方面起到一定的作用。 **Accuracy** refers to the degree to which students' use of the language is structurally correct and their behavior is culturally appropriate. Sociolinguistic factors, vocabulary, syntax, pronunciation, and fluency all play a role in this category.

外语学习阶段准则要素具体内容
Continuum Text

第一阶段 Stage One

阶段准则要素 Continuum Component	阶段准则内容 Continuum Text
功能 Function	1. 学生相互问候 (students greet and respond to greetings) 2. 学生相互介绍 (students introduce and respond to introductions) 3. 学生进行对话 (students engage in conversations) 4. 学生表达喜好和憎恶 (students express likes and dislikes) 5. 学生提出要求 (students make requests) 6. 学生获得信息 (students obtain information) 7. 学生理解某些观点和熟悉的话题 (students understand some ideas and familiar details) 8. 学生开始提供信息 (students begin to provide information)
情景 Context	1. 学生在面对面社交场合时对话 (students converse in face-to-face social interaction) 2. 学生在社交场合中听懂和理解视听材料(students listen during social interaction and listen to audio or video texts) 3. 学生看懂诸如菜单、海报、时刻表、图表、招牌和简短

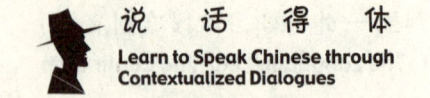

阶段准则要素 Continuum Component	阶段准则内容 Continuum Text
	介绍等原始材料 (students use authentic materials such as menus, photos posters, schedules, charts, signs and short narratives, when reading) 4. 学生写便条、列单、写诗、写明信片以及短信 (students write notes, lists, poems, postcards, and short letters)
形式 Text Type	1. 学生在说与写的时候，使用短句、所学到的词语和词组，以及简单的提问和要求 (students use short sentences, learned words and phrases, and simple questions and commands when speaking or writing) 2. 学生在听的时候，理解某些表达清晰、不复杂的讲话中的某些看法以及熟悉的话题 (students understand some ideas and familiar details presented in clear, uncomplicated speech when listening) 3. 学生在阅读过程中理解有视觉相辅的短小篇章 (students understand short texts enhanced by visual clues when reading)
内容 Content	第一阶段和第二阶段经常包括一些以下话题的组合 (stage I and II often include some combination of the following topics): 1. 学生理解和表达与自己有关的信息，如家庭，朋友，居家，房间，身体，学校，时刻表，休闲活动，校园生活，好恶，购物，衣服，价格，大小和数量，宠物与动物 (students understand and convey information about the self such as family, friends, home, rooms, health, school, schedules, leisure activities, campus life, likes and dislikes, shopping, clothes, prices, size and quantity, and pets and animals) 2. 学生理解和表达超越与自己有关的信息，如地理，地形，方向，建筑物和纪念碑，气象与季节，标记，文化和历史人物，地点和事件，颜色，数字，星期，日期，月份，时间，食物和风俗习惯，交通，旅游，职业和工作 (students understand and convey information beyond self such as geography, topography, directions, buildings and monuments, weather and seasons, symbols, cultural and historical figures, places and events, colors,

附录一 外语学习阶段准则(简介)
Appendix I The Language Learning Continuum

阶段准则要素 Continuum Component	阶段准则内容 Continuum Text
	numbers, days, dates, months, time, food and customs, transportation, travel, professions and work)
准确度 Accuracy	1. 学生作有效的交流，在不影响理解的情况下，允许出现少许的停顿和错误 (students communicate effectively with some hesitation and errors, which do not hinder comprehension) 2. 根据第一阶段的功能要求，学生在文化方面的表现能被接受 (students demonstrate culturally acceptable behavior for Stage I functions) 3. 学生理解大部分重要信息 (students understand most important information)

第二阶段 Stage Two

阶段准则要素 Continuum Component	阶段准则内容 Continuum Text
功能 Function	1. 学生提出要求 (students make requests) 2. 学生表达需求 (students express their needs) 3. 学生理解和发表重要看法以及提出某些细节 (students understand and express important ideas and some details) 4. 学生描述和比较 (students describe and compare) 5. 学生使用和理解表达带有感情色彩的话语 (students use and understand expressions indicating emotion)
情景 Context	1. 学生进行面对面的社交对话 (students speak in face-to-face social interaction) 2. 学生听懂社交对话和视听材料 (students listen during social interaction and using audio or video texts) 3. 学生读懂真实材料，比如短小介绍广告、入场券、说明书以及其他的媒体形式 (students read using authentic materials such as short narratives, advertisements, tickets, brochures, and other media) 4. 学生书信和短小的引导性文章 (students write letter and short guided compositions)

245

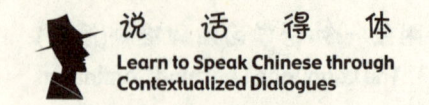

说话得体
Learn to Speak Chinese through Contextualized Dialogues

阶段准则要素 Continuum Component	阶段准则内容 Continuum Text
形式 Text Type	1. 在说与听的过程中，学生使用和理解所学到的词语、句子和连贯句子，提问以及作委婉要求 (students use and understand learned expressions, sentences, and strings of sentences, questions, and polite commands when speaking and listening) 2. 在写作的过程中，学生创作简单的语段 (students create simple paragraphs when writing) 3. 在阅读的过程中，学生理解高层次语境化下的重要信息和细节 (students understand important ideas and some details in highly contextualized authentic texts when reading)
内容 Content	第一阶段和第二阶段经常包括以下一些话题的组合 (stage I and II often include some combination of the following topics): 1. 学生理解和表达有关自己的信息，如家庭，朋友，居家，房间，身体，学校，休闲活动，校园生活，好恶，购物，衣服，价格，大小和数量，宠物与动物 (students understand and convey information about the self such as family, friends, home, rooms, health, school, schedules, leisure activities, campus life, likes and dislikes, shopping, clothes, prices, size and quantity, and pets and animals) 2. 学生理解和表达超越与自己有关的信息，如地理，地形，方向，建筑物和纪念碑，气象与季节，标记，文化和历史人物，地点和实践，颜色，数字，星期，日期，月份，时间，食物和风俗习惯，交通，旅游，职业和工作 (students understand and convey information beyond self such as geography, topography, directions, buildings and monuments, weather and seasons, symbols, cultural and historical figures, places and events, colors, numbers, days, dates, months, time, food and customs, transportation, travel, professions and work)

附录一 外语学习阶段准则(简介)
Appendix I The Language Learning Continuum

阶段准则要素 Continuum Component	阶段准则内容 Continuum Text
准确度 Accuracy	1. 学生表达流畅,并掌握词汇的使用(students demonstrate increasing fluency and control of vocabulary) 2. 根据第一阶段的功能要求,学生没有明显的模式错误(students show no significant pattern of error when performing Stage I functions) 3. 根据第二阶段的功能要求,学生进行有效的交流,少许的错误可能会稍稍影响完全理解(students communicate effectively with some pattern of error, which may interfere slightly with full comprehension when performing Stage II functions) 4. 根据第二阶段的功能要求,学生理解口头的与书面的论述,在阅读时伴有少量理解失误,学生在文化方面的表现能被接受(students understand oral and written discourse, with few errors in comprehension when reading; demonstrate culturally appropriate behavior for Stage II functions)

第三阶段 Stage Three

阶段准则要素 Continuum Component	阶段准则内容 Continuum Text
功能 Function	学生在能够表现所有第一和第二阶段功能项目中所提到的能力基础上继续扩展以外,还得培养以下能力(students expand their ability to perform all the functions developed in Stage I and II. They also develop the ability to): 1. 阐明、要求和理解事实说明(clarify and ask for and comprehend clarification) 2. 表示和理解观点(express and understand opinions) 3. 陈述和理解现在、过去、将来时间的表达(narrate and understand narration in the present, past, and future) 4. 分辨、阐明以及理解感受和心情(identify, state, and understand feelings and emotions)

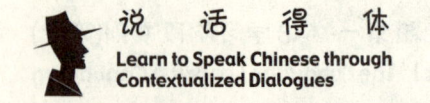

阶段准则要素 Continuum Component	阶段准则内容 Continuum Text
情景 Context	学生能够在下列情况中表现以上功能 (students can perform these functions): 1. 在说的方面，进行面对面社交对话和简单的电话沟通 (when speaking, in face-to-face social interaction and in simple transactions on the phone) 2. 在听的方面，理解社交对话和使用视听材料 (when listening, in social interaction and using audio or video texts) 3. 在阅读方面，阅读短小的故事、诗歌、散文和文章 (when reading short stories, poems, essays, and articles) 4. 在写的方面，书写日记、信件和散文 (when writing journals, letters, and essays)
形式 Text Type	1. 在说的方面，学生能使用连贯的相关句子 (students use strings of related sentences when speaking) 2. 在听的方面，学生理解由习惯与学生打交道的人员精心组织的绝大部分话语 (students understand most spoken language when the message is deliberately and carefully conveyed by a speaker accustomed to dealing with learners when listening) 3. 在写作方面，学生创造简单的语段 (students create simple paragraphs when writing) 4. 在阅读方面，学生从综合的真实材料中获得学问或新的知识 (students acquire knowledge and new knowledge from comprehensive authentic texts when reading)
内容 Content	内容包括文化、个人和社会话题 (content includes cultural, personal, and social topics): 1. 历史、艺术、文学、音乐、时事和文明，在这些领域中偏重重要人物和事件 (history, art, literature, music, current affairs, and civilization, with an emphasis on significant people and events in these fields) 2. 职业选择、环境问题、社会问题和政治问题 (career choices, the environment, social issues, and political issues)

附录一 外语学习阶段准则(简介)
Appendix I The Language Learning Continuum

阶段准则要素 Continuum Component	阶段准则内容 Continuum Text
准确度 Accuracy	1. 随着任务和信息的复杂化，学生出现理解错误，有些错误模式会影响对整体意义的理解 (students tend to become less accurate as the task or message becomes more complex, and some patterns of error may interfere with meaning) 2. 学生通常为自己熟悉的话题选择合适的词汇，可是当难度增加时出现迟疑表现，并出现组词和语音语调方面的错误(students generally choose appropriate vocabulary for familiar topics, but as the complexity of the message increases, there is evidence of hesitation and groping for words, as well as patterns of mispronunciation and intonation) 3. 学生通常在社会环境中表现出适当的文化行为(students generally use culturally appropriate behavior in social situations) 4. 在阅读和听的时候，学生理解并抓住主题思想和一些相辅的细节(students understand and retain most key ideas and some supporting details when reading and listening)

第四阶段 Stage Four

阶段准则要素 Continuum Component	阶段准则内容 Continuum Text
功能 Function	学生在能够表现所有第一、第二和第三阶段功能项目中所提到的能力基础上继续扩展以外，还得培养以下能力(students expand their ability to perform all the functions developed in Stage I, II and III. They also develop the ability to): 1. 提出和理解劝告和建议 (give and understand advice and suggestions) 2. 开始、深入和结束话题 (initiate, engage in, and close a conversation) 3. 比较和对比 (compare and contrast) 4. 解释和支持某观点 (explain and support an opinion)

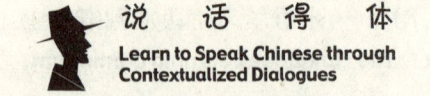

阶段准则要素 Continuum Component	阶段准则内容 Continuum Text
情景 Context	学生能够在下列情况中表现以上功能 (students can perform these functions): 1. 在说的方面，进行面对面社交对话，简单的电话沟通，小组讨论，有准备的辩论以及报告 (when speaking, in face-to-face social interaction and in simple transactions on the phone, and in group discussions, prepared debates, and presentation) 2. 在听的方面，听懂社交对话和使用视听材料包括电视会谈和新闻报导 (when listening, in social interaction and using audio or video texts, including TV interviews and newscasts) 3. 在阅读方面，阅读短小的文学性语段、诗歌和文章 (when reading short literary texts, poems, and articles) 4. 在写作方面，写日记、信件和散文 (when writing journals, letters, and essays)
形式 Text Type	1. 在说的方面，学生使用一系列连贯的语段作简单的论述 (students use simple discourse in a series of coherent paragraphs when speaking) 2. 在听的方面，学生理解大部分真实生活中的口头表达 (students understand most authentic spoken language when listening) 3. 在写的方面，学生创作一系列连贯的语段 (students create a series of coherent paragraphs when writing) 4. 在阅读方面，学生在阅读复杂的真实材料的过程中获取学问和新知识 (students acquire knowledge and new information from comprehensive authentic texts when reading)
内容 Content	1. 内容涉及广义的文化特殊概念，包括诸如目的语文化中的教育体系、政府、政治和社会等问题 (content embraces concepts of broader cultural significance, including institutions such as the education system, the government, and political and social issues in the target culture) 2. 内容也涉及诸如与社会及个人有关的音乐、文学、艺术和科学等话题 (content also embraces topics of social and personal interest such as music, literature, the arts, and the sciences)

附录一 外语学习阶段准则(简介)
Appendix I The Language Learning Continuum

阶段准则要素 Continuum Component	阶段准则内容 Continuum Text
准确度 Accuracy	1. 学生对话时使用大量合适的词汇，伴有少量明显错误 (students engage in conversation with few significant patterns of error and use a wide range of appropriate vocabulary) 2. 虽然随着任务和信息的复杂化，学生出现理解错误，但是他们对恰当的文化行为表现出极强的意识 (students demonstrate a heightened awareness of culturally appropriate behavior, although, as the task or messages become more complex, they tend to become less accurate) 3. 在读和听的时候，学生能够理解和汇报最主要的观点以及相辅的细节 (students are able to understand and report most key ideas and some supporting detail when reading and listening)

第五阶段 Stage Five

阶段准则要素 Continuum Component	阶段准则内容 Continuum Text
功能 Function	学生在能够表现所有第一、第二、第三和第四阶段功能项目中所提到的能力基础上继续拓展以外，还得培养以下能力 (students expand their ability to perform all the functions developed in Stage I, II, III and IV. They also develop the ability to): 1. 交换意见和谈判 (conduct transactions and negotiations) 2. 举证解释和详尽阐述观点 (substantiate and elaborate opinions) 3. 确信和使人信服 (convince and persuade) 4. 分析和评判 (analyze and critique)
情景 Context	几乎在任何场合，包括很多复杂的情况中，学生都能够表现上述功能 (students can perform above functions in almost any context, including many complex situations)
形式 Text Type	学生能够在适当的情况下，在更大范围内作论述时表现上述功能 (students can perform above functions in extended discourse when appropriate)

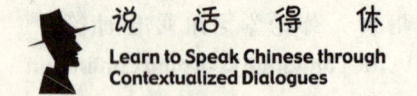

阶段准则要素 Continuum Component	阶段准则内容 Continuum Text
内容 Content	1. 内容涉及广义的文化特殊概念，包括诸如目的语文化中的环境保护和人权等社会问题 (content embraces concepts of broader cultural significance, including social issues in the target culture, such as the environment and human rights) 2. 内容也涉及有关艺术、文学和社会学等的抽象概念 (content also embraces abstract ideas concerning art, literature, politics, and society)
准确度 Accuracy	1. 学生使用符合目的语文化的语言，虽然可能出现一些迟疑和正常的停顿，但是表现出词汇量丰富的特点，很少出现句型错误 (students use culturally appropriate language, characterized by a wide range of vocabulary, with few patterns of error, although speech may contain some hesitation and normal pauses) 2. 学生理解主题思想以及大部分的辅助细节 (students comprehend significant ideas and most supporting details)

附录一 外语学习阶段准则(简介)
Appendix I The Language Learning Continuum

外语学习阶段准则阶段与四个用法参考对照表
Language Learning Continuum Comparison Chart

《说话得体》中的四个用法是按照《加州公立学校外语学习准则》的"外语学习五个阶段"的前四个准则所编排的。

外语学习五个阶段 Five Stages of Language Learning Continuum	《说话得体》中的四个用法 Four Deliveries in the textbook
外语学习第一阶段 （结构性学习） Stage I (Formulaic)	《说话得体》中的基本用法： 要求学生能熟练运用 Essential Delivery requires skillful application.
外语学习第二阶段 （自创性学习） Stage II (Created)	《说话得体》中的实用用法： 要求学生理解、运用 Practical Delivery requires comprehension and application.
外语学习第三阶段 （规划性学习） Stage III (Planned)	《说话得体》中的复杂用法： 要求学生知道、理解 Complex Delivery requires introduction and comprehension.
外语学习第四阶段 （拓展性学习） Stage IV (Extended)	《说话得体》中的特殊用法： 要求学生了解，知道 Special Delivery requires introduction.
外语学习第五阶段 （特适性学习） Stage V (Tailored)	专业用法：范围非本课本所涉及 Professional Delivery is not included in this textbook.

附录二 Appendix II

《说话得体》教学安排
Instructional Plan for Speaking Chinese through Contextualized Dialogues

第一阶段：开启思路
Stage I: Brainstorming

分小组或对子讨论、设计场景，并选择用于对话的词句
Possible situations, words and expressions (group or pair work)

对话地点 Setting	中心话题 Topic	对话者相互关系 Relationship between Speakers	甲可能说的话 What A might say	乙可能说的话 What B might say

场景设计表
Possible situations, words and expressions

对话地点 Setting	中心话题 Topic	对话者相互关系 Relationship between Speakers	甲可能说的话 What A might say	乙可能说的话 What B might say

（小组或对子活动 group or pair work）

附录二《说话得体》教学安排
Appendix II Instructional Plan for Speaking Chinese through Contextualized Dialogues

第二阶段：词句比照
Stage II: Matching up

1. 词句对比：比较常用词句中的表达法，从中选出意思接近的词或者句子（参见：常用词句部分）

   Matching up: Compare Brainstorming Ideas with Common Expressions found in the textbook and select the most appropriate words and expressions (Refer to Common Expressions Section)

	开启思路的词句 Brainstorming Ideas		常用词句中的表达法 Common Expressions in the Textbook
1		1	
2		2	
3		3	
4		4	
5		5	
6		6	
7		7	
8		8	
9		9	
10		10	

（供学生比较时用 for students to take notes and compare)

2. 选用合适的中文词句用于学生选定的三个场景

   Sentence Structures: Choose the most appropriate Chinese expressions for 3 mini-dialogues students selected

3. 试着回应选择的句子

   Application: Provide selected expressions with proper responses

说 话 得 体
Learn to Speak Chinese through Contextualized Dialogues

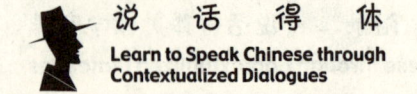

《说话得体》短小对话场景设计及汉语表达
Mini Dialogue Designing and Chinese Expressions

主题 Theme

预设场景 Proposed Setting	人物关系 Relationship between Characters	汉语表达 Chinese Expressions	可能的回应 Possible Responses
		A:	B:

主题 Theme

预设场景 Proposed Setting	人物关系 Relationship between Characters	汉语表达 Chinese Expressions	可能的回应 Possible Responses
		A:	B:

主题 Theme

预设场景 Proposed Setting	人物关系 Relationship between Characters	汉语表达 Chinese Expressions	可能的回应 Possible Responses
		A:	B:

（小组或对子活动 group or pair work）

附录二《说话得体》教学安排
Appendix II Instructional Plan for Speaking Chinese through Contextualized Dialogues

第三阶段：课文学习
Stage III: Text Study

1	基本用法 Essential Delivery	Sentence Patterns 根据课文定	1. 2. 3. 4.	课文（对话范本）： A: B: A: B:
		Useful Expressions 老师选择	1. 2. 3. 4. 5. 6. 7. 8. 9. 10.	学生练习： A: B: A: B:
2	实用用法 Practical Delivery	Sentence Patterns 根据课文定	1. 2. 3. 4.	课文（对话范本）： A: B: A: B:
		Useful Expressions 老师选择	1. 2. 3. 4. 5. 6. 7. 8. 9. 10.	学生练习： A: B: A: B:
3	复杂用法 Complex Delivery	Sentence Patterns 根据课文定	1. 2. 3. 4.	课文（对话范本）： A: B: A: B:
		Useful Expressions 老师选择	1. 2. 3. 4. 5. 6. 7. 8. 9. 10.	学生练习： A: B: A: B:
4	特殊用法 Special Delivery	Sentence Patterns 根据课文定	1. 2. 3. 4.	课文（对话范本）： A: B: A: B:
		Useful Expressions 老师选择	1. 2. 3. 4. 5. 6. 7. 8. 9. 10.	学生练习： A: B: A: B:
5	看图说话 Narrative Presentation	Sentence Patterns 根据图画定	1. 2. 3. 4.	理解与描述
		Useful Expressions 老师选择	1. 2. 3. 4. 5. 6. 7. 8. 9. 10.	学生练习：

说 话 得 体
Learn to Speak Chinese through Contextualized Dialogues

	为适应不同水平的学生达到同一交流目的所设定的四个层次 There are four delivery levels designed to meet the requirements of students at various levels.
1	基本用法：要求熟悉、理解、操练、熟练运用 Essential Delivery requires familiarization, comprehension, practice and skillful application.
2	实用用法：要求熟悉、理解、操练、运用 Practical Delivery requires familiarization, comprehension, practice and application.
3	复杂用法：要求熟悉、理解、操练 Complex Delivery requires familiarization, comprehension, and practice.
4	特殊用法：要求熟悉、理解 Special Delivery requires familiarization and comprehension.

教学过程：

1	词汇学习 Vocabulary Study
2	基本句型 Sentence Structures
3	课文理解 Text Comprehension
4	文化特性解释 Explanation of Cultural Characteristics
5	小品构思和准备 Skits Preparation
6	练笔 Writing Exercises

1. 词汇学习 Vocabulary Study

1		11	
2		12	
3		13	
4		14	
5		15	
6		16	
7		17	
8		18	
9		19	
10		20	

（教师根据学生需要，从"对话部分"中挑选
Selected from the Texts section by instructors）

Appendix II Instructional Plan for Speaking Chinese through Contextualized Dialogues

2. 基本句型 Sentence Structures

基本句型 Sentence Structures	造句 Sentence Composition

(教师根据学生需要，从"对话部分"中挑选 Selected from the Texts section by instructors)

3. 课文理解 Text Comprehension

(由教师根据学生具体情况安排 Arranged by instructors)

4. 文化特性解释 Cultural Perspectives

(由教师根据学生具体情况安排 Arranged by instructors)

5. 小品构思和准备 Skit Preparation

情景 Situations	小品构思 Authentic and Critical Thinking for Skit Development	新学词句的运用 Application of What have been learned

(小组或对子活动 group or pair work)

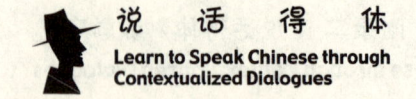

第四阶段：反馈测评
Stage IV: Feedback and Assessment

1. 看图说话 Story Narration

按照以下图画顺序及各幅图画所提示的情景，叙述一个有始有终的完整故事。
Based on the order of the following pictures and the situations presented in each, narrate a story including a beginning and an end.

Appendix II Instructional Plan for Speaking Chinese through Contextualized Dialogues

2. 小品表演 Skit Performance

学生创作对话小品时尽可能使用本单元列出的和学生学到的新词、新句。小品主题选择应得到老师首肯，以免重复。

Create situational dialogues with topics approved by the teacher. Use as many expressions listed/learned in this unit as possible.

情景与中心话题 Setting & Topic	对话时间与地点 Time & Place	对话者相互关系 Relationship between Speakers

甲可能说的话 What A Might Say	乙可能说的话 What B Might Say
A:	B:
A:	B:
A:	B:
A:	B:
A:	B:
A:	B:
A:	B:
A:	B:
A:	B:
A:	B:

（参见每课课文后面的场景提示 Refer to the Skit Hints section）

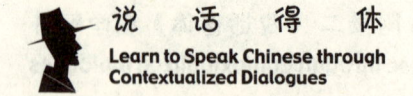

说 话 得 体
Learn to Speak Chinese through Contextualized Dialogues

3. 听力练习 Listening Comprehension (1)
（每个单元有 10 句话或语段 10 sentences or paragraphs for each unit）

（参见"听力练习"部分 Refer to the Listening Comprehension section）

	听写内容 Sentence(s) Given	1. 理解提示 Comprehension Hints	2. 情景识别 Context Identification	3. 学生回应 Student Response
1				
2				
3				
4				
5				
6				
7				
8				
9				
10				

（学生用 for student's use）

附录二 《说话得体》教学安排
Appendix II Instructional Plan for Speaking Chinese through Contextualized Dialogues

听力练习 Listening Comprehension (2)
（学生在观摩小品表演时必须做笔记 Students are required to take notes or messages while watching skit performances）

人物 who	时间 when	地点 where	事件 what	原因 why	过程 how	结果 result

（学生用 for student's use）

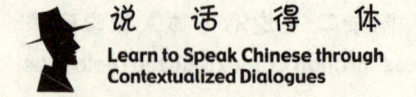

说话得体 Learn to Speak Chinese through Contextualized Dialogues

听力练习 Listening Comprehension (3)

对话地点 Place of dialogue	对话情景 Situation of Dialogue	对话者关系 Relationship between Speakers	对话内容 Dialogue Content	最感兴趣部分 What interests you most?

(学生用 for student's use)

Appendix II Instructional Plan for Speaking Chinese through Contextualized Dialogues

听力练习 Listening Comprehension(4)
(录像及讲评 Video-taping and Discussion)

学生姓名 Student's Name	设计构思 Originality 20%	对话内容 Content 20%	发音发声 Pronunciation & Tones 20%	流畅表达 Fluent Delivery 20%	总体表现 Overall Performance 20%

(教师用 for instructor's use)

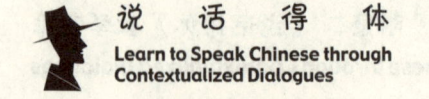

说话得体
Learn to Speak Chinese through Contextualized Dialogues

4. 练笔 Writing Exercises

(根据要求写短文，尽可能用上本单元学到的词句。Write a short passage on the given topic. Do your best to use words and expressions from the sentence patterns you have learned.)

第一单元 Unit 1	第一课 问候 Lesson 1 Greetings	留言 (Write a short message for someone who can't be reached at the moment.)
	第二课 告别 Lessone 2 Saying Farewell	告别高中时代演说辞 (Write a commencement speech to bid farewell to your high school.)
第二单元 Unit 2	第一课 介绍 Lesson 1 Introducing	竞选学生会主席的演说辞 (Write a speech on the topic of running for the president of the student union.)
	第二课 推荐 Lesson 2 Recommending	推荐我的学校 (Write a letter recommending the school you attend.)
第三单元 Unit 3	第一课 询问 Lesson 1 Inquiring	写信打听去中国留学的规定 (Write a letter to inquire about the detailed rules regarding studying in China.)
	第二课 要求 Lesson 2 Requesting	委托朋友预订飞机票 (Write a note asking your friend to help you book airline tickets.)
第四单元 Unit 4	第一课 拒绝 Lesson 1 Refusing	无法应邀看歌剧的回条 (Write a reply memo to decline an invitation to an opera.)
	第二课 接受 Lesson 2 Accepting	接受同学毕业舞会邀请的回条 (Write a reply memo to accept an invitation from your classmate to the senior prom.)
第五单元 Unit 5	第一课 告诫 Lesson 1 Cautioning	给邻居写一张警告条，他家的宠物又咬人了 (Write a warning note to your neighbor that his/her pet had attacked people again.)
	第二课 建议 Lesson 2 Suggesting	对有作弊习惯的同学提出建议 (Write a suggestion to your classmate who has a bad habit of cheating.)
第六单元 Unit 6	第一课 许诺 Lesson 1 Promising	写信给老师保证不再旷课 (Write a letter to the teacher promising to no longer cut class.)
	第二课 致歉 Lesson 2 Apologizing	错怪了同屋，写信致歉 (Write a letter apologizing for having blamed a roommate wrongly.)
第七单元 Unit 7	第一课 同情 Lesson 1 Showing Sympathy	老师被校方解雇了，写信表示同情 (Write a letter to your teacher who has been laid off by the school.)
	第二课 安慰 Lesson 2 Giving Comfort and Reassurance	同学出车祸住医院，写慰问信 (Write a note to express your consolation to a classmate who had a car accident.)
第八单元 Unit 8	第一课 恭维 Lesson 1 Complimenting	祝贺朋友上大学 (Write a letter to congratulate your friend who is going to college.)
	第二课 抱怨 Lesson 2 Complaining	写一篇日记抱怨生不逢时 (Write a dairy entry complaining that everything is going against your wishes.)

附录三 Appendix III

《说话得体》教学课时安排
（仅供参考）

Daily Agenda for Teaching and Learning (for reference only)

1. 正常课时安排 Regular Schedule (50 分钟 50 Minutes)
（十个课时完成一个单元 10 class hours for completion of one unit）

	准备活动 Warm-up	常用词句学习 Common Expressions	分析理解 Analysis/Comprehension	语境操练 Contextualized Practice	检测评估 Assessment	作业选择 Homework Options
第一天 Day 1	第一课：开启思路 Brainstorming (Lesson 1) 设计十个场景 Designing 10 Scenes	常用词句介绍 Common Expressions	词句对照 Expression Comparison	为自设场景配话 Provide Lines for 10 Scenes	准备小对话 Prepare for 3 Mini-Dialogues	准备小对话 Prepare for 3 Mini-Dialogues
第二天 Day 2	场景重现 10 Scenes Review	常用词句操练 Vocabulary/Sentence Practice	课文理解（对话 1-2） Text Comprehension Dialogues 1-2	结合课文理解做小对话练习 3 Mini-Dialogues Exercise	新字择选 15 New Characters Applied in Sentences (Selected from Common Expressions) 小对话演示 3 Mini-Dialogues Presentation	准备一个短小语段 1 Short Paragraph 写字练习 New Characters Applied in Sentences

267

续上表

	准备活动 Warm-up	常用词句学习 Common Expressions	分析理解 Analysis/Comprehension	语境操练 Contextualized Practice	检测评估 Assessment	作业选择 Homework Options
第三天 Day 3	语段汇报 Paragraph Report	常用词句操练 Vocabulary/Sentence Practice	课文理解（对话 3-4） Text Comprehension Dialogues 3-4	结合课文理解做小对话练习 3 Mini-Dialogues Exercise 根据小品提示设计小品 Prepare for Skits	小对话演示 3 Mini-Dialogues Presentation	练笔 Writing Exercise
第四天 Day 4	看图说话（开启思路） Story Narration Brainstorming from Pictures	常用词句复习 Vocabulary/Sentence Review 小品词汇搜寻 Skit Vocabulary Exploration	准备小品表演 Prepare for Skits	看图说话练习 Story Narration Exercise	小品表演 Skit Performance 看图说话 Story Narration Report	常用词句总结 Summarization for Common Expressions
第五天 Day 5	第二课：开启思路 Brainstorming (Lesson 2) 设计十个场景 Designing 10 Scenes	常用词句介绍 Common Expressions	词句对照 Expression Comparison	为自设场景配话 Provide Lines for 10 Scenes	准备小对话 Prepare for 3 Mini-Dialogues	准备小对话 Prepare for 3 Mini-Dialogues
第六天 Day 6	场景重现 10 Scenes Review	常用词句操练 Vocabulary/Sentence Practice	课文理解（对话 1-2） Text Comprehension Dialogues 1-2	结合课文理解做小对话练习 3 Mini-Dialogues Exercise	新字择选 15 New Characters Applied in Sentences (Selected from Common Expressions) 小对话演示 3 Mini-Dialogues Presentation	准备一个短小语段 1 Short paragraph 写字练习 New Characters Applied in Sentences

268

续上表

	准备活动 Warm-up	常用词句学习 Common Expressions	分析理解 Analysis/Comprehension	语境操练 Contextualized Practice	检测评估 Assessment	作业选择 Homework Options
第七天 Day 7	语段汇报 Paragraph Report	常用词句操练 Vocabulary/Sentence Practice	课文理解（对话 3-4） Text Comprehension Dialogues 3-4	结合课文理解做小对话练习 3 Mini-Dialogues Exercise 根据小品提示设计小品 Prepare for Skits	小对话演示 3 Mini-Dialogues Presentation	练笔 Writing Exercise 准备小品表演 Prepare for Skits
第八天 Day 8	看图说话（开启思路） Story Narration Brainstorming from Pictures	常用词句复习 Vocabulary/Sentence Review 小品词汇搜寻(5') Skit Vocabulary Exploration	准备小品表演 Prepare for Skits	看图说话练习 Story Narration Exercise	小品表演 Skit Performance 看图说话 Story Narration Report	常用词句总结 Summarization for Common Expressions
第九天 Day 9	看图说话复习 Review Story Narration	单元常用词复习 Review Unit Common Expressions	单元听力练习理解回应 Unit Listening Comprehension and Possible Response		单元听力练习 Unit Listening Comprehension	
第十天 Day 10	重温单元听力练习 Review Unit Listening Comprehension 看图说话复习 Review Story Narration	单元听力练习词句讲解 Explanation of Expressions in Unit Listening Comprehension		单元听力练习理解与操练 Unit Listening Comprehension and Practice	讲评与总结 Evaluation and Summarization	检查文字作业： 10-3-1 课堂笔记 练笔 Writing Exercise Listening Test worksheet 新字择选 New Characters Applied in Sentences

269

2. 组合课时安排 Block Schedule (90 分钟 90 minutes)
(五个双课时完成一个单元 5 double class hours for completion of one unit)

	准备活动 Warm-up	常用词句学习 Common Expressions	分析理解 Analysis/Comprehension	语境操练 Contextualized Practice	检测评估 Assessment	作业选择 Homework Options
第一天 Day 1	第一课: 开启思路 Brainstorming (Lesson 1) 设计十个场景 Designing 10 Scenes	常用词句介绍 Common Expressions 常用词句操练 Vocabulary/Sentence Practice	词句对照 Expression Comparison 课文理解(对话 1-2) Text Comprehension Dialogues 1-2	为自设场景配话 Provide Lines for 10 Scenes 结合课文理解作小对话练习 3 Mini-Dialogues Exercise	准备小对话 Prepare for 3 Mini-Dialogues 新字择选 15 New Characters Applied in Sentences (Selected from Common Expressions)	准备一个短小语段 1 Short Paragraph 写字练习 New Characters Applied in Sentences
第二天 Day 2	语段汇报 Paragraph report 看图说话(开启思路) Story Narration Brainstorming from Pictures	常用词句操练 Vocabulary/Sentence Practice	课文理解(对话 3-4) Text Comprehension Dialogues 3-4 准备小品表演 Prepare for Skits	根据小品提示设计小品 Prepare for Skits 看图说话 Story Narration Report	小品对话演示 3 Mini-Dialogues Presentation 小品表演 Skit Performance 练笔 Writing Exercise	常用词句总结 Summarization for Common Expressions
第三天 Day 3	第二课: 开启思路 Brainstorming (Lesson 2) 设计十个场景 Designing 10 Scenes	常用词句介绍 Common Expressions 常用词句操练 Vocabulary/Sentence Practice	词句对照 Comparison 课文理解(对话 1-2) Text Comprehension Dialogues 1-2	为自设场景配话 Provide Lines for 10 Scenes	小对话演示 3 Mini-Dialogues Presentation 新字择选 15 New Characters Applied in Sentences (Selected from Common Expressions)	准备一个短小语段 1 Short Paragraph 写字练习 New Characters

续上表

	准备活动 Warm-up	常用词句学习 Common Expressions	分析/理解 Analysis/Comprehension	语境操练 Contextualized Practice	检测评估 Assessment	作业选择 Homework Options
第四天 Day 4	语段汇报 Paragraph Report 看图说话(开启思路) Story Narration Brainstorming from Pictures	常用词句操练 Vocabulary/Sentence Practice	课文理解(对话 3-4) Text Comprehension Dialogues 3-4 准备小品表演 Prepare for Skits	根据小品提示设计小品 Prepare for Skits 看图说话 Story Narration Report	小对话演示 3 Mini-Dialogues Presentation 小品表演 Skit Performance 练笔 Writing Exercise	准备小品表演 Prepare for Skits
第五天 Day 5	单元常用词复习 Review Unit Common Expressions	单元听力练习词句讲解 Explanation of Expressions in Unit Listening Comprehension	单元听力练习理解回应 Unit Listening Comprehension and Possible Responses 重温单元听力练习 Review Unit Listening Comprehension	单元听力练习理解与操练 Unit Listening Comprehension and Practice	单元听力练习 Unit Listening Comprehension 讲评与总结 Evaluation and Summarization	检查文字作业： 10-3-1 课堂笔记 练笔 Writing Exercise Listening Test Worksheet 新词(字)择选 New Characters Applied in Sentences

271

附录四 Appendix IV

《说话得体》总体教学要求参考与自我检测
General Instructional Requirement and Self-Evaluations

学生自测 Student Self-Evaluation

课前我所知道的 What did I know before the class?	课前我期待能学到的 What did I expect to learn?	老师在课上所讲的 What has the teacher taught?	我在课堂上学到的 What have I learned?	我还需要学的 What do I need for further work?

教师自测 Teacher Evaluation

需要学生知道的 What is it that I want students to know?	学生能够做到的 What should they be able to do?	能帮助学生学习的教学活动 What activities will help them learn these things?	老师和学生是如何知道学习进展的 How will we (teachers and students) know how well we are doing?

* A well-balanced assessment is embedded in instruction and does not exist in isolation. Assessment should be standards-based and respond to the above questions.

附录四 《说话得体》总体教学要求参考与自我检测
Appendix IV General Instructional Requirement and Self-Evaluations

语言/文化功能主题 Language/Culture Functional Theme	中心课文参考 Core Text Reference	外语学习阶段准则 Continuum Stages	教学目标 Instructional Objective		
			介绍 Introduction	练习 Practice	熟练掌握 Mastery
1.1 问候 Greetings	您说着了 You Are Right	1 / 2		X	X
	恭喜，贺喜 Congratulations	1 / 2		X	X
	欢迎光临 Welcome	2 / 3	X	X	
	稀客 What a Rare Visitor	3 / 4	X	X	
1.2 告别 Saying Farewell	时间不早了 It's Getting Late.	1 / 2		X	X
	接着聊 Continue to Talk	1 / 2		X	X
	保持联系 Keep in Touch	2 / 3	X	X	
	尽管来找我 Feel Free to Visit Me	2 / 3	X	X	
2.1 介绍 Introducing	不必客套 No Need to Be So Formal.	1 / 2		X	X
	听好消息 Hearing Good News	1 / 2		X	X
	自我介绍 Self-Introducing	2 / 3	X	X	
	逛商场 Shopping	2 / 3	X	X	
2.2 推荐 Recommending	读个痛快 Read with Pleasure	1 / 2		X	X
	不会让你失望 You Won't Be Disappointed.	1 / 2		X	X
	北京特产 Beijing Specialties	2 / 3	X	X	
	必不可少 Absolutely Necessary	2 / 3	X	X	

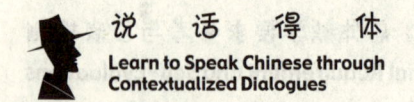

说 话 得 体
Learn to Speak Chinese through Contextualized Dialogues

语言/文化功能主题 Language/Culture Functional Theme	中心课文参考 Core Text Reference	外语学习阶段准则 Continuum Stages	教学目标 Instructional Objective		
			介绍 Introduction	练习 Practice	熟练掌握 Mastery
3.1 询问 Inquiring	对不起，请问 Excuse Me, May I Ask …	1 / 2		X	X
	有何贵干 What Kind of Business Do You Have?	1 / 2		X	X
	申请工作 Applying for a Job	2 / 3	X	X	
	你几岁了？ How Old Are You?	2 / 3	X	X	
3.2 要求 Requesting	家常饭菜 Homemade Meal	1 / 2		X	X
	洗耳恭听 Listening Devoutly and Respectfully	1 / 2		X	X
	请你转告 Please, Pass the Word	2 / 3	X	X	
	赏光 Will You Honor Me?	2 / 3	X	X	
4.1 拒绝 Refusing	恕不远送 Sorry for not Escorting You any Further	1 / 2 / 3		X	X
	看你怎么办 What Will You Do?	1 / 2 / 3		X	X
	情我领了 Appreciate the Kindness	2 / 3	X	X	
	销售代理 Becoming a Sales Representative	2 / 3	X	X	
4.2 接受 Accepting	多买便宜 The More, the Cheaper	1 / 2 / 3		X	X
	祝贺生日 Celebrating a Birthday	1 / 2 / 3		X	X

附录四《说话得体》总体教学要求参考与自我检测
Appendix IV General Instructional Requirement and Self-Evaluations

语言/文化功能主题 Language/Culture Functional Theme	中心课文参考 Core Text Reference	外语学习阶段准则 Continuum Stages	教学目标 Instructional Objective		
			介绍 Introduction	练习 Practice	熟练掌握 Mastery
	接受任职 Accepting a Job Offer	3/4	X	X	
	接受建议 Taking a Suggestion	3/4	X	X	
5.1 告诫 Cautioning	预防万一 Prepare for the Worst	2/3		X	X
	第一次开车 First Time Driving	2/3		X	X
	别惹麻烦 Don't Look for Trouble	3/4	X	X	
	权衡得失 Weighing Gains and Losses	3/4	X	X	
5.2 建议 Suggesting	我感冒了 I Have a Cold	2/3		X	X
	去哪儿玩 Where to Have Fun	2/3		X	X
	温故而知新 Review What has been Learned so as to Learn Something New	3/4	X	X	
	减肥要领 Key to Dieting	3/4	X	X	
6.1 许诺 Promising	不再失信 No More Breaking Promises	2/3	X	X	
	修理电脑 Repairing a Computer	2/3	X	X	
	额外加分 Extra Credit	3/4	X	X	
	促销期间 Sales Promotion	3/4	X	X	
6.2 致歉 Apologizing	隐私权 Right to Privacy	2/3	X	X	
	坏记性 A Poor Memory	2/3	X	X	

275

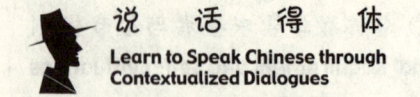

说 话 得 体
Learn to Speak Chinese through Contextualized Dialogues

语言/文化功能主题 Language/Culture Functional Theme	中心课文参考 Core Text Reference	外语学习阶段准则 Continuum Stages	教学目标 Instructional Objective		
			介绍 Introduction	练习 Practice	熟练掌握 Mastery
7.1 同情 Showing Sympathy	又迟到了 Being Late Again	3 / 4	X	X	
	收回所说的话 Taking Back What was Said	3 / 4	X	X	
	谈学业 Talking about College Study	2 / 3	X	X	
	探望受伤者 Visiting the Injured	2 / 3	X	X	
	等待大学入学通知 Waiting for College Admission	3 / 4	X	X	
	最需要的关心 The Most Needed Care	3 / 4	X	X	
7.2 安慰 Giving Comfort and Reassurance	违规受罚 Fine for Traffic Violation	2 / 3	X	X	
	发挥正常 Performing Normally	2 / 3	X	X	
	你们尽力了 You Did All You Could	3 / 4	X	X	
	振作起来 Pull Yourself Together	3 / 4	X	X	
8.1 恭维 Complimenting	托你的福 Thanks to You	2 / 3	X	X	
	找舞伴 Looking for a Prom Date	2 / 3	X	X	
	乔迁之喜 Congratulations on Moving to a New Home	3 / 4	X	X	
	名师出高徒 A Great Master Brings up Brilliant Disciples.	3 / 4	X	X	

276

附录四 《说话得体》总体教学要求参考与自我检测
Appendix IV General Instructional Requirement and Self-Evaluations

语言/文化功能主题 Language/Culture Functional Theme	中心课文参考 Core Text Reference	外语学习阶段准则 Continuum Stages	教学目标 Instructional Objective		
			介绍 Introduction	练习 Practice	熟练掌握 Mastery
8.2 抱怨 Complaining	不能随便 Can't Do as You Wish	2 / 3	X	X	
	怎么回事 What's the matter?	2 / 3	X	X	
	人影都没有 Can't Find Him	3 / 4	X	X	
	习惯了就行 You Will Get Used to It	3 / 4	X	X	
补充词句 Supplementary Common Expressions	120 Expressions	1 / 2 / 3 / 4	X		

277

语言/文化功能主题 Language/Culture Functional Theme	中心课文参考 Core Text Reference	外语学习阶段准则 Continuum Stages	介绍 Introduction	练习 Practice	熟练掌握 Mastery

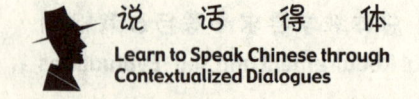

AP中文教学标准核查表
Assessment Standards Information for AP Chinese Instruction:

语言技能 Language Skills	核查方法 Assessment Means	自我检测评估（选择符合要求的选项） Self Evaluation (You may check one or all for each item.)
听 Listening	单元听力训练 Listening Comprehension	1　2　3　4.1　4.2　4.3　4.4　4.5　5.1　5.2　5.3　5.4　5.5
说 Speaking	小品表演/看图说话 Skit Performance / Story Narration	1　2　3　4.1　4.2　4.3　4.4　4.5　5.1　5.2　5.3　5.4　5.5
读 Reading	课文/讲义理解 Texts / Handouts	1　2　3　4.1　4.2　4.3　4.4　4.5　5.1　5.2　5.3　5.4　5.5
写 Writing	10-3-1练习/小品 10-3-1 Work/Skit Lines 练笔 Writing Exercises	1　2　3　4.1　4.2　4.3　4.4　4.5　5.1　5.2　5.3　5.4　5.5
创造性思维 Creative Thinking	开启思路/情景识别及回应 Brainstorming/Context Indentifications and Responses	1　2　3　4.1　4.2　4.3　4.4　4.5　5.1　5.2　5.3　5.4　5.5
参与 Participation	课堂活动/团队精神 Classroom Activities/ Group Work	1　2　3　4.1　4.2　4.3　4.4　4.5　5.1　5.2　5.3　5.4　5.5

▲三个学习模式 3 Modes
1. 互动交流 Interpersonal
2. 理解诠释 Interpretive
3. 表达演示 Presentational

▲五个教学目标 5 Cs
4.1 沟通 Communication
4.2 文化 Culture
4.3 连贯 Connection
4.4 比较 Comparison
4.5 社区 Communication

▲语言能力评定 Language Ability Assessment
5.1 综合 Synthesizing
5.2 分析 Analyzing
5.3 假设 Hypothesizing
5.4 概括 Concluding
5.5 总体结构 Organization（开始，中间和结束 a beginning, middle & an end）

附录五 Appendix V

听力练习文本
Text for Listening Comprehension

第一单元 Unit 1

	录音文本 Sentence(s) Given
1	李先生，你好！你这是去吃饭吧？
2	稀客，稀客！是什么风把您吹来的？
3	好久不见。你最近身体怎么样？
4	欢迎您来我们学校指导工作。
5	见到你真高兴。一路上好吗？
6	欢迎你再来我家做客。
7	有困难，尽管来找我。我很乐意帮助你。
8	再见了。祝你学习顺利！
9	我是来向你告别的。
10	请多保重。一路顺风！

第二单元 Unit 2

	录音文本 Sentence(s) Given
1	我在华美高中二年级中文班念书。
2	我来为你们俩介绍一下。这是老李，这是小张。
3	我叫李友朋，是星巴克连锁咖啡馆的公关代表，初次见面，请多关照。
4	这双运动鞋，式样新，耐穿，价格适中，赶快买吧。
5	这本书讲的是美国教育制度。你想了解美国大学吗？这本书值得你读一读。
6	请问，你是不是本田汽车公司的王经理？我是《洛杉矶时报》的记者，想了解一下贵公司的销售业绩。
7	我们今天有幸邀请到了斯坦福大学的格林教授。现在请格林教授谈谈申请大学的注意事项。
8	我们餐厅是以正宗中国北方菜而闻名的。我们的招牌菜是北京烤鸭。你不妨叫一份试试看，你一定会喜欢的。
9	郑聪明同学是电脑专业三年级学生。这是他第三年跟我学中文了。这个同学勤奋好

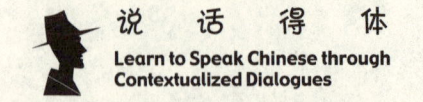

说 话 得 体
Learn to Speak Chinese through Contextualized Dialogues

	学，办事认真负责，很值得信赖。
10	东方明珠塔位于上海黄浦江畔，建成于1994年10月1日，塔高468米，是仅次于加拿大多伦多电视塔和俄罗斯的莫斯科电视塔的世界第三高塔，也是上海新的标志性建筑。

第三单元 Unit 3

	录音文本 Sentence(s) Given
1	请到这儿来一下，我需要你帮我一个忙。
2	不知道能否借你的笔用一下？
3	这个问题，我要求你立即答复。
4	麻烦你帮我叫一辆计程车，好吗？
5	成龙先生，门外有几个人说他们都喜欢看你的表演，都是你的影迷，想请你为他们签名留念，不知道你是否愿意？
6	这本书很有意思，写得也不错，适合高中程度的学生，你们不妨借去读一读。
7	我明天有考试，现在要去图书馆查资料。你不会出去吧？如果有人打电话找我，请给我记一下留言，好吗？
8	陈先生，你好！我是怀特。我想请您为我写一封申请奖学金的推荐信。我会在明天上午把我的简历和有关材料送到您办公室去。要是不方便，请给我打个电话，我再另找时间，谢谢！
9	龙凤餐厅吗？我要预订一张十个人的桌子，时间是今晚七点。请准备一个生日蛋糕。还有，我们不抽烟。
10	我要预订两张联合航空公司三月二十一日星期六早上八点从洛杉矶直达纽约的普通舱单程飞机票。

第四单元 Unit 4

	录音文本 Sentence(s) Given
1	谢谢你的好意，请我参加生日晚会。不过，我已经跟朋友约好了明天晚上去看电影，真对不起！
2	我只是做了我应该做的事，不值得一提。现在你送我这么贵重的礼物，我受之有愧。你还是留着自己用吧。
3	抱歉，这种运动服我们刚刚卖完，一时还进不了货。今天是没法子满足你了。要不，你留下一个电话号码，我们一有货就通知你。
4	我坦率地告诉你，我是不会同意让你一个人去外州上大学的。当然啦，要是你的好朋友跟你一块儿去，那我就赞成。
5	你提出的建议很中肯，设想也很有创意。我们在制定计划的时候一定会认真考虑的。

附录五 听力练习文本
Appendix V Text for Listening Comprehension

6	你上次借我的车出了车祸,害得我花了一大笔钱修理,保险也涨了,我再也不会把车借给你了。不管你怎么说,我就是不借。
7	我们研究了你的申请和你的工作经验,决定聘请你担任我们公司营销部门的主任助理。祝贺你!
8	你这次的作业大有进步,字写得很清楚,格式也符合要求了。你把作业放在桌子上吧。我明天抽时间看一下,再和你讨论。
9	根据你的工作表现,我个人同意给你加薪。但是,很遗憾,主管今天不在。等他回来以后,我们商量一下再决定,好不好?
10	鹿死谁手还不知道呢!我愿意接受你的挑战,我不信我得不到这位小姐的芳心。

第五单元 Unit 5

	录音文本 Sentence(s) Given
1	我们老师明天过生日。我觉得她喜欢花,不如送她一束康乃馨,表表我们的心意。
2	我建议你报考洛杉矶大学的生物系,不过,如果我是你的话,我会去伯克利大学学医。
3	看你的身材,没有必要减肥。就是要减肥,你也应该先去医生那儿咨询一下。
4	既然大多数同学都来了,我们就不等小王了,先开始讨论今天的工作,大家说好不好?
5	孩子们都长大了,都学会照顾自己的生活了,你何必再操心呢?
6	他在生气,我劝你还是别去他那儿惹他为好,否则会自讨没趣。
7	你最好别外出,按时服药,多喝水,少说话,多休息。请多保重!
8	张教授出的考题肯定不会容易,你不好好准备是很难通过的。今天晚上你非得下工夫不可。
9	你要小心了。下一个路口是单行道,车子只能左拐,不能右转。警察常常等在那儿拦车、开罚单。
10	外面已经开始下雨了,路上滑,开车走路都要当心。还有,别忘了带一把伞,淋到雨,生了病就麻烦了。

第六单元 Unit 6

	录音文本 Sentence(s) Given
1	我对天发誓,我没有偷看你的日记。
2	我很后悔,没有及时通知你我们改变了计划,给你工作带来那么多不便。我保证这是最后一次,一定改正。
3	你就放心吧。我明天一早就把功课交给你。
4	这台电脑没有什么大问题。我答应你明天开始修理,星期五下午你就可以来取了。

281

5	我昨天说的话伤了你的自尊心,我现在正式向你道歉。你也别太计较了。我请你去喝咖啡,怎么样?
6	真该死!是我不小心,弄脏了你的衣服。脱下来吧,我帮你洗一洗。
7	真不好意思!我把地址搞错了,让你白跑一趟。
8	我不是故意的,但这是因为我疏忽才闯下的大祸。我愿意接受任何处罚。
9	这件事小菜一碟,包在我身上了。
10	大丈夫一言既出,驷马难追。难道你还信不过我吗?

第七单元 Unit 7

	录音文本 Sentence(s) Given
1	听到他出车祸的消息,我简直不敢相信自己的耳朵。那是一场飞来横祸。幸运的是他人没事儿。
2	这次考试,你没有发挥出应有的水平,考砸了,我们都为你惋惜。不过,凭你的实力,我肯定你下次会考出好成绩的。
3	请允许我向你表示最深切的慰问。事情已经发生了,你不要过分悲伤。有些事情我们是无法抗拒的。我们会永远记住他的。
4	他家昨天遭窃了,所有值钱的东西都被偷走了。我知道他现在一定很不好受。可怜的人哪!
5	怎么?加州大学没有录取你?太不幸了。不过,没关系,车到山前必有路。也许更好的大学在向你招手呢!
6	小李告诉我,今天你超速被警察开了罚单。别太在意了,一时的疏忽罢了,以后注意些就是了。
7	听说你女朋友跟你分手了。别太难过了,想想究竟是什么原因,看看有没有挽救的可能。
8	千万别泄气。常言说得好:道路是曲折的,前途是光明的。只要坚持到底,你一定会成功的。
9	这次比赛,你们没能获胜,真替你们可惜。这也不能全怨你们,对方占尽天时地利,你们已经尽力了。
10	朱老师,您被学校免职了,这不完全是您的过错,您也没必要为此不安。您还是我们的老师,我们仍然尊敬您。希望你在不久的将来找到一份更好的工作。

第八单元 Unit 8

	录音文本 Sentence(s) Given
1	你不会唱歌,不会跳舞,凭什么来参加"偶像选拔赛"?
2	你去看朋友,为什么出门前不打一个电话通知他?结果他一点儿准备都没有,多尴尬啊!这事都得怨你。

附录五 听力练习文本
Appendix V Text for Listening Comprehension

3	这是怎么回事?我定的是大号蓝色西装,你却给我一件超大号黑色的。型号、颜色都不对。现在退换已经来不及了,我原计划是今天晚上有事要穿的。把你们的经理找来,我要投诉。
4	你是怎么搞的?这个学期已经第三次旷课了,而且你还有三次作业没交。要是你继续旷课、不做功课,除了成绩不好以外,学校还会作出严肃处理,到那时,你后悔都来不及了。
5	哎哟!瞧你走路连蹦带跳的,兴高采烈的样子。一定是得到了什么好消息吧?是不是北京大学给你发来了录取通知书?我早就知道你会有出息的,会给你爸爸妈妈争光的。
6	这是图书馆,是看书学习的地方。你们要是想聊天,请小声一点。要是想吸烟,请到别处去。公共场所最好不要抽烟。你们没有看到这块牌子上"禁止吸烟"四个字吗?
7	没想到你还有这么一手绝活,能在这么短的时间里烘烤出这样色香味俱佳的蛋糕。单凭这蛋糕的造型,要是有做蛋糕比赛,你一定能得冠军。
8	这件红色上衣配这条披肩,看上去非常典雅,特别适合你这样年龄的女性,你的确很有品味。
9	你买的新车是今年最流行的越野休闲车,外形美观,车内宽敞、舒适,耐久性强,省油,你真是好眼力。听说你买车的价格也不贵,是在哪儿买的?
10	你不仅人长得英俊潇洒,而且书又念得好,能说两种外语,还在学校学生会担任领导。像你这样的人才不多见啊。要是你能参加我的毕业舞会,做我的舞伴,那该多好啊!

词语总表
Vocabulary

A

安慰	ānwèi	condolence; to comfort; to console	7-2-4
按（照）	àn(zhào)	according to	4-1-4
按时	ànshí	on time; on schedule	5-2-1
熬	áo	to stew; to cook	2-2-3
熬夜	áoyè	stay up late; work until deep into the night	5-1-4

B

把握	bǎwò	assurance; confidence	5-1-2
办公用品	bàngōng yòngpǐn	office supply	2-1-4
办理	bànlǐ	to process	4-1-4
棒球	bàngqiú	baseball	5-1-4
薄饼	báobǐng	pancake	2-2-3
饱	bǎo	have eaten one's fill; be full	2-1-4
保持	bǎochí	to keep; to maintain	5-1-2
保暖	bǎonuǎn	keep warm	5-2-1
保证	bǎozhèng	guarantee	6-1-1
保重	bǎozhòng	take care	1-2-4
报警	bàojǐng	call (report to) the police	8-2-1
悲伤	bēishāng	painfully sad	7-2-4
北加州	Běi Jiāzhōu	Northern California	8-2-4
背	bèi	to recite from memory; learn by heart	5-1-4
被盗	bèi dào	be stolen	8-2-1
本地	běndì	local	5-2-2
本季	běnjì	this season	5-1-4
比赛	bǐsài	game; competition	5-1-4
彼此	bǐcǐ	each other	4-1-4
必不可少	bì bù kě shǎo	indispensable; essential	2-2-4
必胜	bìshèng	will most certainly win; be sure to win	7-2-2
必要	bìyào	essential; necessary	5-1-1
毕竟	bìjìng	after all	4-1-4

词语总表
Vocabulary

毕业	bìyè	to graduate	3-1-3
毕业舞会	bìyè wǔhuì	graduation prom; graduation dancing party	8-1-2
闭门不出	bì mén bù chū	be confined to the house	7-1-4
变	biàn	change	8-1-1
表现	biǎoxiàn	performance; presentation	8-1-4
别家	biéjiā	others; other stores	4-2-1
别具一格	bié jù yī gé	have a style of one's own; having a distinctive style	8-1-3
别人	biéren	other people, others	6-2-4
别致	biézhì	unique	8-1-2
并不是	bìng bù shì	actually not	6-1-3
伯母	bómǔ	aunt	8-1-1
博物馆	bówùguǎn	museum	2-2-4
补	bǔ	to make up	6-1-3
不必	bùbì	needn't	2-1-1
不错	bùcuò	pretty well; not bad	1-1-4
不对劲	bùduìjìn	(feeling) awkward; inappropriate	8-2-2
不妨	bùfáng	there is no harm (in doing sth.)	3-2-2
不敢(当)	bùgǎn (dāng)	It's very kind of you.	1-1-3
不管	bùguǎn	no matter how (what)	8-2-1
不好使	bù hǎo shǐ	be inconvenient to use; do not work well	8-1-1
不好受	bù hǎoshòu	find oneself beset (with difficulties)	7-1-4
不好意思	bù hǎoyìsi	feel embarrassed; impolite (to do something)	3-1-1
不见不散	bùjiàn bùsàn	not leave without seeing each other	1-2-2
不景气	bù jǐngqì	depressing	8-2-4
不久	bùjiǔ	before long	1-2-3
不可思议	bù kě sīyì	inconceivable; unthinkable; beyond comprehension	7-1-3
不如	bùrú	not as	4-1-1
不行	bùxíng	no way; doesn't work	4-1-2
不幸	bùxìng	unfortunately	7-1-3
不争气	bù zhēngqì	fail to live up to expectations	7-2-3
布局	bùjú	arrangement; layout	8-1-3
布置	bùzhì	assign; make arrangements for	5-2-4
步行	bùxíng	go on foot; walk	3-1-1
部门	bùmén	department; division; section	2-1-2

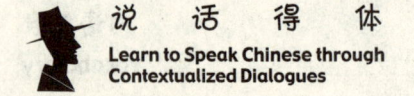

C

猜	cāi	to guess	2-1-1
裁判	cáipàn	referee	7-2-3
踩油门	cǎi yóumén	to step on the gas (accelerator)	5-1-2
菜肴	càiyáo	cooked dishes	5-2-2
参观	cānguān	to visit	2-2-4
参谋	cānmóu	give advice	6-1-4
操作	cāozuò	to operate	3-1-3
查	chá	to check; to look up	3-2-3
差	chà	poor; not up to standard	8-2-2
产品	chǎnpǐn	product	4-1-4
忏悔	chànhuǐ	repent; confess (one's sin)	6-2-4
尝	cháng	to taste	3-2-1
常言	chángyán	common saying; as the saying goes	7-2-3
厂商	chǎngshāng	manufacturer; firm	2-2-2
场	chǎng	quantifier (measure word) for sports games	7-2-3
超速	chāosù	speeding	7-2-1
朝	cháo	towards	8-1-2
(朝)代	(cháo)dài	dynasty	2-2-1
车到山前必有路	chē dào shān qián bì yǒu lù	things will eventually sort themselves out	7-1-3
车祸	chēhuò	car accident	7-1-2
车站	chēzhàn	bus stop	3-1-1
趁	chèn	take advantage of	6-1-4
称	chēng	to weigh	4-2-1
称呼	chēnghu	call; form of address	3-1-4
成功	chénggōng	success	8-1-4
成绩	chéngjì	grade; achievement; progress	6-1-3
成就	chéngjiù	achievement; accomplishment; success	2-2-1
诚恳	chéngkěn	sincere; earnest	4-2-4
诚挚	chéngzhì	sincere	7-1-4
吃法	chīfǎ	eating method	2-2-3
吃亏	chīkuī	suffer losses; in an unfavorable situation	5-1-3
迟到	chídào	be late; arrive late; tardy	6-2-3
充分	chōngfēn	sufficient; abundant	5-1-4
重犯	chóngfàn	repeat (an error or offense)	6-2-4
重新	chóngxīn	again; anew; afresh	7-1-3
重做	chóng zuò	cook again	8-2-2

Vocabulary

抽时间	chōu shíjiān	to seize an opportunity; find time	5-2-3
出点子	chū diǎnzi	make suggestions	6-1-4
出门	chūmén	get out; leave home	7-2-1
出人意料	chū rén yì liào	exceeding all expectations	7-1-3
出色	chūsè	outstanding; remarkable	8-1-4
出席	chūxí	be present; to attend	4-2-3
初犯	chūfàn	first offense	6-2-2
初级	chūjí	elementary; primary; initial	3-1-3
初期	chūqī	prime; initial stage	2-2-1
厨师	chúshī	chef; cooker	8-2-2
处理	chǔlǐ	to handle; to settle	6-1-3
处在	chǔzài	be in a certain situation	7-2-4
处	chù	place	3-1-1
传统	chuántǒng	tradition; traditional	2-1-4
吹	chuī	blow	1-1-4
词汇	cíhuì	vocabulary	5-2-3
葱	cōng	scallion	2-2-3
聪明	cōngmíng	intelligent; clever; bright	7-2-2
从来不(没)	cónglái bù(méi)	never	8-2-3
从命	cóngmìng	comply with someone's wish	4-1-1
促销	cùxiāo	sales promotion	6-1-4
错不了	cuò bù liǎo	unlikely to go wrong	2-2-2
错怪	cuòguài	to blame wrongly or unjustly	6-2-4
错过	cuòguò	to miss; let slip	5-1-4

D

答应	dāying	assent; consent; to promise	6-1-2
答题	dátí	to answer questions; to solve problems	5-2-3
打包票	dǎ bāopiào	guarantee; vouch for	6-1-4
打交道	dǎ jiāodao	to come into contact; have dealings with	2-1-1
打搅	dǎjiǎo	disturb; trouble	3-1-2
打扰	dǎrǎo	to bother	4-1-1
打扫	dǎsǎo	to clean	4-1-2
大概	dàgài	perhaps; probably	3-1-1
大好人	dàhǎorén	person of fine quality	3-2-3
大家	dàjiā	everyone	4-2-2
大驾光临	dàjià guānglín	Your gracious presence	1-1-3
大考	dàkǎo	final; important test	5-2-3
大量	dàliàng	a great quantity; abundant; enormous	8-1-4

287

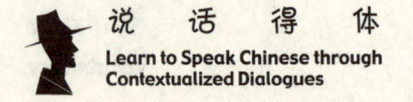

说话得体
Learn to Speak Chinese through Contextualized Dialogues

代	dài	in place of; on behalf of	1-1-2
代表	dàibiǎo	representative; to represent; on behalf of	2-1-1
代理	dàilǐ	agent; agency	4-1-4
带	dài	bring; bring to someone	3-1-2
待	dài	to treat	6-2-4
担保	dānbǎo	warrant; guarantee	6-1-4
担心	dānxīn	worry; feel anxious	6-1-3
担忧	dānyōu	to worry; be concerned	7-2-2
耽搁	dānge	delay; hold up; stop over	3-1-1
耽误	dānwu	to delay; to waste	5-1-4
但愿	dànyuàn	if only; wish	8-1-3
当面	dāngmiàn	in sb's presence; face to face	3-1-2
当然	dāngrán	of course	2-1-3
档案	dàng'àn	files; archives; record	7-1-3
导购图	dǎogōutú	shopping guide; directory	2-1-4
导师	dǎoshī	tutor or supervisor (at high learning institutes)	3-1-2
导游	dǎoyóu	tour guide	3-1-3
倒霉	dǎoméi	have bad luck; fall on hard time	7-2-1
倒	dào	used to denote a transition or concession	3-2-2
道	dào	course (of cooked dishes)	8-2-2
道路	dàolù	road; the way	7-2-3
道歉	dàoqiàn	to apologize; make an apology	6-2-4
登门拜访	dēngmén bàifǎng	come (go) on a visit to sb's house	3-1-2
地利	dìlì	favorable geographical conditions	7-2-3
递	dì	to pass	3-2-1
电脑	diànnǎo	computer	2-2-2
电梯	diàntī	elevator	2-1-4
电讯	diànxùn	telecommunication	4-2-3
电子邮件	diànzǐ yóujiàn	email	2-1-1
吊死	diàosǐ	to hang oneself; to hang by the neck (committing suicide)	7-2-4
丁字路口	dīngzì lùkǒu	T-shaped road junction	5-1-2
鼎足三分	dǐngzú sān fēn	a situation dominated by three powerful rivals	2-2-1
东部	dōng bù	eastern part; in the east	7-1-3
懂	dǒng	to understand	3-1-3
动手	dòngshǒu	start work; get to work	6-1-2
动心	dòngxīn	touched; moved	6-1-4
读后感	dúhòugǎn	impression of a book or an article	3-2-2

独家	dújiā	exclusive; sole	4-1-4
端	duān	hold something level with both hands	8-2-2
段	duàn	section; part; cut	2-2-3
锻炼	duànliàn	to exercise; have physical training	5-2-4
对待	duìdài	to treat; to deal with	7-2-4
对方	duìfāng	opponent; the other side	7-2-3
顿	dùn	a measure word for meal	5-2-2
多余	duōyú	more than what is due; unnecessary	7-2-2

E

额外	éwài	extra; additional	6-1-3

F

发挥	fāhuī	bring into play	7-2-2
发誓	fāshì	to swear	6-1-1
罚单	fádān	ticket (notice) for penalty	7-2-1
罚酒	fá jiǔ	be made to drink as punishment	6-2-3
罚款	fákuǎn	fine; penalty	7-2-1
翻	fān	to search	6-2-1
凡是	fánshì	any; all; every	4-1-4
烦恼	fánnǎo	be worried	7-1-3
反而	fǎn'ér	on the contrary	5-2-4
反应	fǎnyìng	reaction; reflection	8-1-4
反映	fǎnyìng	to reflect	4-2-4
犯	fàn	to do; to offend; to commit a wrong doing	6-2-2
饭菜	fàncài	food	3-2-1
方便	fāngbiàn	convenient	3-1-1
方向盘	fāngxiàngpán	steering wheel	5-1-2
防人	fáng rén	to take precautions against (harmful) people	5-1-3
房产经济	fángchǎn jīngjì	real estate agent	8-1-3
放心	fàngxīn	feel at ease	3-2-3
飞机场	fēijīchǎng	airport	8-2-1
非 不可	fēi...bùkě	must; have to (no other alternative)	5-1-4
分不开	fēn bù kāi	can not be separated	8-1-4
分手	fēnshǒu	part (company); say goodbye; break up	7-2-4
风	fēng	wind	1-1-4
风格	fēnggé	style; manner (attitude)	8-1-4
奉劝	fèngquàn	to give a piece of advice	5-1-3
否则	fǒuzé	otherwise	5-2-4

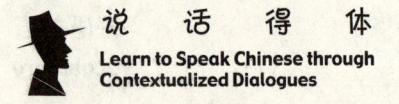

夫人	fūrén	Lady; Madame; Mrs.	3-1-4
服务员	fúwùyuán	waiter (waitress); attendant	8-2-2
服务质量	fúwù zhìliàng	service quality	8-2-2
服药	fúyào	take medicine	5-2-1
服用	fúyòng	take (medicine)	5-2-4
服装	fúzhuāng	clothing; fashion	2-1-4
府上	fǔshàng	your home (family)	3-1-2
负责	fùzé	be in charge of; responsible for	2-1-3
附近	fùjìn	vicinity; nearby	3-1-1
复查	fùchá	check; double-check; reexamine	7-1-3
复习	fùxí	review	5-1-4

G

该死	gāisǐ	deserve death	6-2-1
改日	gǎirì	some other day	2-1-2
改善	gǎishàn	to improve	4-1-4
改天	gǎitiān	another day; some other day	4-1-1
干吗	gànmá	what to do; why; why on earth	5-1-2
感到	gǎndào	feel; to sense	7-1-2
感冒	gǎnmào	catch a cold; cold	5-2-1
感受	gǎnshòu	to feel; feelings; experience	7-1-4
感谢	gǎnxiè	be grateful	4-2-4
高级	gāojí	advanced; senior; high-ranking; superb	2-2-2
高手	gāoshǒu	master-hand	8-1-3
高寿	gāoshòu	long life; longevity	3-1-4
告辞	gàocí	take leave; farewell	2-1-2
格调	gédiào	(literary or artistic) style	8-1-3
格外	géwài	exceptionally; especially	8-1-2
个案	gè'àn	individual case	8-1-4
个人隐私	gèrén yǐnsī	privacy	6-2-1
公交车	gōngjiāochē	public bus	3-1-1
公共场所	gōnggòng chǎngsuǒ	public place	5-2-1
公平	gōngpíng	fair; justice	8-2-3
公式	gōngshì	formula	5-1-4
公元	gōngyuán	the Christian era; AD	2-2-1
公园	gōngyuán	park	5-1-3
功劳	gōngláo	contribution; meritorious service (deed)	8-1-3
功能	gōngnéng	function	6-1-4

供应	gōngyìng	to supply	2-1-4
宫殿	gōngdiàn	palace	2-2-4
恭敬	gōngjìng	respectful; with great respect	4-1-1
恭喜	gōngxǐ	congratulate	1-1-2
沟通	gōutōng	communicate	2-2-2
古代	gǔdài	ancient	2-2-4
古典	gǔdiǎn	classical	2-2-1
古董	gǔdǒng	antique	2-1-4
骨头	gǔtou	bone	2-2-3
鼓励	gǔlì	to encourage	7-2-3
故宫	GùGōng	the Palace Museum	2-2-4
故事	gùshi	story	2-2-1
故意	gùyì	on purpose; deliberately	6-1-3
顾客	gùkè	customer	8-2-2
拐	guǎi	turn	3-1-1
关键	guānjiàn	key; crux	5-1-4
关心	guānxīn	be concerned with; show solicitude for	7-1-2
关照	guānzhào	look after	4-2-3
观看	guānkàn	to watch	3-2-4
管	guǎn	a preposition (like "把") used with "叫"	3-1-4
光明	guāngmíng	bright	7-2-3
光线	guāngxiàn	light; ray of light	8-1-3
广	guǎng	wide; broad	8-1-4
逛	guàng	stroll; wander about	2-1-4
规矩	guīju	established practice	6-1-1
贵	guì	expensive	4-2-1
果然	guǒrán	really; as expected	3-2-1
过	guò	cross; pass	5-1-2
过错	guòcuò	fault	6-2-3
过奖	guòjiǎng	over praise; "You flatter me."	8-1-4
过时	guòshí	out of date; out of fashion	6-1-4
过于	guòyú	excessive	7-2-4

H

孩子头	háizitóu	king of children	8-2-4
海鲜	hǎixiān	sea food	5-2-2
害人	hài rén	to harm others	5-1-3
害羞	hàixiū	shy; bashful	2-2-2
行家	hángjia	expert; connoisseur	3-2-4

291

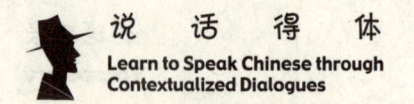

豪宅	háozhái	splendid house	8-1-3
好极了	hǎo jí le	extremely good	2-2-3
好玩儿	hǎowánr	to have fun; amusing; interesting	5-1-1
好学	hàoxué	be good at learning	2-2-2
合理	hélǐ	reasonable; rational	8-1-3
合群	héqún	be gregarious; get on well with others	2-2-2
合作	hézuò	cooperation	8-2-3
何必	hébì	why must	7-2-4
何况	hékuàng	much less; let alone	8-2-1
何乐而不为	hé lè ér bù wéi	I don't see any reason why not.	3-2-4
和解	héjiě	become reconciled	6-2-4
恨	hèn	to hate; regret	7-2-3
红绿灯	hónglǜdēng	traffic light	3-1-1
宏大	hóngdà	grand; immense; vast	2-2-1
后顾之忧	hòu gù zhī yōu	fear of disturbance in the rear; trouble back at home	7-2-2
后悔	hòuhuǐ	to regret	5-1-4
厚爱	hòu'ài	great kindness	4-2-4
华夏	Huáxià	China; Cathay	3-1-1
化妆品	huàzhuāngpǐn	cosmetics	2-1-4
欢迎会	huānyínghuì	a party (meeting) to welcome someone	4-2-3
环境	huánjìng	environment	8-1-3
换	huàn	to change; to exchange	5-1-2
慌	huāng	flustered; confused	5-1-2
皇宫	huánggōng	imperial palace	2-2-4
回头见	huítóujiàn	see you later	1-2-2
回心转意	huí xīn zhuǎn yì	turn back one's heart and change one's mind	6-2-4
回音	huíyīn	reply; response; echo	7-1-3
会议室	huìyìshì	conference room	4-2-3
货真价实	huò zhēn jià shí	genuine goods at a fair price	6-1-4
获得	huòdé	to obtain; achieve	3-1-3
获奖	huòjiǎng	win an award	8-1-4
获胜	huòshèng	to win victory	7-2-3
祸不单行	huò bù dān xíng	mishaps always come in battalions; misfortunes never come singly	7-1-2

词语总表
Vocabulary

J

机会	jīhuì	opportunity	1-2-4
机智	jīzhì	resourceful; quick-witted	8-1-4
基本功	jīběngōng	basic training; essential technique	8-1-4
即日起	jírì qǐ	from today on	4-2-3
急	jí	urgent; pressing; nervous; anxious	6-1-2
急需	jíxū	be badly in need of	2-2-2
计算机专业	jìsuànjī zhuānyè	computer science	2-2-2
记	jì	to write down	3-2-3
记性	jìxing	memory	6-2-2
记住	jìzhù	to keep in mind	6-2-1
既然	jìrán	since	6-1-2
继续	jìxù	to continue; to go on	7-2-3
加把劲	jiā bǎ jìn	put on a spurt; put forth strength	6-1-3
加分	jiā fēn	to give extra credit	6-1-3
加州	Jiāzhōu	California	7-1-3
家常	jiācháng	the daily life of a family	3-2-1
家具	jiājù	furniture	2-1-4
家用电器	jiāyòng diànqì	household electrical appliances	2-1-4
价格	jiàgé	price	6-1-4
假日宾馆	Jiàrì Bīnguǎn	Holiday Inn	3-1-1
坚持	jiānchí	persist in; uphold; stick to	5-2-4
坚持到底	jiānchí dàodǐ	hold on straight to the end	7-2-3
坚定	jiāndìng	firm; steadfast	7-2-3
减肥	jiǎnféi	on diet; reduce weight; weight-loss	5-2-4
检查	jiǎnchá	to examine; to check up	4-2-4
简单	jiǎndān	simple; easy to handle	2-2-2
见鬼	jiànguǐ	see the ghost; absurd; fantastic	5-2-4
见面	jiànmiàn	to meet	2-1-1
建	jiàn	build; establish	2-2-4
建设性	jiànshèxìng	constructive	4-2-4
建议	jiànyì	suggestion	4-2-4
建筑群	jiànzhùqún	building complex	2-2-4
健康	jiànkāng	health	5-2-4
健身房	jiànshēnfáng	gym; fitness center	5-2-4
健身器材	jiànshēn qìcái	fitness facilities	2-1-4
将就	jiāngjiu	to make the best of it	8-2-4

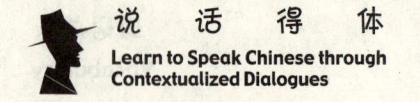

讲话	jiǎnghuà	to speak; speech	2-1-3
讲解员	jiǎngjiěyuán	guide; interpreter	2-2-2
讲师	jiǎngshī	lecturer	2-1-2
讲授	jiǎngshòu	to lecture on	2-1-3
讲述	jiǎngshù	tell about; give an account of	2-2-1
酱油	jiàngyóu	soy sauce	3-2-1
交	jiāo	turn in; hand in	6-1-2
交叉口	jiāochākǒu	cross roads	3-1-1
交代	jiāodài	to give an account of; to make clear	3-2-3
交朋友	jiāo péngyou	to make friends with	4-1-3
交通	jiāotōng	traffic	7-2-1
交往	jiāowǎng	associate with; contact	2-2-2
叫醒	jiàoxǐng	to awake	3-1-2
教训	jiàoxun	lesson	6-2-2
教育	jiàoyù	education	3-2-2
接触	jiēchù	get in touch	4-1-4
接受	jiēshòu	to accept	4-2-3
接着	jiēzhe	go on; continue	1-2-2
街	jiē	street; block	3-1-1
街对面	jiē duìmiàn	cross the street	8-2-2
街口	jiē kǒu	street corner	1-1-1
节哀	jié'āi	restrain one's grief	7-1-4
结构	jiégòu	structure	2-2-1
结果	jiéguǒ	result	8-1-4
结婚	jiéhūn	to marry; marriage	3-1-4
结束	jiéshù	to end	7-1-1
截止日期	jiézhǐ rìqī	deadline	7-1-3
介绍	jièshào	to introduce	2-1-2
届时	jièshí	at the appointed time; on the occasion	4-2-3
斤	jīn	a unit of weight (=1/2 kilogram)	4-2-1
紧张	jǐnzhāng	nervous; tense; intense	5-1-2
尽管	jǐnguǎn	feel free; not hesitate to	1-2-4
尽量	jǐnliàng	do all one can; to the best of one's ability	7-1-3
尽心尽责	jìnxīn jìnzé	fulfill one's duty whole-heartedly	4-2-3
进口	jìnkǒu	import	4-1-4
进行	jìnxíng	to conduct; to carry on; to carry out	4-2-4
经济	jīngjì	economy; economic situation	8-2-4
经手	jīngshǒu	to handle; go through someone's hands	4-1-4
经验	jīngyàn	experience	7-2-2

经营能力	jīngyíng nénglì	management competence	4-1-4
精彩	jīngcǎi	exciting	8-1-4
精练	jīngliàn	refine; concise	2-2-1
精神	jīngshen	spirit and energy	8-1-1
精致	jīngzhì	fine; delicate	2-2-3
景色	jǐngsè	scenery; view; landscape	8-1-3
警察	jǐngchá	police officer	7-2-1
警觉	jǐngjué	(to arouse) vigilance	7-2-1
敬意	jìngyì	heartfelt respect	4-2-2
久等	jiǔděng	wait for long time	6-2-3
久仰	jiǔyǎng	It's a pleasure to finally meet you.	1-1-3
居住	jūzhù	to reside; to live	2-2-4
举行	jǔxíng	to hold	4-2-3
具体	jùtǐ	concrete; specific	2-2-2
距离	jùlí	distance	5-1-2
聚	jù	to get together	3-2-4
卷	juǎn	roll	2-2-3
绝对	juéduì	absolutely	2-2-2

K

开车	kāi chē	to drive (a vehicle)	5-1-2
开幕	kāimù	open; inaugurate	2-2-2
开玩笑	kāi wánxiào	joke; to play a trick; to jest	5-1-4
开张	kāizhāng	open (for business)	5-2-4
看医生	kàn yīshēng	visit a doctor	5-2-1
康复	kāngfù	recovery; restored to health	7-1-2
考量	kǎoliáng	for the benefit of; consideration	5-2-4
考虑	kǎolǜ	to consider	4-1-4
烤鸭	kǎoyā	roast duck	2-2-3
烤炙	kǎozhì	to roast; to bake	2-2-3
靠近	kàojìn	close to	5-2-1
可怜	kělián	pitiful; to have pity on	7-1-1
可怕	kěpà	fearful; frightening; horrible	7-1-1
可惜	kěxī	It's a pity; unfortunately	7-1-1
可信赖	kě xìnlài	reliable; dependable	2-2-2
刻薄	kèbó	mean; harsh	8-2-2
客户	kèhù	customer; client; business connection	4-2-4
客气	kèqi	polite; courteous	4-2-2

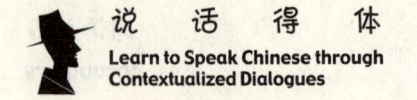

客套	kètào	courteous	2-1-1
课程	kèchéng	course (for learning); curriculum	3-1-3
课堂笔记	kètáng bǐjì	notes taken during the class	5-2-3
课题	kètí	project; a question for study or discussion	8-2-3
课业	kèyè	study; course work	5-2-4
肯定	kěndìng	surely	6-1-2
恐怕	kǒngpà	(I am) afraid	4-1-4
枯燥	kūzào	boring; uninteresting	8-2-4
夸奖	kuājiǎng	praise; compliment	8-1-3
会计师	kuàijìshī	accountant	3-1-3
快乐	kuàilè	happy; cheerful	4-2-2
宽敞	kuānchang	spacious; capacious	8-1-3
宽宏大量	kuānhóng dàliàng	kind and generous	6-2-2
昆剧	kūnjù	Kunqu opera	3-2-4
扩大	kuòdà	to expand	4-1-4

L

辣	là	(spicy) hot	3-2-1
来不及	láibují	there is not enough time	5-1-4
拦住	lánzhù	to block; hold back	5-1-3
老年人	lǎoniánrén	the aged; old people	3-1-4
老样子	lǎoyàngzi	the same appearance (manner, air)	8-1-1
乐于	lèyú	be happy to; to take delight in	4-2-4
愣着	lèng zhe	absent-minded; distracted; blank	5-1-2
冷静	lěngjìng	calm; to keep calm	7-2-4
礼物	lǐwù	gift; present	4-2-2
理解	lǐjiě	to understand	7-1-4
理由	lǐyóu	reason	7-2-2
历史	lìshǐ	history	7-1-1
俩	liǎ	two	6-2-2
脸色	liǎnsè	face; look	8-2-4
练习题	liànxítí	exercise	5-1-4
凉	liáng	cool	8-2-2
辆	liàng	classifier (measure word) for vehicles	5-1-2
聊	liáo	to chat	1-2-2
了解	liǎojiě	to know; understand	4-1-4
列入	lièrù	to be placed in	6-1-3
临时	línshí	at the time when sth. happens	6-2-3

临时抱佛脚	línshí bào fójiǎo	embrace Buddha's feet and pray for help in time of emergency; take measures only when in urgency	5-2-3
淋雨	línyǔ	be caught in the rain	5-1-1
领带	lǐngdài	tie	8-1-2
流行	liúxíng	epidemic	5-2-1
留步	liúbù	don't bother to come any further	1-2-4
留神	liúshén	be careful; look sharp; lookout for	5-1-2
留言	liúyán	words (message) written; to leave message	3-2-3
留得青山在，不怕没柴烧	liú dé qīng shān zài, bù pà méi chái shāo	As long as the green hills are there, one need not worry about firewood.	7-1-2
龙门	lóngmén	Dragon Gate	3-1-1
录取	lùqǔ	enrollment; to recruit; admit to	7-1-3
旅游	lǚyóu	tour; tourism	3-1-3
轮(到)	lún(dào)	it's someone's turn	4-1-2

M

麻烦	máfan	trouble	5-1-3
马路	mǎlù	street; road	5-1-2
马上	mǎshàng	immediately	1-2-2
麦当劳快餐店	Màidāngláo kuàicāndiàn	McDonalds fast food restaurant	8-2-2
满意	mǎnyì	satisfactory; satisfaction	2-2-2
贸易	màoyì	trade	2-1-3
没门儿	méiménr	have no access; have no means	6-2-4
没意思	méiyìsi	not promising; good for nothing	8-2-4
弥补	míbǔ	to make up; to smooth over	6-2-3
迷	mí	fans	3-2-4
免不了	miǎnbuliǎo	be bound to be; be unavoidable	5-2-3
免了	miǎn le	excuse someone from something; exempt from	4-1-3
勉强	miǎnqiǎng	be forced; to do with difficulty	7-2-4
面试	miànshì	interview	7-1-2
妙	miào	excellent	5-2-1
敏捷	mǐnjié	quick-witted	8-1-4
名单	míngdān	name list	6-1-3
名师出高徒	míngshī chū gāotú	an accomplished disciple owes his accomplishment to his great teacher	8-1-4
名著	míngzhù	masterpiece; famous work	2-2-1

明白	míngbai	to understand	7-2-4
明显	míngxiǎn	obvious; evident	7-2-3
抹	mǒ	to put on; to spread	2-2-3
《牡丹亭》	Mǔdān Tíng	*Peony Pavilion* (a traditional Chinese drama)	3-2-4
木柴	mùchái	firewood	2-2-3

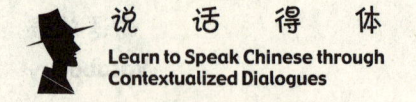

N

哪里	nǎlǐ	not really	3-2-3
哪里，哪里	nǎlǐ, nǎlǐ	a polite expression responding a compliment	8-1-4
内向	nèixiàng	reticent; uncommunicative	3-1-3
难怪	nánguài	no wonder	5-2-4
难过	nánguò	have a hard time; upset	7-1-1
难以启齿	nányǐ qǐchǐ	too embarrassing to say	7-2-4
年纪	niánjì	age	3-1-4
年龄	niánlíng	age	3-1-4
年轻人	niánqīngrén	young people	8-1-1
您	nín	you (polite)	1-1-1
宁可	nìngkě	would rather	7-1-1
努力	nǔlì	make great efforts; try hard; hard-working	6-1-3
女士	nǚshì	Ms.; Miss	3-1-4

P

怕	pà	afraid of	5-2-2
派	pài	send	7-1-2
派往	pàiwǎng	be sent to/for	2-1-3
旁征博引	páng zhēng bó yǐn	well-provided with extensive supporting materials	8-1-4
陪	péi	accompany; escort	5-1-3
培养	péiyǎng	to train; to cultivate	8-1-4
佩服	pèifú	admire; have admiration (respect) for	8-1-2
佩服，佩服	pèifú, pèifú	a polite way to express admiration	8-1-4
配	pèi	to match	8-1-2
捧	pěng	hold or carry in both hands	6-2-2
碰面	pèngmiàn	to meet	5-1-3
皮	pí	skin	2-2-3
皮革制品	pígé zhìpǐn	leatherwear	2-1-4
脾气	píqi	temperament; characteristics	8-2-3

词语总表
Vocabulary

偏	piān	deliberately; on purpose	4-1-2
偏护	piānhù	have a bias towards; show partiality	7-2-3
便宜	piányi	inexpensive; let (sb) off (without punishment)	4-2-1
片刻	piànkè	a short while	8-2-2
票友	piàoyǒu	amateur performer (of traditional Chinese theater)	3-2-4
拼命	pīnmìng	to risk one's life; put up a desperate fight	7-1-1
平安	píng'ān	safe and sound	1-2-4
平常心	píngchángxīn	normal state of mind	7-2-2
平时	píngshí	in normal times; at ordinary times	4-1-3
凭	píng	to go by; to depend on	7-2-2
苹果	píngguǒ	apple	4-2-1
破财消灾	pòcái xiāozāi	suffer unexpected personal financial losses to remove ill fortune	7-2-1
破费	pòfèi	go to some expense	4-2-2

Q

妻子	qīzi	wife	3-1-4
期间	qījiān	during; period; time	6-1-4
期末考试	qīmò kǎoshì	finals; final examination	7-1-1
齐全	qíquán	complete; all in readiness	6-1-4
其实	qíshí	in fact	2-1-1
企业管理	qǐyè guǎnlǐ	business management	2-1-3
起来	qǐlái	to get up; to rise	5-1-1
千万	qiānwàn	be sure to	5-2-3
谦虚谨慎	qiānxū jǐnshèn	be modest and prudent; humble and cautious	8-1-4
前方	qiánfāng	front; the place ahead	5-1-2
前景	qiánjǐng	prospect; vista	2-1-3
前途	qiántú	prospect; future	7-2-3
强	qiáng	strong	8-1-4
乔迁之喜	qiáoqiān zhī xǐ	best wishes for moving to a new residence	8-1-3
瞧	qiáo	to look	3-2-3
巧	qiǎo	coincidental; as luck would have it	5-1-1
切片	qiēpiàn	slice	2-2-3
亲戚	qīnqi	relative	7-2-4
勤奋	qínfèn	diligent	2-2-2
轻巧	qīngqiǎo	easy; light	7-2-2

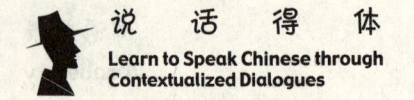

轻松	qīngsōng	relaxed; light	5-2-4
清楚	qīngchu	clear; clearly	5-1-2
情	qíng	kindness	4-1-3
情节	qíngjié	plot; story; details	2-2-1
请教	qǐngjiāo	ask for advice; consult	1-2-4
请求	qǐngqiú	request	7-1-3
请示	qǐngshì	to request instructions	4-1-4
请问	qǐng wèn	May I ask...	3-1-1
求	qiú	to beg	6-1-3
曲折	qūzhé	tortuous; complicated; twists and turns	2-2-1
取	qǔ	to pick up	6-1-2
取药	qǔ yào	get medicine; fill the prescription	5-2-1
权衡	quánhéng	judge and weigh; to balance	5-1-4
缺点	quēdiǎn	defect; weakness	2-2-2
缺少	quēshǎo	lack; be short of	7-1-4
确实	quèshí	in deed	6-1-4

R

让	ràng	let; allow; make	4-2-2
饶	ráo	to forgive	6-2-2
热	rè	warm; hot	8-2-2
人事处	rénshìchù	human resources department	3-1-3
认为	rènwéi	to think; to believe	5-2-3
认真	rènzhēn	earnest; serious	2-2-2
日记	rìjì	diary; journal	6-2-1
荣幸	róngxìng	be honored	2-1-3
如何	rúhé	how; what	5-1-4
如意	rúyì	as one wishes	7-2-1
入学	rùxué	enter a school	7-1-3
入座	rùzuò	be seated	3-2-1

S

撒	sǎ	spread; scatter	2-2-3
赛程	sàichéng	schedule for the game	5-1-4
伞	sǎn	umbrella	5-1-1
散步	sànbù	to take a walk; go for a stroll	5-1-3
傻	shǎ	stupid; silly	6-2-2
姗姗来迟	shānshān lái chí	be long (slow) in coming; arrive late	6-2-3

词语总表
Vocabulary

伤人	shāng rén	to hurt other people	7-2-1
商城	shāngchéng	shopping center; mall	2-1-4
商量	shāngliang	consult; discuss	7-1-4
商品	shāngpǐn	product	6-1-4
赏脸	shǎngliǎn	do one the honor	4-1-3
上(下)班	shàng (xià) bān	go to work (get off work)	1-2-1
上(下)课	shàng (xià) kè	go to or attend class (dismiss or finish class)	1-2-1
上车	shàng chē	get on/into vehicle	3-1-1
上机	shàng jī	to run (machine); to work with a computer	3-1-3
稍等	shāo děng	wait a moment	3-1-2
设计师	shèjìshī	designer; creator	8-1-3
申请	shēnqǐng	to apply for	3-1-3
身材	shēncái	stature; figure	5-2-4
身体	shēntǐ	health; body	1-1-4
深入浅出	shēn rù qiǎn chū	explain the profound in simple terms	8-1-4
神秘兮兮	shénmì xīxī	kind of mysterious	8-2-3
审题	shěntí	to examine the questions (in a test)	5-2-3
生	shēng	unacquainted; new; strange(r)	1-2-3
生病	shēngbìng	fall ill	5-1-1
生活	shēnghuó	life; living	7-1-4
生日	shēngrì	birthday	4-2-2
声誉	shēngyù	reputation; fame	6-1-4
胜败乃兵家常事	shèngbài nǎi bīngjiā chángshì	victory and defeat are both common in battle	7-2-3
失败是成功之母	shībài shì chénggōng zhī mǔ	failure is the mother of success	7-2-3
失望	shīwàng	disappoint	2-2-2
师傅	shīfu	master	6-1-2
师傅领进门，修行在个人	shīfu lǐng jìn mén, xiūxíng zài gèrén	the master teaches the trade, but the apprentice's skill is self-made	8-1-4
石头落地	shítou luòdì	lift (take) a weight off one's mind; fully relieved	7-1-2
时间	shíjiān	time	1-2-1
实话	shíhuà	truth	8-2-4
实验报告	shíyàn bàogào	lab report	6-1-2
实在	shízài	really; dependable; down to earth	5-1-2
食品	shípǐn	food	2-1-4
食言	shíyán	eat one's own words; break one's promise	6-1-3
世纪	shìjì	century	2-2-1

301

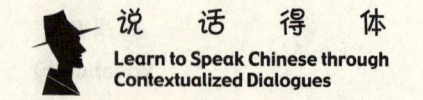

市场调查	shìchǎng diàochá	market research	2-1-3
市内	shì nèi	in the city; downtown	6-2-2
式样	shìyàng	fashion; style	8-1-2
事出有因	shì chū yǒu yīn	it is by no means accidental; there is no smoke without fire	7-2-2
事先	shìxiān	before hand; in advance	5-1-4
视窗	shìchuāng	Windows	3-1-3
试	shì	to try	3-2-1
试读	shìdú	on probation; academic probation	6-1-3
试用期	shìyòngqī	probationary period; trial stage	8-2-4
室内装潢	shìnèi zhuānghuáng	interior designing and decoration; upholster	8-1-3
适合	shìhé	suitable for	3-1-3
收回	shōuhuí	take back	6-2-4
收入	shōurù	income; gain	8-2-4
手工艺品	shǒugōngyìpǐn	arts and crafts product	2-1-4
首先	shǒuxiān	first	2-1-2
售后服务	shòuhòu fúwù	after sale service	6-1-4
舒服	shūfu	comfortable	5-2-4
输	shū	to lose	7-2-3
熟	shú	familiar; experienced	1-2-3
恕不远送	shù bù yuǎn sòng	sorry not to escort you further	1-2-4
数码	shùmǎ	digital	6-1-4
数学	shùxué	mathematics	5-1-4
顺利	shùnlì	smoothly; successfully	7-2-2
说服力	shuōfúlì	persuasion	8-1-4
说明	shuōmíng	explanation; illustration	8-1-4
说着了	shuō zháo le	What you say is correct.	1-1-1
私自	sīzì	without permission	6-2-1
思想准备	sīxiǎng zhǔnbèi	mental preparation	7-2-4
送	sòng	to escort	4-1-1
算了	suànle	leave it at that, never mind	6-1-1
虽然	suīrán	although	3-1-3
虽说	suīshuō	although	2-1-1
随便	suíbiàn	informal; do as one pleases	3-2-1
随和	suíhé	amiable; easy going; easy to get along with	2-2-2
所谓	suǒwèi	so-called	3-1-4
所在地	suǒzàidì	site; location	2-2-4

T

太极拳	tàijíquán	Tai-Chi, traditional Chinese shadowboxing	1-1-1
太平洋	Tàipíng Yáng	the Pacific Ocean	4-2-3
袒护	tǎnhù	give biased favor to	8-2-3
探望	tànwàng	to visit	7-1-4
掏	tāo	speak (from the bottom of the heart); take out	6-2-4
讨论	tǎolùn	to discuss	3-2-2
讨厌	tǎoyàn	nuisance; to loathe	8-2-4
特别	tèbié	special	3-2-1
特产	tèchǎn	special product	2-2-3
提供	tígōng	to provide	4-1-4
天赋	tiānfù	inborn; innate; endowed by nature	7-2-2
天气	tiānqì	weather	5-1-1
天气预报	tiānqì yùbào	weather forecast	5-1-1
天时	tiānshí	favorable climate (situation)	7-2-3
甜	tián	sweet	3-2-1
甜面酱	tiánmiànjiàng	a sweet sauce made of fermented flour	2-2-3
挑剔	tiāotī	picky; find fault with	8-2-2
挑选	tiāoxuǎn	select; choose	2-2-2
调剂	tiáojì	exchange and sell	2-1-4
贴切	tiēqiē	appropriate; suitable	3-1-4
听说	tīngshuō	it is said that	7-1-2
停车	tíngchē	to stop the car; to park	5-1-2
停止	tíngzhǐ	to stop	5-2-4
通得过	tōng de guò	able to pass (the test)	5-1-4
通过	tōngguò	pass (test)	3-1-3
通知	tōngzhī	to inform; to notify; notice; circular; message	4-2-3
同样	tóngyàng	the same	8-1-4
同意	tóngyì	permission	8-2-1
统治	tǒngzhì	to rule; to dominate	2-2-4
痛快	tòngkuài	joyful; to one's great satisfaction	2-2-1
偷懒	tōulǎn	be lazy; to loaf on the job	4-1-2
透	tòu	fully; extremely	7-1-1
推荐	tuījiàn	recommend	2-2-2
推销	tuīxiāo	to promote sales	4-1-4
托	tuō	entrust	3-1-2
托福	tuōfú	thanks to you	8-1-1

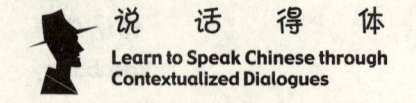

W

外观	wàiguān	appearance; exterior	6-1-4
完全	wánquán	absolutely; whole; complete	2-2-3
完整	wánzhěng	intact; complete	2-2-4
万一	wànyī	just in case; if by any chance	5-1-1
网球	wǎngqiú	tennis	7-1-1
往后	wǎnghòu	from now on; in the future	7-2-4
忘了	wàng le	forgot	5-1-1
为时过早	wéi shí guò zǎo	it's not time yet; it's not ready	4-1-4
唯一	wéiyī	only	2-2-2
味道	wèidào	taste	2-2-3
慰问	wèiwèn	to express sympathy and solicitude for; to console	7-1-2
温故而知新	wēn gù ér zhī xīn	review what you have learned in order to learn sth. new	5-2-3
温习	wēnxí	review	5-2-3
文化	wénhuà	culture	2-1-3
文具	wénjù	stationery	2-1-4
文字	wénzì	characters; script; writing	2-2-1
闻名	wénmíng	well-known; famous	2-2-3
问候	wènhòu	send one's regards (respects) to; extend greetings to	7-1-4
握	wò	to hold; grasp; to take by the hand	5-1-2
无论	wúlùn	no matter what (how); regardless of	5-1-4
午睡	wǔshuì	nap	3-1-2
舞伴	wǔbàn	dancing partner	8-1-2
物尽其用	wù jìn qí yòng	to make the best use of everything	2-2-3
物理	wùlǐ	physics	7-1-1

X

西餐	xīcān	Western style food	4-1-3
吸取	xīqǔ	to draw a lesson	6-2-3
希望	xīwàng	to hope	1-2-3
稀客	xīkè	rare guest	1-1-4
习惯	xíguàn	be accustomed to; habit; custom	8-2-4
洗耳恭听	xǐ ěr gōng tīng	listen respectfully	3-2-2
喜事	xǐshì	joyous occasion; happy event	1-1-2

词语总表
Vocabulary

戏	xì	theatrical play; drama	3-2-4
下不为例	xià bù wéi lì	not to be repeated	6-2-2
下车	xià chē	get off/out of vehicle	3-1-1
下工夫	xià gōngfu	devote time and energy; concentrate one's efforts	5-1-4
下回(次)	xiàhuí(cì)	next time	6-2-1
下雨	xiàyǔ	to rain	5-1-1
先后	xiānhòu	successively; one after another	2-2-4
鲜	xiān	tasty; delicious	3-2-1
鲜花	xiānhuā	fresh flower	6-2-2
咸	xián	salty	8-2-2
显(得)老	xiǎn(de) lǎo	look older (than one's real age)	8-1-1
现存	xiàncún	be extant	2-2-4
羡慕	xiànmù	to admire; to envy	8-1-3
相互	xiānghù	mutually	4-1-4
相依为伴	xiāng yī wéi bàn	depend on each other's company	7-1-4
相知(见)恨晚	xiāng zhī(jiàn) hèn wǎn	too late to know each other	1-2-3
详细	xiángxì	detailed	2-1-4
项链	xiàngliàn	necklace	8-1-2
消息	xiāoxi	news; information	2-1-2
销售	xiāoshòu	to sell; marketing	4-1-4
销售计划	xiāoshòu jìhuà	sales plan	4-1-4
小孩儿	xiǎoháir	little kids	3-1-4
小心	xiǎoxīn	be careful; watch out	5-1-1
小意思	xiǎoyìsi	small gift; small token of kindly feelings	4-2-2
小组讨论	xiǎozǔ tǎolùn	group discussion	7-1-1
协调	xiétiáo	harmonize; integrate; cohere with	8-1-3
鞋帽	xiémào	shoes and hats	2-1-4
泄气	xièqì	be discouraged; to lose heart	7-2-3
谢天谢地	xiè tiān xiè dì	Thank goodness!	7-1-3
心动	xīndòng	touched; moved	6-1-4
心里话	xīnlihuà	words from the bottom of the heart	6-2-4
心理	xīnlǐ	psychology; mentality	5-2-4
心领	xīnlǐng	to understand; to appreciate	4-1-3
辛苦	xīnkǔ	effort; hardworking	2-1-2
辛勤	xīnqín	diligently; hard working	8-1-4
欣慰	xīnwèi	feel delighted and pleased; pleasure	7-1-2
新华书店	Xīnhuá Shūdiàn	Xinhua Bookstore	2-1-4

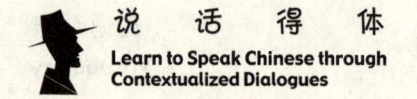

新居	xīnjū	new residence; new home	8-1-3
新式	xīnshì	new fashion; new style	2-1-4
薪金	xīnjīn	salary	8-2-4
信念	xìnniàn	faith; belief; conviction	7-2-2
信誉	xìnyù	honor	4-1-4
行	xíng	fine; be all right	6-1-2
行动	xíngdòng	take action	6-1-4
行人	xíngrén	pedestrian	5-1-2
行事	xíngshì	to handle matters; to act	8-2-4
幸会	xìnghuì	It's great to meet you.	1-1-3
幸运	xìngyùn	fortunate; lucky	1-2-3
性格	xìnggé	temperament; character	3-1-3
休息	xiūxi	to rest	3-1-2
修	xiū	to take (courses)	3-1-3
需要	xūyào	in need	4-1-4
许可	xǔkě	permission	4-1-4
旋转餐厅	xuánzhuǎn cāntīng	rotating cafeteria	2-1-4
选购	xuǎngòu	pick out and buy; selective purchasing	6-1-4
选择	xuǎnzé	to select; to choose	8-1-2
学乖	xué guāi	learn to be well-behaved	7-2-1
学科	xuékē	subjects	8-2-4
学问	xuéwen	scholarship; knowledge	8-1-4
迅速	xùnsù	rapidly	4-1-4

Y

压力	yālì	pressure	5-2-4
押	yā	give as security	6-1-1
烟酒	yānjiǔ	tobacco and alcoholic drinks	2-1-4
严重	yánzhòng	serious	5-2-1
研发部	yánfābù	department of research and developmen	4-2-3
盐	yán	salt	8-2-2
颜色	yánsè	color	8-1-3
眼力	yǎnlì	have good taste and judgement	8-1-2
演示	yǎnshì	to demonstrate	3-1-3
演说	yǎnshuō	speech	8-1-4
要求	yāoqiú	require; requirement	2-2-2
邀请	yāoqǐng	to invite	8-1-2
药物	yàowù	medicine; drug	5-2-4

词语总表
Vocabulary

要不	yàobù	otherwise; or else	3-2-3
也许	yěxǔ	perhaps	3-2-3
业务	yèwù	business; transaction	4-1-4
一般	yībān	common; ordinary; general	3-1-4
一定	yīdìng	surely; certainly	1-1-2
一干二净	yī gān èr jìng	clean out completely; cleared up without reminder	6-2-2
一面之词	yī miàn zhī cí	one-sided story; one-sided statement	6-2-4
一下	yīxià	once (measure word for verb)	3-1-3
一早	yīzǎo	early in the morning	6-1-3
一阵风	yīzhènfēng	a gust of wind	8-1-1
医学院	yīxuéyuàn	medical school	7-2-2
医药	yīyào	medicine	2-1-4
依我看	yī wǒ kàn	from my point of view	5-2-3
遗憾	yíhàn	regretful; sorry	7-1-3
艺术	yìshù	art	2-2-1
艺术中心	yìshù zhōngxīn	art center	5-2-2
意见	yìjiàn	opinion; suggestion	4-2-4
意思	yìsi	meaning	3-1-4
意义	yìyì	significance	3-2-2
因病故世	yīn bìng gùshì	die of an illness	7-1-4
因人而异	yīn rén ér yì	vary with each individual	3-1-4
因素	yīnsù	factor; element	5-2-4
阴	yīn	cloudy	5-1-1
音乐会	yīnyuèhuì	concert	5-2-2
应该	yīnggāi	should; must	1-2-1
应酬	yìngchou	engage in social activities	5-2-2
硬	yìng	insist	8-2-3
硬朗	yìnglang	strong and healthy; springtly	1-1-4
拥有	yōngyǒu	possess	8-1-3
佣金	yòngjīn	commission	4-1-4
用	yòng	to eat or drink	3-2-1
用料	yòngliào	condiments; seasoning; ingredient	2-2-3
优秀	yōuxiù	brilliant; excellent	8-1-4
幽雅	yōuyǎ	(of a place) quiet and tastefully laid out	8-1-3
尤其	yóuqí	especially; particularly	8-2-4
友谊	yǒuyì	friendship	2-1-4
有道理	yǒu dàolǐ	reasonable; to have sense	4-1-4
有关	yǒuguān	to have relations with; concerned	4-2-4

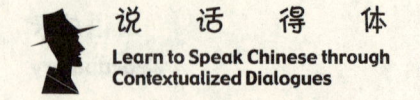

有何贵干	yǒu hé guì gàn	What can I do for you?	3-1-2
有劲	yǒujìn	energetic; interesting	2-1-4
有品味	yǒu pǐnwèi	have good taste (savour)	8-1-2
有意	yǒuyì	intentionally; on purpose	8-2-1
又嫩又脆	yòu nèn yòu cuì	both tender and crispy	2-2-3
右手边	yòushǒubiān	right (hand) side	3-1-1
于	yú	in (the year of)	2-2-4
愉快	yúkuài	happy; pleasant	6-2-4
与众不同	yǔ zhòng bù tóng	different from others	8-1-2
预备	yùbèi	to prepare	4-1-2
预防	yùfáng	to prevent; take precautions against	5-1-1
遇到	yùdào	to encounter; to come across	6-2-4
原谅	yuánliàng	to excuse	6-2-1
原因	yuányīn	cause	5-2-4
缘故	yuángù	reason; cause; for the reason of	5-2-4
怨	yuàn	to complain; to blame	7-2-3
愿望	yuànwàng	wish	4-1-4
愿意	yuànyì	be willing to	3-2-4
约	yuē	to make an appointment	4-1-3
允许	yǔnxǔ	allow; permit	2-1-3
运动	yùndòng	exercise; sports; athletics	5-2-4

Z

在乎	zàihu	care about	7-2-1
咱们	zánmen	we; us (including the addressed)	5-1-3
赞成	zànchéng	agree with	4-1-4
糟	zāo	in a mess	5-1-4
糟糕	zāogāo	What a mess! What bad luck!	7-1-1
早点	zǎodiǎn	breakfast	1-1-1
怎么回事	zěnme huíshì	What's the matter?	6-2-1
怎么啦	zěnme la	What's wrong?	6-2-2
扎实	zhāshi	solid; have a good grasp of	8-1-4
展览会	zhǎnlǎnhuì	exhibition	2-2-2
展销	zhǎnxiāo	sales exhibition	2-1-4
占	zhàn	to occupy; to own; to hold	7-2-3
丈夫	zhàngfu	husband	3-1-4
招牌菜	zhāopaicài	house special (at restaurants)	2-2-3
招惹	zhāorě	to provoke; stir up (trouble)	5-1-3
招手	zhāoshǒu	wave; welcome	7-1-3

词语总表
Vocabulary

找借口	zhǎo jièkǒu	make an excuse for	4-1-2
照相机	zhàoxiàngjī	camera	6-1-4
折磨	zhémó	cause physical or mental suffering	7-2-4
这不	zhè bù	that is why	7-1-2
这阵子	zhèzhènzi	these days; a spell	5-2-1
真是的	zhēnshi de	(used in a complaint or an apology) indeed; really	6-2-1
真心	zhēnxīn	heartfelt; sincere; true intention	6-2-4
振作	zhènzuò	pull oneself together; bestir oneself; display vigour	7-2-4
整理	zhěnglǐ	to put things in order	4-1-2
整体	zhěngtǐ	whole; entirety; overall	8-1-3
正	zhèng	just; exactly; precisely	2-1-1
正常	zhèngcháng	normal	7-2-2
正式	zhèngshì	formally; officially	1-2-3
正值	zhèngzhí	right at the time of	6-1-4
证明	zhèngmíng	certificate	4-1-4
芝加哥	Zhījiāgē	Chicago	5-2-2
知识面	zhīshimiàn	range of knowledge	8-1-4
直接	zhíjiē	directly	3-1-4
值得	zhídé	worthy; worth	2-2-1
职	zhí	position	3-1-3
指	zhǐ	to indicate; to mean	3-1-4
指导	zhǐdǎo	to direct; to instruct	1-2-4
质量	zhìliàng	quality	4-2-4
中级	zhōngjí	intermediate	3-1-3
种种好	zhǒngzhǒng hǎo	good deeds of all kinds	6-2-4
众多	zhòngduō	numerous; multitudinous	2-2-1
重话	zhònghuà	harsh words	6-2-4
周到	zhōudào	thoughtful; considerate	3-2-4
周围	zhōuwéi	around; vicinity	8-1-3
周转	zhōuzhuǎn	turnover	4-1-4
诸位	zhūwèi	everybody; all of you	6-2-3
主菜	zhǔcài	main course; main dish	2-2-3
主场	zhǔchǎng	host; home ground (court)	7-2-3
主管	zhǔguǎn	person in charge	3-1-3
主任	zhǔrèn	director	4-2-3
注视	zhùshì	look attentively	5-1-2
祝	zhù	express good wishes	4-2-2

309

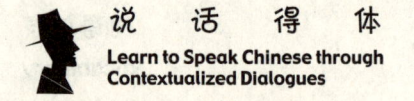

祝贺	zhùhè	congratulation	8-1-3
著作	zhùzuò	literary works	2-2-1
抓紧	zhuājǐn	firmly grasp; make the best of (one's time)	5-1-4
专科学校	zhuānkē xuéxiào	vocational college	3-1-3
转	zhuǎn	to turn	5-1-2
转达	zhuǎndá	pass on	7-1-4
转告	zhuǎngào	to pass on	3-2-3
转行	zhuǎnháng	change professions	8-2-4
装饰	zhuāngshì	(interior) decoration	8-1-3
准备	zhǔnbèi	prepare	5-1-4
准时	zhǔnshí	on time	4-2-3
捉摸不透	zhuōmō bù tòu	unpredictable; difficult to ascertain	8-2-3
酌情	zhuóqíng	take the circumstance into consideration	6-1-3
咨询	zīxún	consult; seek advice from	5-2-4
资格证书	zīgé zhèngshū	certificate of qualification	3-1-3
资金	zījīn	capital; fund	4-1-4
资料	zīliào	data; material	3-2-3
滋味	zīwèi	flavor; taste	7-1-1
仔细	zǐxì	careful; carefully	5-2-3
紫禁城	Zǐjìn Chéng	Forbidden City	2-2-4
自认倒霉	zì rèn dǎoméi	accept bad luck without complaint	8-2-3
自讨没趣	zì tǎo méiqù	look for trouble	8-2-3
自我	zìwǒ	oneself; self	2-1-3
自学	zìxué	self-taught; self-learning	3-1-3
自言自语	zì yán zì yǔ	talk (murmur) to oneself	8-2-2
自由	zìyóu	freedom	8-2-4
总结经验	zǒngjié jīngyàn	learn from the experience	7-2-3
总经理	zǒngjīnglǐ	general manager	4-1-4
走好	zǒuhǎo	walk with care	1-2-4
走运	zǒuyùn	have one's moment; be lucky	7-1-2
足	zú	sufficient	2-1-4
最初	zuìchū	first; prime	2-2-4
最多	zuìduō	at most; maximum	4-2-1
最好	zuìhǎo	best; had better	5-2-1
最近	zuìjìn	recently	1-1-2
尊姓大名	zūnxìng dàmíng	What is your name?	1-1-3
作者	zuòzhě	writer; author	2-2-1